plan graphics

SECOND EDITION

DRAWING · DELINEATION · LETTERING

THEODORE D. WALKER

Additional copies may be ordered from: **P D A PUBLISHERS**
Box 3075
West Lafayette, Indiana
47906

Copyright © 1975, 1977 by Theodore D. Walker

Library of Congress Catalog Card Number: 75-12051

ISBN 0-914886-07-X

Printed in the United States of America

CONTENTS

INTRODUCTION   1

SITE ANALYSIS   7

DESIGN CONCEPTS   29

MASTER PLANS   51

FREEHAND PLANS   139

FULL SIZE PLANS   155

ELEVATIONS AND SECTIONS   179

LETTERING   201

SECOND EDITION SUPPLEMENT   211

INTRODUCTION

This book resulted from a need which became apparent following the publication of *Perspective Sketches* in 1972. Professionals and students alike requested additional visuals beyond the sketches for reference. Even though the central focus of this book is on plans it also includes elevations and sections.

Good graphics are impressive to clients whether we like it or not. Sharp, clean, crisp work creates a more positive impression than work which is dull and sloppy.

Graphic skills, in the language of the educator, are *perceptual motor skills*. They are easiest to learn when an individual is young and such skill development is easiest to achieve. The many hours of effort spent early in life will provide many rewards, including self satisfaction and a sense of achievement, later in one's career.

There is very little text in this book as *perceptual motor skills* are almost impossible to describe in words. One who has these skills can demonstrate them to another, after which the latter must practice to master them. The approach in this book is to provide many different examples which can be used by anyone as he experiments with the development of his own skills. To master any *perceptual motor skill* whether it is graphics, surgery, or performing on a musical instrument, many long patient hours of practice are required. Some will find it easier and quicker to learn than others as we are all different.

In its organization, this book begins with several different graphic techniques for site analysis. In sequence this chapter is followed by design concepts, master plans of various sizes and scale, plans drawn completely freehand, and a chapter of plans at full size or unreduced which will be explained later. Other chapters include elevations and sections, and lettering. The final chapter lists the sources and credits for all the plans shown and in some cases additional information is provided.

The process of reducing plans photograph-ically (as was done for most of those in this book) reduces the width of the lines, eliminates some white space and fuzziness, and makes the drawings sharper and crisper than at their full size. Chapter Six, a group of full size drawings, includes work in ink, pencil and felt tip. These have been provided to illustrate work not reduced. You may wish to refer to this chapter frequently as you review plans in other chapters in order to observe the contrast and change created during reduction. The following pages may be helpful in this review:

FULL SIZE	REDUCTION
166	60
167	88
168	53
169	57
172	90
173	94

David Linstrum has prepared the following illustrations especially for this book to compare pencil, marker, and ink techniques side by side. He suggests testing various media, techniques, and paper in this manner before launching a final presentation drawing to insure getting the results you want.

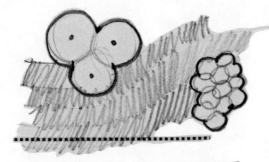

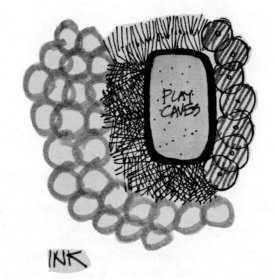

INK

PENCIL

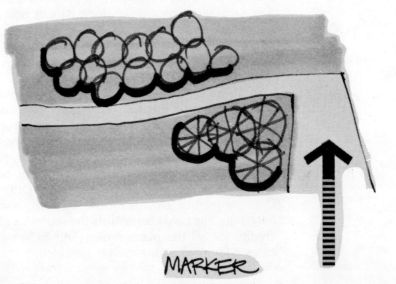

MARKER

4

SECOND EDITION

Added to the first edition are several more plans in black and white and a group of plans in color. These form Chapter Nine. The color plans vary in scale, character, technique, and colors to provide as much diversity as possible under the economic restraints of reproduction.

PLEASE NOTE

Since the principal intent of this book is to serve as a reference for graphic techniques, no design should be copied. The rights to each illustration herein belong to the individual or firm who originally designed it.

ACKNOWLEDGEMENTS

The author gratefully acknowledges the assistance and generosity of many individuals and offices who contributed examples for this book. Each is listed below his work. In most cases these individuals and firms are landscape architects unless otherwise identified. Where the name of a firm is followed by the name of an individual, the latter prepared the drawing for that firm.

SITE ANALYSIS

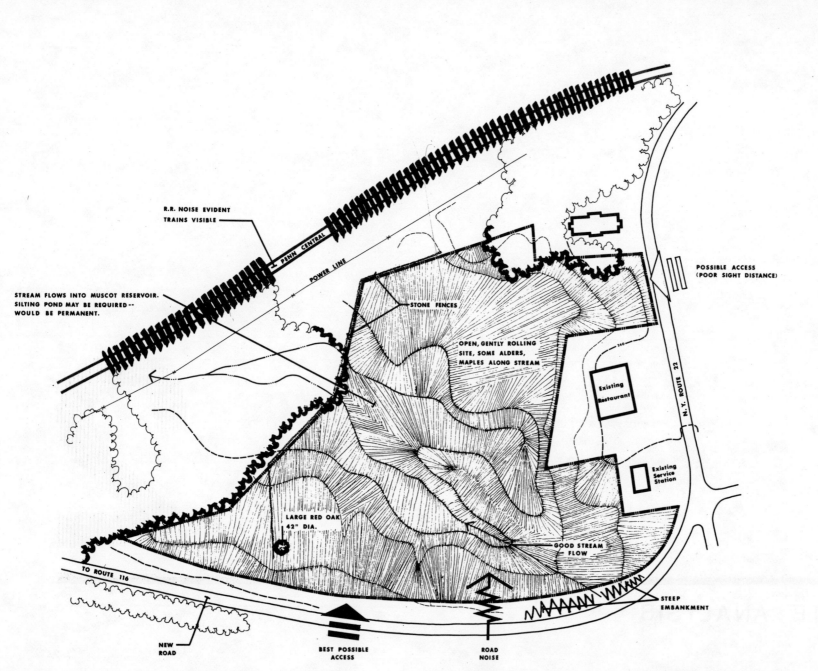

R.R. NOISE EVIDENT
TRAINS VISIBLE

STREAM FLOWS INTO MUSCOT RESERVOIR.
SILTING POND MAY BE REQUIRED --
WOULD BE PERMANENT.

PENN CENTRAL

POWER LINE

STONE FENCES

OPEN, GENTLY ROLLING
SITE, SOME ALDERS,
MAPLES ALONG STREAM

POSSIBLE ACCESS
(POOR SIGHT DISTANCE)

N. Y. ROUTE 22

Existing
Restaurant

Existing
Service
Station

LARGE RED OAK
42" DIA.

GOOD STREAM
FLOW

TO ROUTE 116

STEEP
EMBANKMENT

NEW
ROAD

BEST POSSIBLE
ACCESS

ROAD
NOISE

Site Analysis, North Salem, UDC. The Saratoga Associates.

8

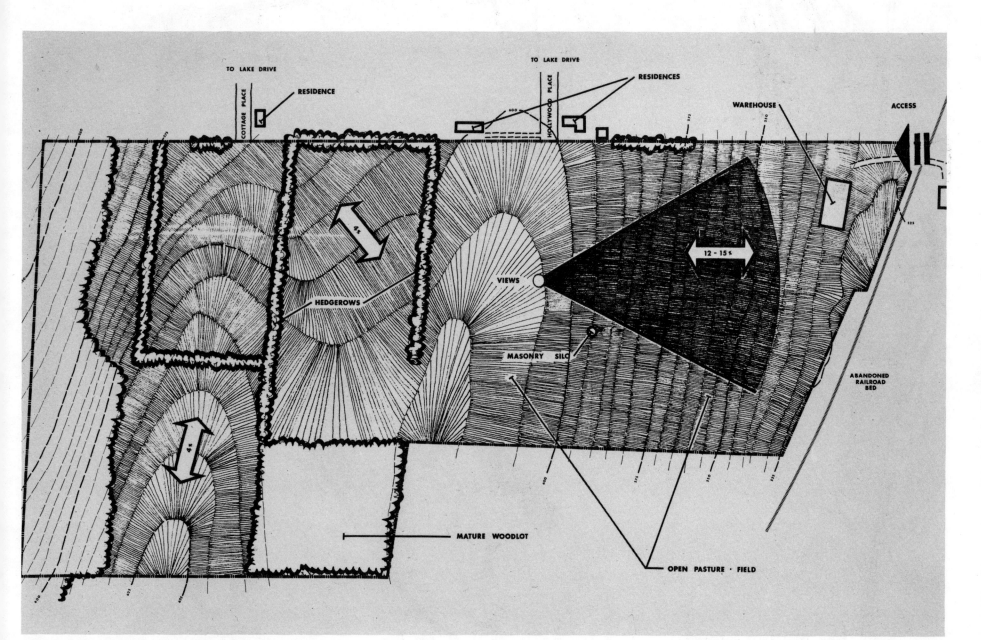

TO LAKE DRIVE

RESIDENCE

COTTAGE PLACE

TO LAKE DRIVE

RESIDENCES

HOLLYWOOD PLACE

WAREHOUSE

ACCESS

HEDGEROWS

VIEWS

12 - 15 %

MASONRY SILO

ABANDONED
RAILROAD
BED

MATURE WOODLOT

OPEN PASTURE · FIELD

Site Analysis, Somers, UDC. The Saratoga Associates.

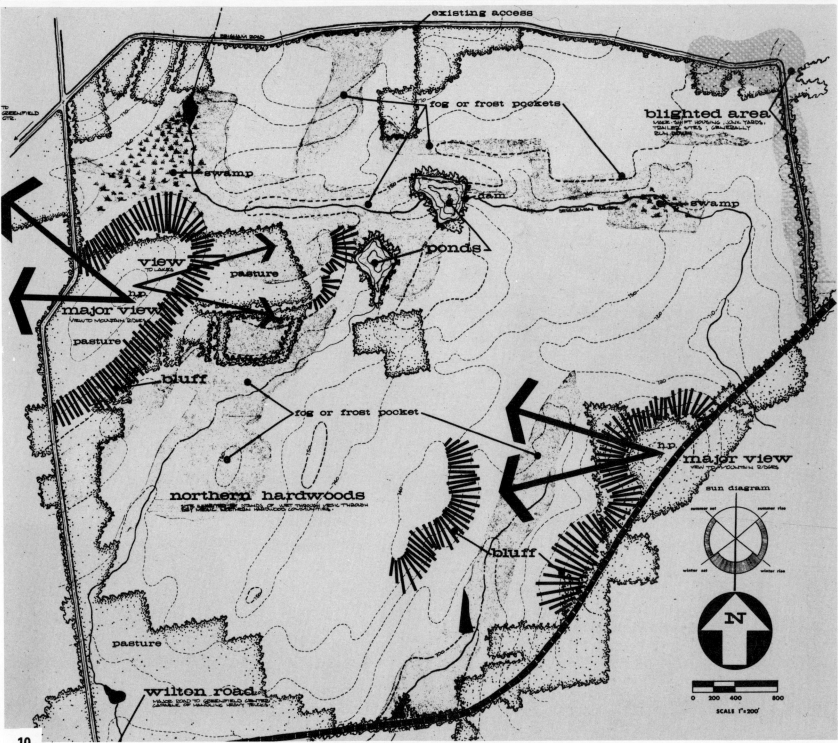

existing access

fog or frost pockets

blighted area
MAKE-SHIFT HOUSING, JUNK YARDS,
TRAILER SITES, GENERALLY
RUN DOWN

swamp

dam

swamp

ponds

view
TO LAKES

pasture

major view
VIEW TO MOUNTAIN RIDGES

pasture

bluff

fog or frost pocket

n.p.

major view
VIEW TO MOUNTAIN RIDGES

sun diagram

northern hardwoods

bluff

pasture

wilton road
MAJOR ROAD TO GREENFIELD CENTER
CAPABLE OF HANDLING HEAVY TRUCKS

N

SCALE 1"=200'

0   200   400   800

10

Existing Site Features, New Town. The Saratoga Associates.

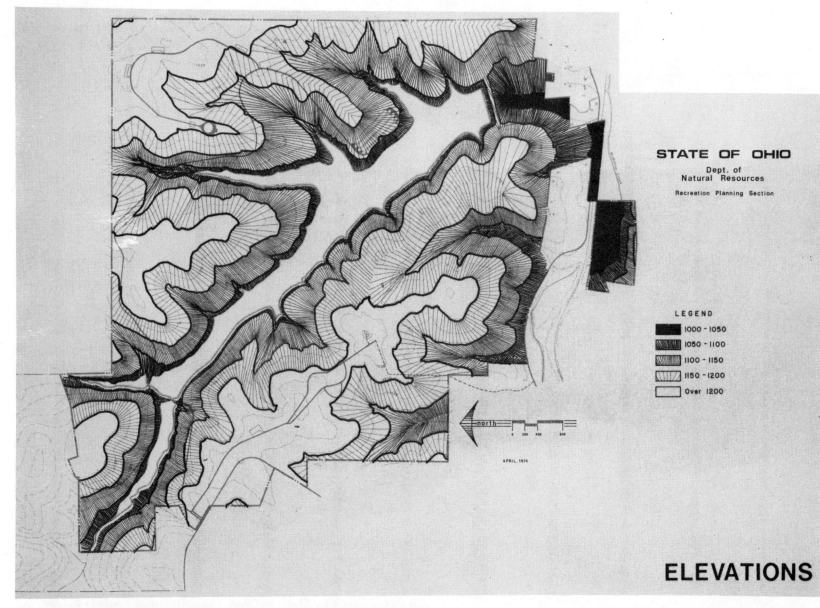

ELEVATIONS

Plans contracted by State of Ohio, Department of Natural Resources.

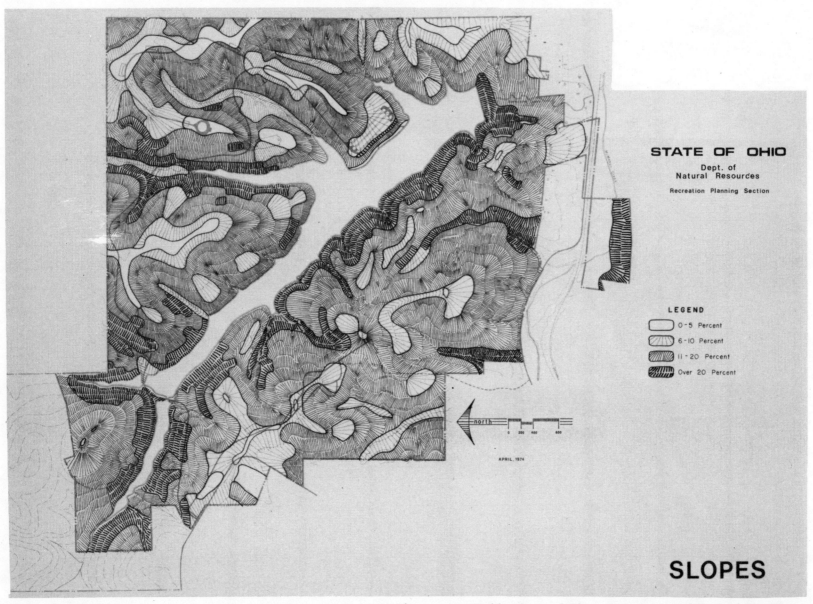

STATE OF OHIO
Dept. of
Natural Resources
Recreation Planning Section

LEGEND
0-5 Percent
6-10 Percent
11-20 Percent
Over 20 Percent

north

0   200   400   800

APRIL, 1974

SLOPES

Plans contracted by State of Ohio, Department of Natural Resources.

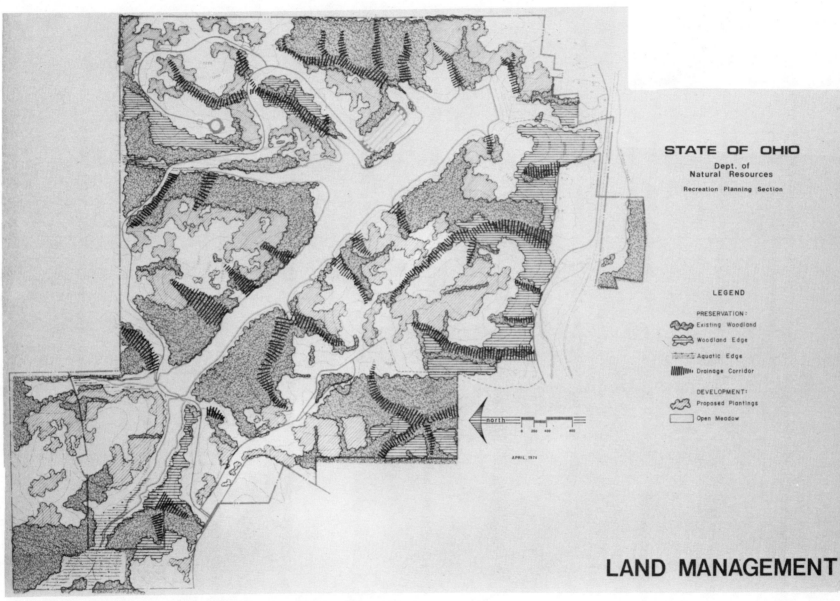

STATE OF OHIO
Dept. of
Natural Resources
Recreation Planning Section

LEGEND

PRESERVATION:
Existing Woodland
Woodland Edge
Aquatic Edge
Drainage Corridor

DEVELOPMENT:
Proposed Plantings
Open Meadow

north

0   200   400   800

APRIL, 1974

LAND MANAGEMENT

Plans contracted by State of Ohio, Department of Natural Resources.

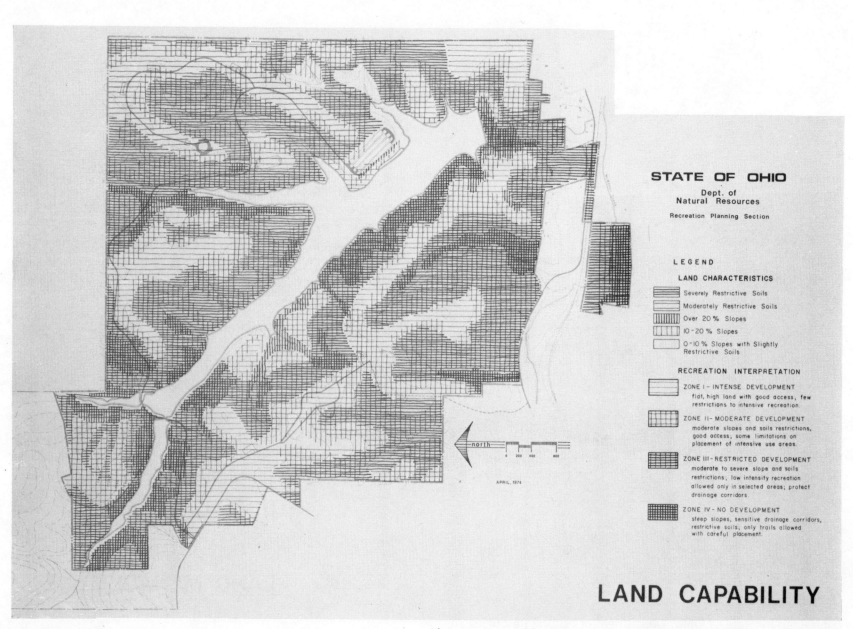

STATE OF OHIO
Dept. of
Natural Resources
Recreation Planning Section

LEGEND

LAND CHARACTERISTICS

Severely Restrictive Soils
Moderately Restrictive Soils
Over 20 % Slopes
10-20 % Slopes
0-10 % Slopes with Slightly
Restrictive Soils

RECREATION INTERPRETATION

ZONE I - INTENSE DEVELOPMENT
flat, high land with good access, few
restrictions to intensive recreation.

ZONE II - MODERATE DEVELOPMENT
moderate slopes and soils restrictions,
good access; some limitations on
placement of intensive use areas.

ZONE III - RESTRICTED DEVELOPMENT
moderate to severe slope and soils
restrictions; low intensity recreation
allowed only in selected areas; protect
drainage corridors.

ZONE IV - NO DEVELOPMENT
steep slopes, sensitive drainage corridors,
restrictive soils, only trails allowed
with careful placement.

north   0   200   400   800

APRIL, 1974

LAND CAPABILITY

Plans contracted by State of Ohio, Department of Natural Resources.

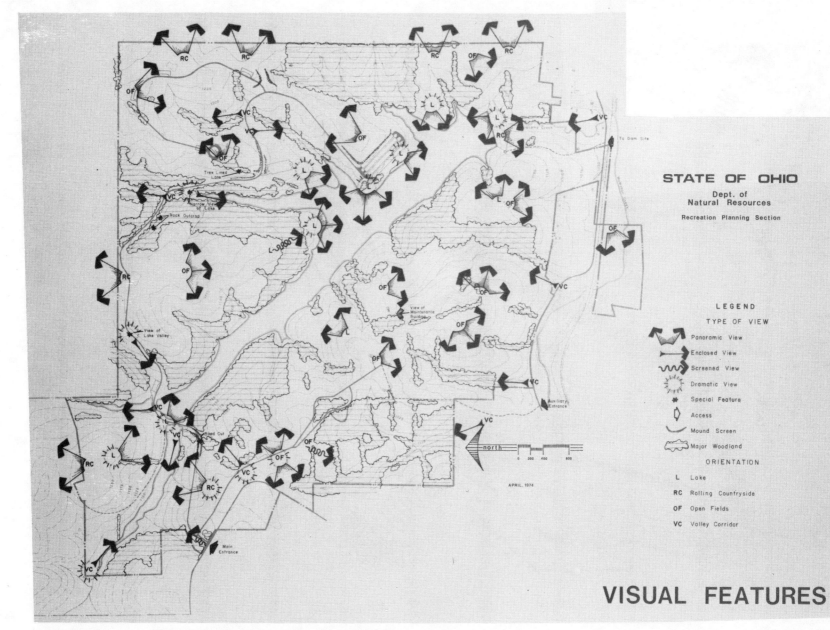

STATE OF OHIO
Dept. of
Natural Resources
Recreation Planning Section

LEGEND

TYPE OF VIEW

Panoramic View
Enclosed View
Screened View
Dramatic View
Special Feature
Access
Mound Screen
Major Woodland

ORIENTATION

L   Lake
RC Rolling Countryside
OF Open Fields
VC Valley Corridor

APRIL, 1974

north

VISUAL FEATURES

Plans contracted by State of Ohio, Department of Natural Resources.

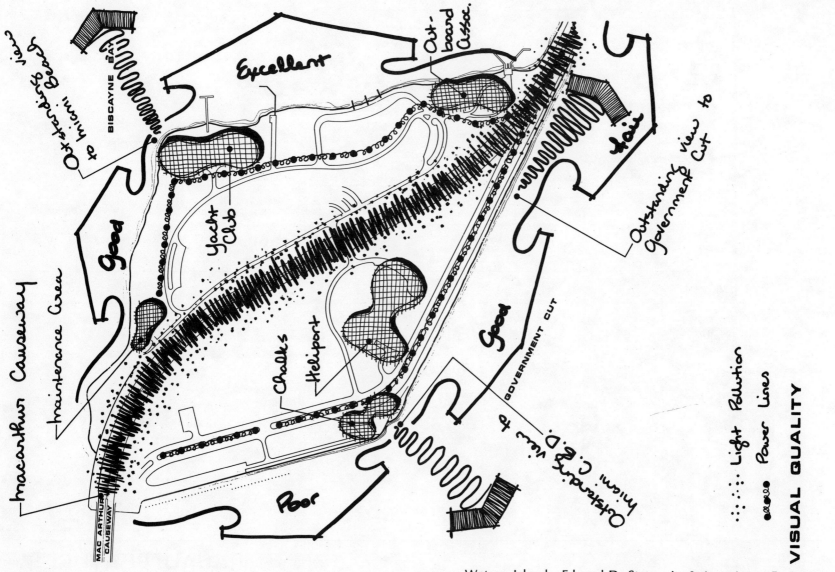

Watson Island.   Edward D. Stone, Jr. & Associates, P. A.

VISUAL QUALITY

16

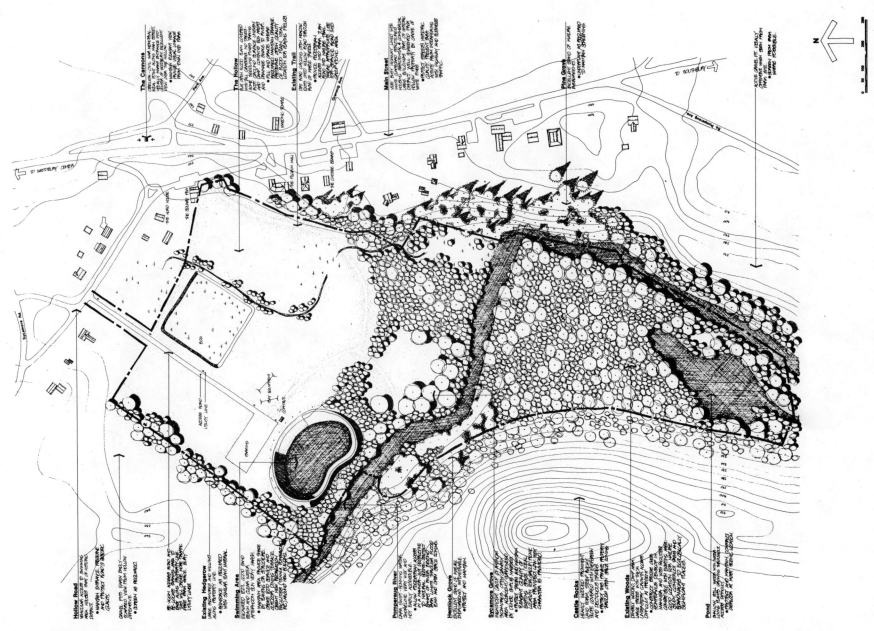

Site Analysis — Land Use. Miceli, Weed, Kulik.

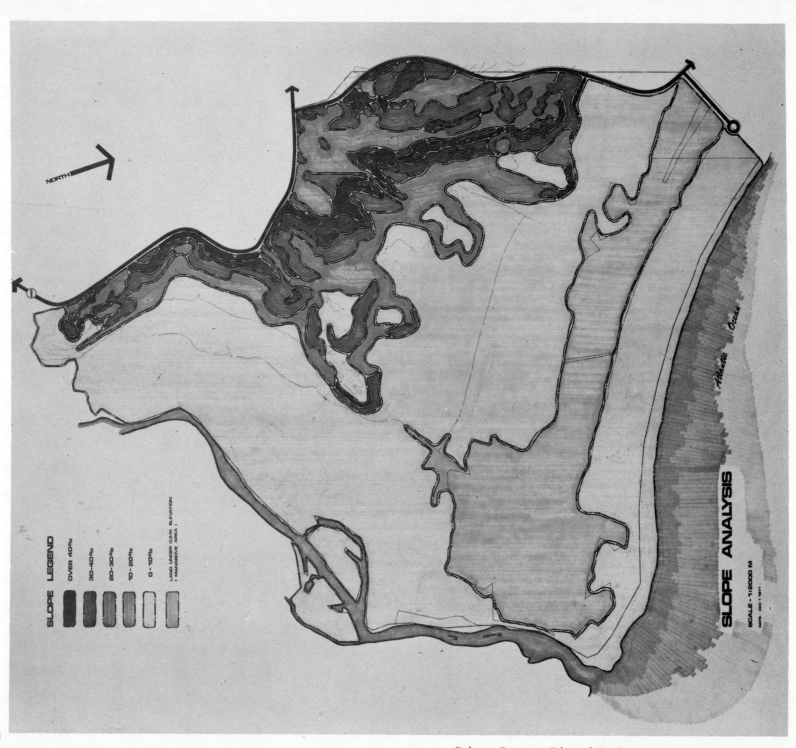

NORTH

SLOPE ANALYSIS

SCALE - 1:12000 M

DATE : DEC 1, 1971

Atlantic Ocean

18

Palmer Resort. Edward D. Stone, Jr. & Associates, P. A.

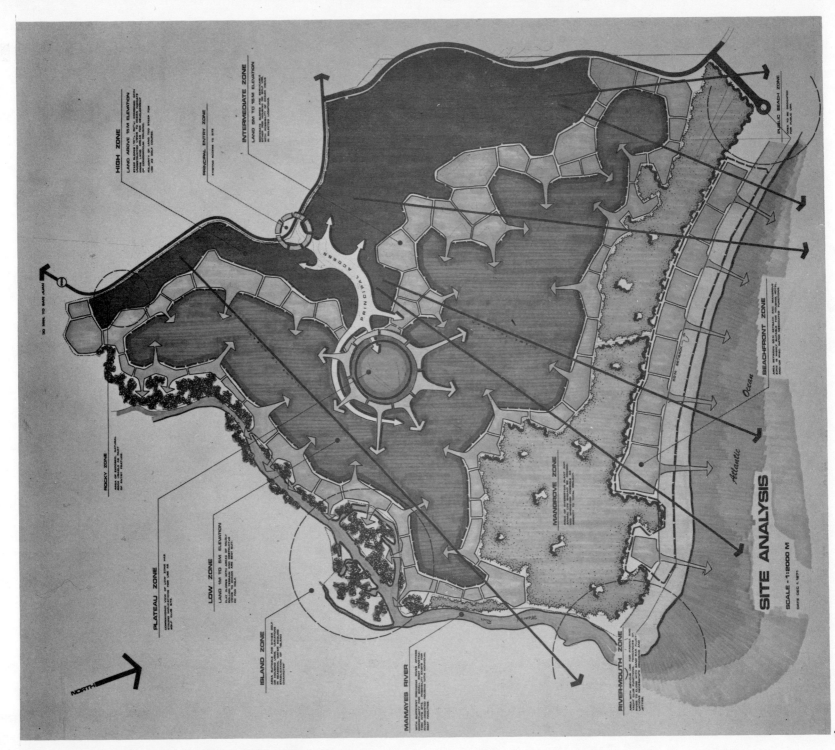

SITE ANALYSIS

SCALE - 1:12000 M

DATE DEC. 1, 1971

NORTH

130 MILES TO SAN JUAN

HIGH ZONE
LAND ABOVE 15 M ELEVATION

PRINCIPAL ENTRY ZONE

INTERMEDIATE ZONE
LAND 5 M TO 15 M ELEVATION

ROCKY ZONE

PLATEAU ZONE

LOW ZONE
LAND 1 M TO 5 M ELEVATION

ISLAND ZONE

MAMAYES RIVER

RIVER-MOUTH ZONE

MANGROVE ZONE

PUBLIC BEACH ZONE

BEACHFRONT ZONE

PRINCIPAL ACCESS

Atlantic Ocean

19

Palmer Resort. Edward D. Stone, Jr. & Associates, P. A.

PERCENT OF SLOPE

0–5
5–10
10–15
15–30

Western Connecticut State College. CR3, Inc., by Jeffrey A. Gebrian.

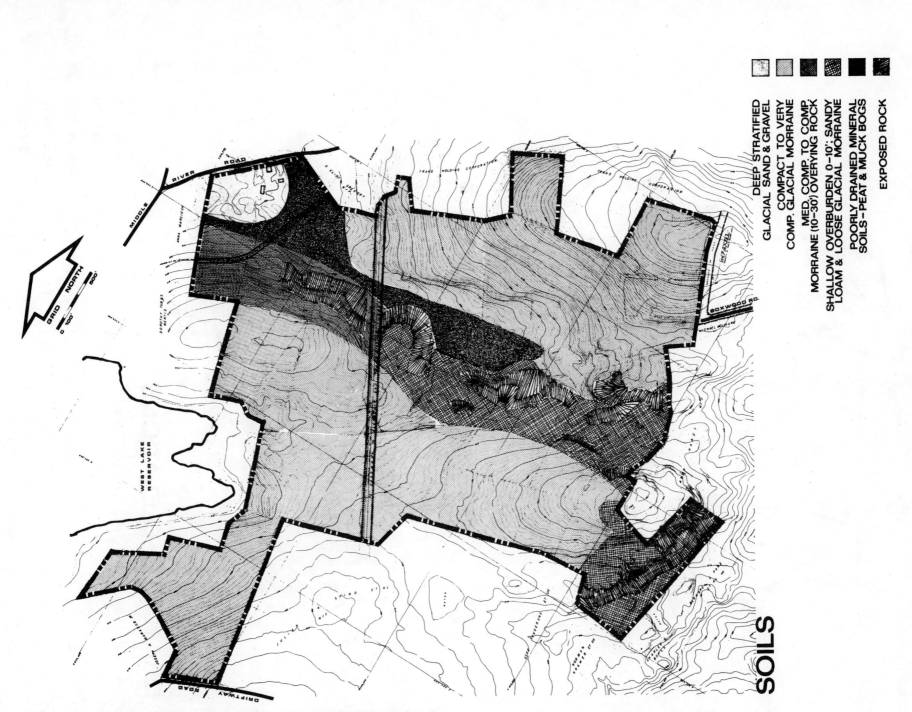

SOILS

Legend:
- DEEP STRATIFIED GLACIAL SAND & GRAVEL
- COMPACT TO VERY COMP. GLACIAL MORRAINE
- MED. COMP. TO COMP. MORRAINE (10–30') OVERYING ROCK
- SHALLOW OVERBURDEN 0–10': SANDY LOAM & LOOSE GLACIAL MORRAINE
- POORLY DRAINED MINERAL SOILS – PEAT & MUCK BOGS
- EXPOSED ROCK

Western Connecticut State College. CR3, Inc., by Jeffrey A. Gebrian.

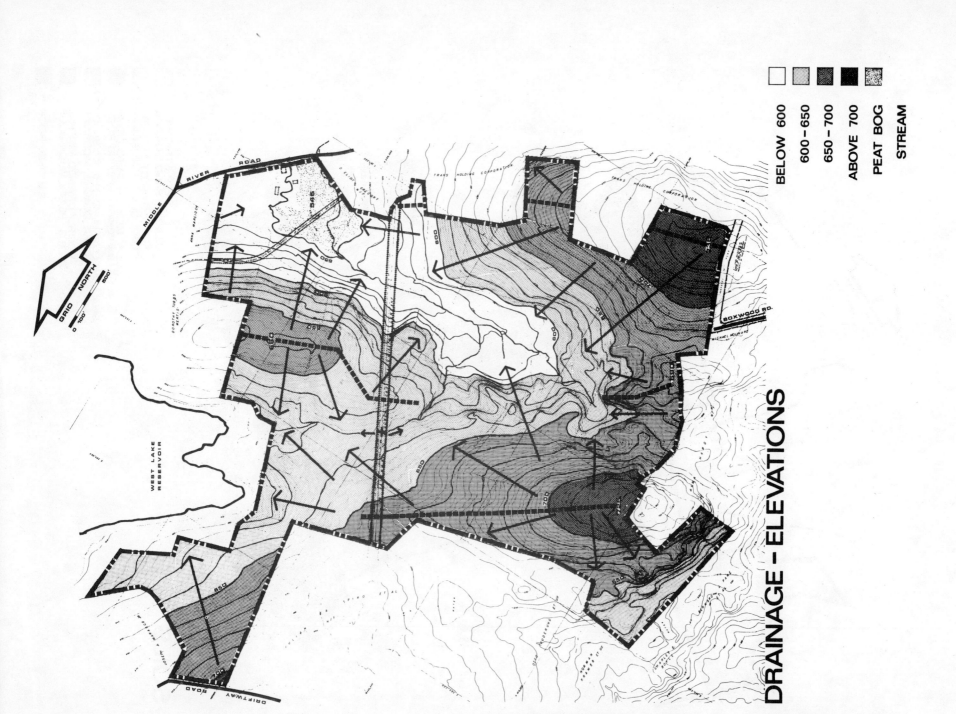

DRAINAGE - ELEVATIONS

BELOW 600
600 - 650
650 - 700
ABOVE 700
PEAT BOG
STREAM

Western Connecticut State College. CR3, Inc., by Jeffrey A. Gebrian.

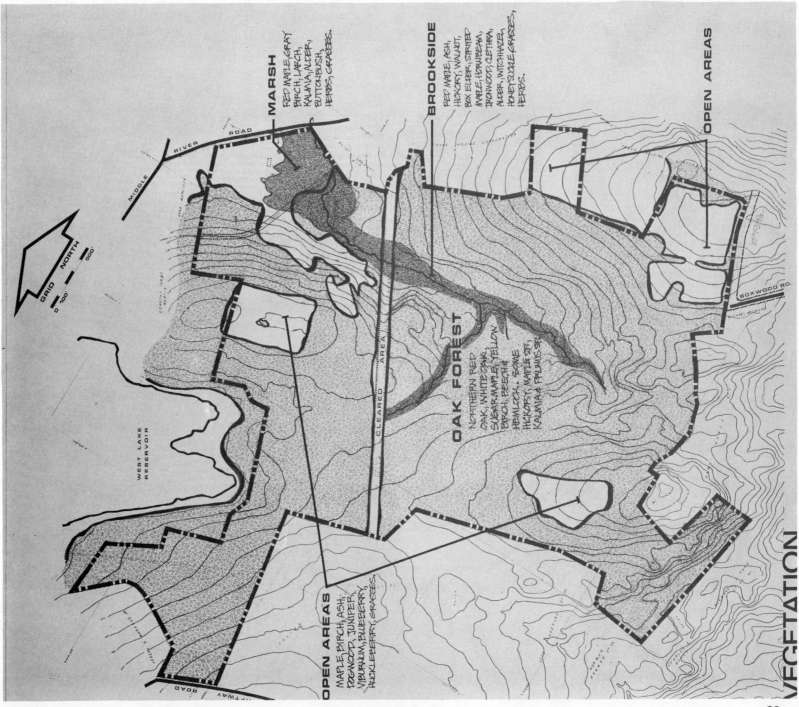

MARSH
RED MAPLE, GRAY BIRCH, LARCH, KALMIA, ALDER, BUTTONBUSH, HERBS, GRASSES.

BROOKSIDE
RED MAPLE, ASH, HICKORY, WALNUT, BOX ELDER, STRIPED MAPLE, HORNBEAM, IRONWOOD, CLETHRA, ALDER, WITCHHAZEL, HONEYSUCKLE, GRASSES, HERBS.

OPEN AREAS

OAK FOREST
NORTHERN RED OAK, WHITE OAK, SUGAR MAPLE, YELLOW BIRCH, BEECH, HEMLOCK. SOME HICKORY, MAPLE SP., KALMIA & PRUNUS SP.

OPEN AREAS
MAPLE, BIRCH, ASH, DOGWOOD, JUNIPER, VIBURNUM, BLUEBERRY, HUCKLEBERRY, GRASSES.

CLEARED AREA

WEST LAKE RESERVOIR

MIDDLE RIVER ROAD

BOXWOOD RD.

GRID NORTH
0 100 500

VEGETATION

Western Connecticut State College. CR3, Inc., by Jeffrey A. Gebrian.

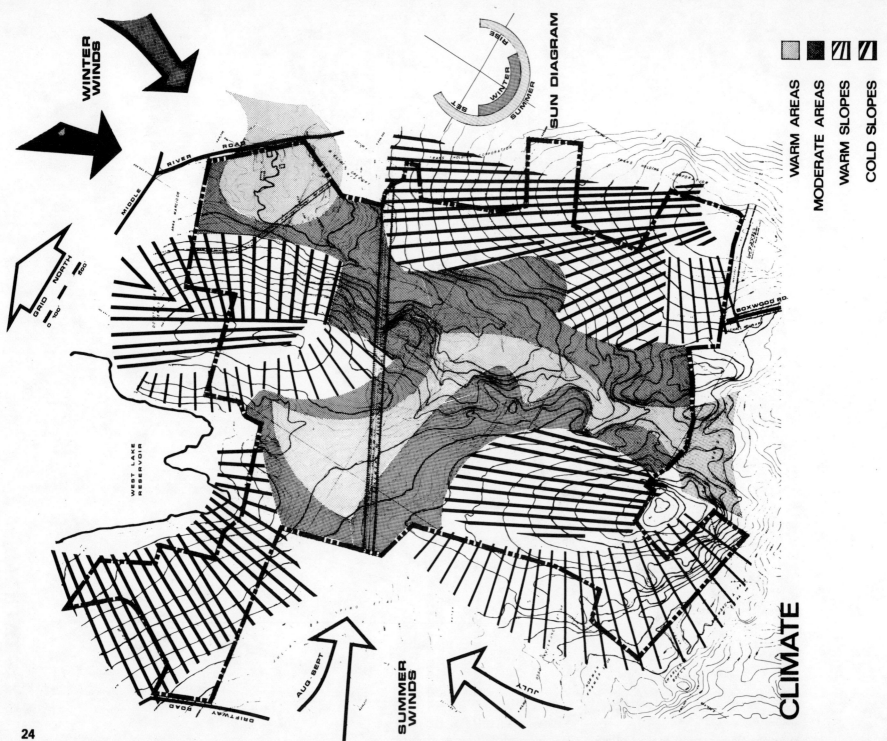

WINTER WINDS

SUN DIAGRAM

RISE

SET

WINTER

SUMMER

WARM AREAS

MODERATE AREAS

WARM SLOPES

COLD SLOPES

RIVER ROAD

MIDDLE ROAD

GRID NORTH

0   100'   500'

WEST LAKE RESERVOIR

BOXWOOD RD.

SUMMER WINDS

AUG-SEPT

JULY

CLIMATE

DRIFTWAY ROAD

Western Connecticut State College. CR3, Inc., by Jeffrey A. Gebrian.

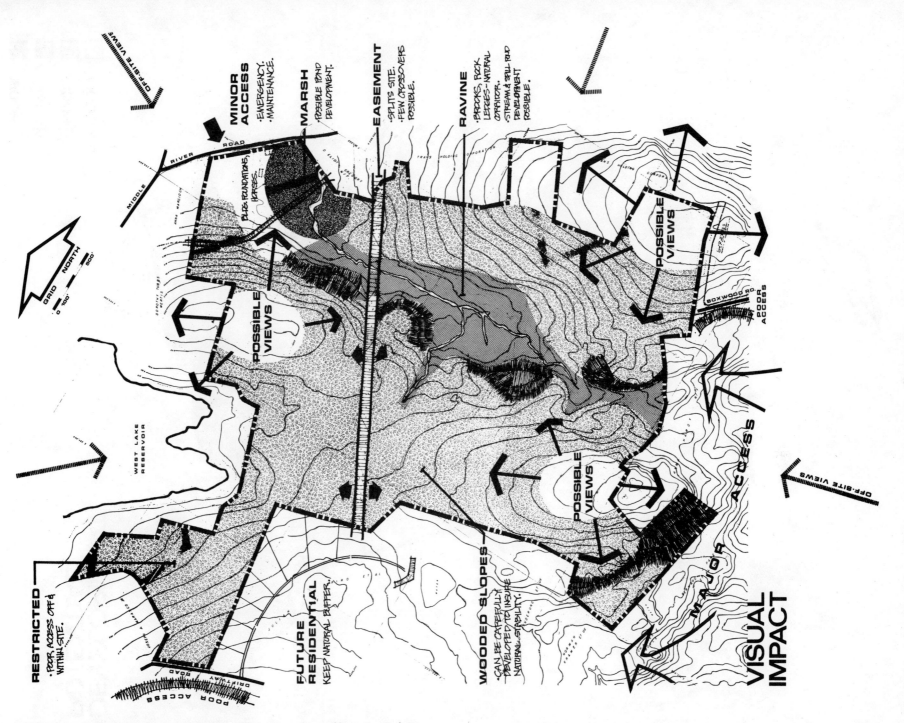

Western Connecticut State College. CR3, Inc., by Jeffrey A. Gebrian.

25

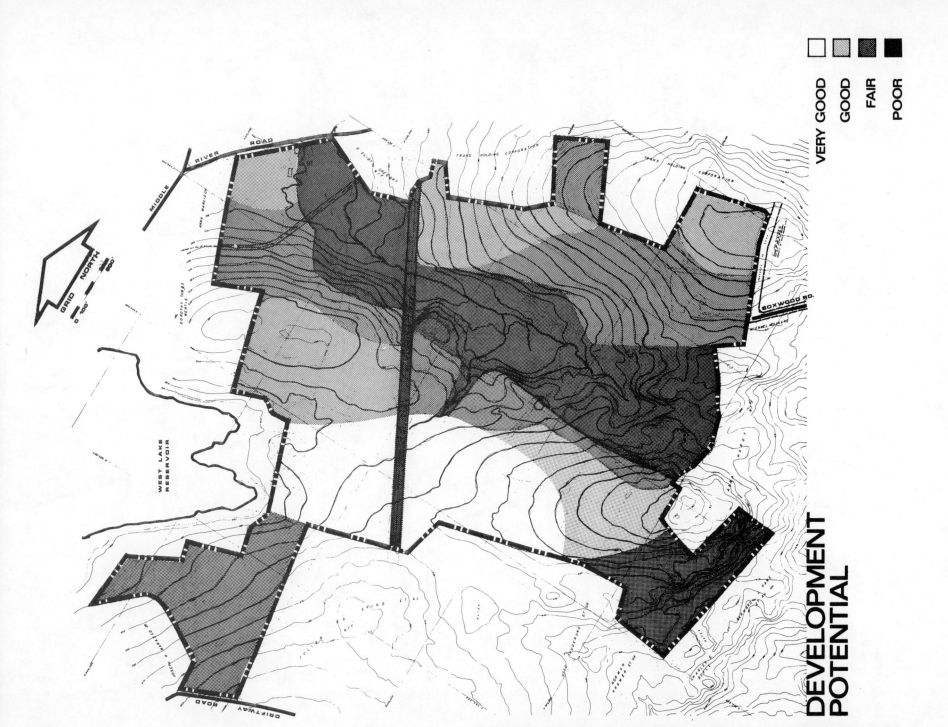

DEVELOPMENT POTENTIAL

VERY GOOD
GOOD
FAIR
POOR

Western Connecticut State College. CR3, Inc., by Jeffrey A. Gebrian.

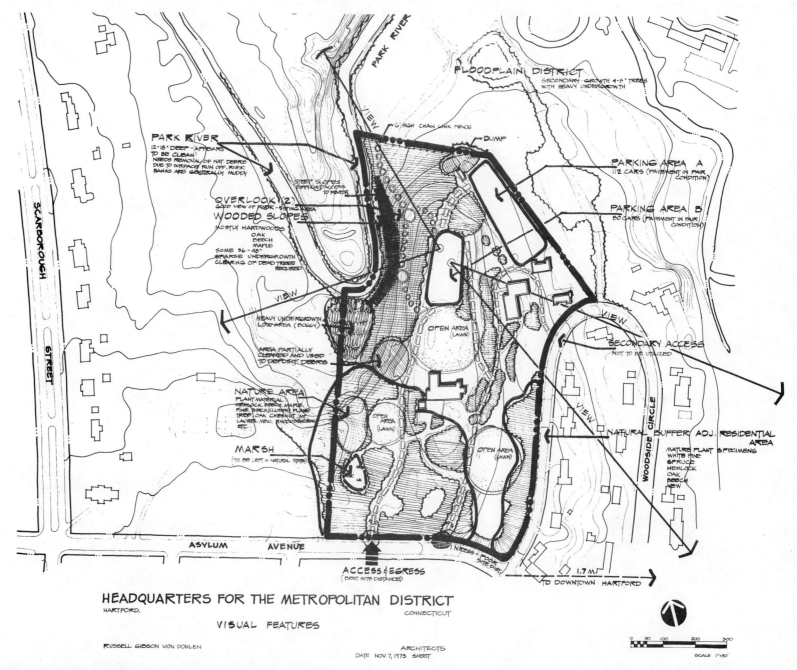

PARK RIVER

FLOODPLAIN DISTRICT
SECONDARY GROWTH 4-8" TREES
WITH HEAVY UNDERGROWTH

6' HIGH CHAIN LINK FENCE

DUMP

PARK RIVER
12-18" DEEP - APPEARS
TO BE CLEAN
NEEDS REMOVAL OF NAT. DEBRIS
DUE TO SURFACE RUN OFF, RIVER
BANKS ARE GENERALLY MUDDY

STEEP SLOPES
DIFFICULT ACCESS
TO RIVER

PARKING AREA A
112 CARS (PAVEMENT IN FAIR CONDITION)

OVERLOOK #2
GOOD VIEW OF RIVER - SITTING AREA

WOODED SLOPES
MOSTLY HARDWOODS
OAK
BEECH
MAPLE
SOME 36-48"
SPARSE UNDERGROWTH
CLEARING OF DEAD TREES
REQUIRED

PARKING AREA B
80 CARS (PAVEMENT IN FAIR CONDITION)

VIEW

SCARBOROUGH STREET

HEAVY UNDERGROWTH
LOW AREA (BOGGY)

OPEN AREA
(LAWN)

VIEW

SECONDARY ACCESS
NOT TO BE UTILIZED

AREA PARTIALLY
CLEARED AND USED
TO DEPOSIT DEBRIS

NATURE AREA
PLANT MATERIAL
HEMLOCK, BEECH, MAPLE,
PINE, BIRCH (CLUMPS) PLANE
TREE, OAK, CHESTNUT, MT.
LAUREL, YEW, RHODODENDRON
ETC.

OPEN AREA
(LAWN)

VIEW

NATURAL BUFFER ADJ. RESIDENTIAL
AREA

MARSH
(TO BE LEFT IN NATURAL STATE)

OPEN AREA
(LAWN)

MATURE PLANT SPECIMENS
WHITE PINE
SPRUCE
HEMLOCK
OAK
BEECH
VIEW

WOODSIDE CIRCLE

ASYLUM AVENUE

INGRESS - POOR
SITE DIST.

ACCESS & EGRESS
(BEST SITE DISTANCE)

1.7 M.

TO DOWNTOWN HARTFORD

HEADQUARTERS FOR THE METROPOLITAN DISTRICT
HARTFORD,   CONNECTICUT
VISUAL FEATURES

RUSSELL GIBSON VON DOHLEN   ARCHITECTS
                                             DATE NOV. 7, 1973 SHEET

0 50 100   200   300
SCALE 1"=80'

Visual Features, Headquarters for Metropolitan District,
Hartford, Connecticut. CR3, Inc., by Dainis Lazda.

DESIGN CONCEPTS

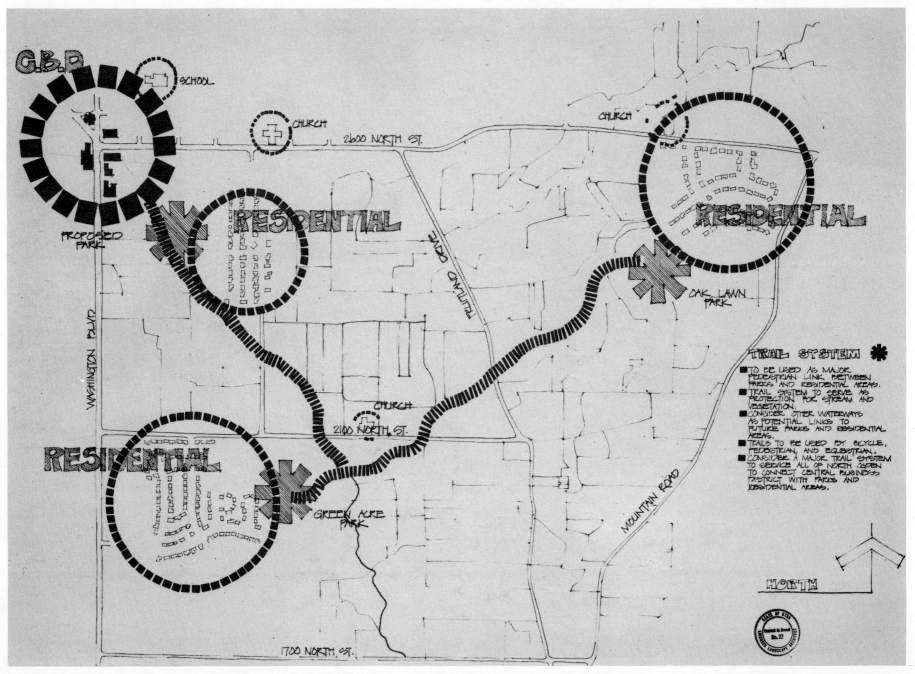

G.B.D.

SCHOOL

CHURCH

2600 NORTH ST.

CHURCH

PROPOSED PARK

RESIDENTIAL

RESIDENTIAL

WASHINGTON BLVD

RUTLAND DRIVE

OAK LAWN PARK

RESIDENTIAL

CHURCH

2100 NORTH ST.

GREEN ACRE PARK

MOUNTAIN ROAD

TRAIL SYSTEM ✳

■ TO BE USED AS MAJOR PEDESTRIAN LINK BETWEEN PARKS AND RESIDENTIAL AREAS.
■ TRAIL SYSTEM TO SERVE AS PROTECTION FOR STREAM AND VEGETATION.
■ CONSIDER OTHER WATERWAYS AS POTENTIAL LINKS TO FUTURE PARKS AND RESIDENTIAL AREAS.
■ TRAILS TO BE USED BY BICYCLE, PEDESTRIAN, AND EQUESTRIAN.
■ CONSIDER A MAJOR TRAIL SYSTEM TO SERVICE ALL OF NORTH OGDEN TO CONNECT CENTRAL BUSINESS DISTRICT WITH PARKS AND RESIDENTIAL AREAS.

1700 NORTH ST.

NORTH

Green Acre Park. Maas and Grassli.

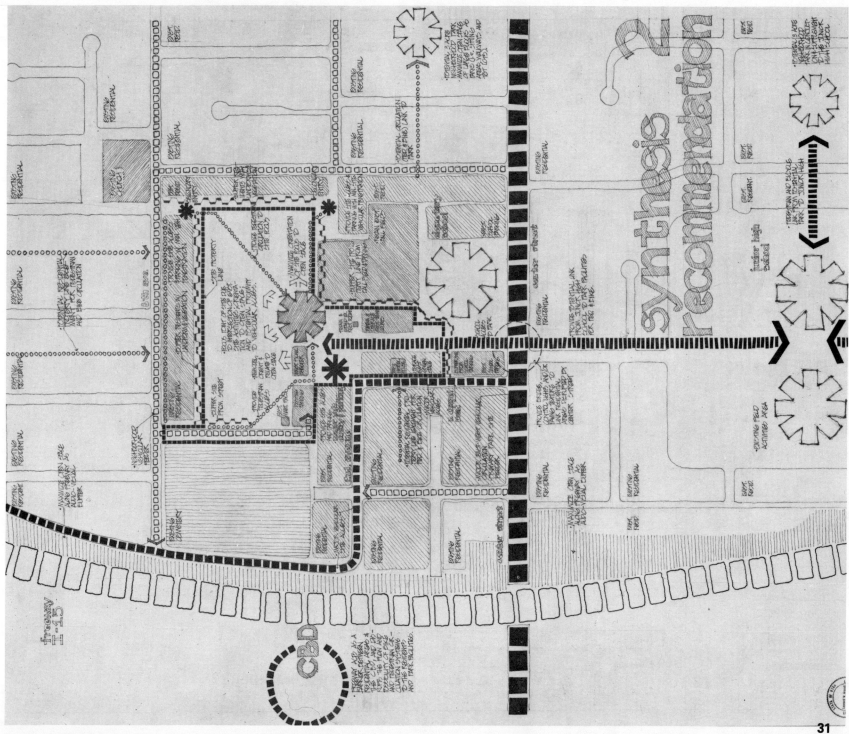

Maas and Grassli.

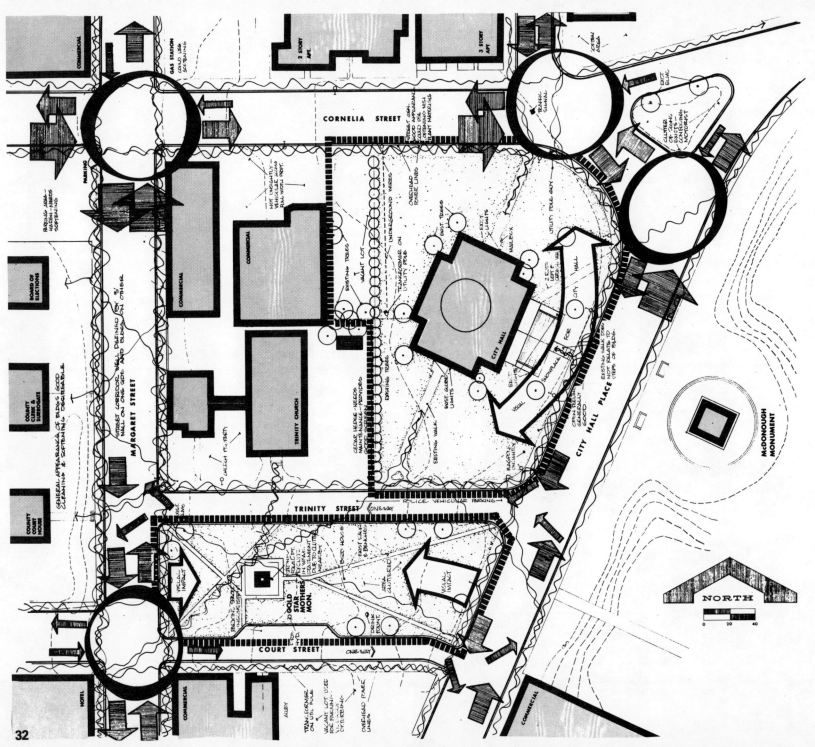

Master plan for City Hall and Trinity Park. The Saratoga Associates.

32

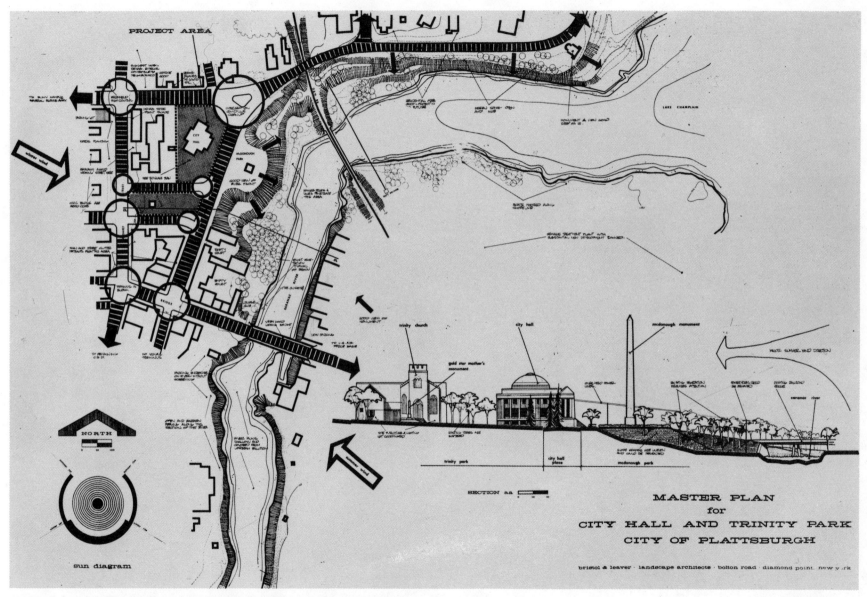

Master plan for City Hall and Trinity Park. The Saratoga Associates.

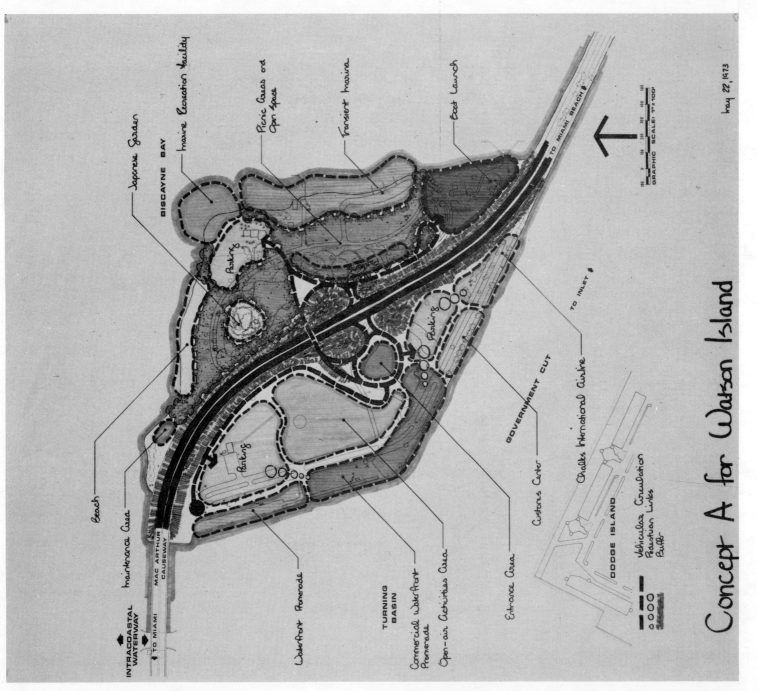

Watson Island.   Edward D. Stone, Jr. & Associates, P.A.

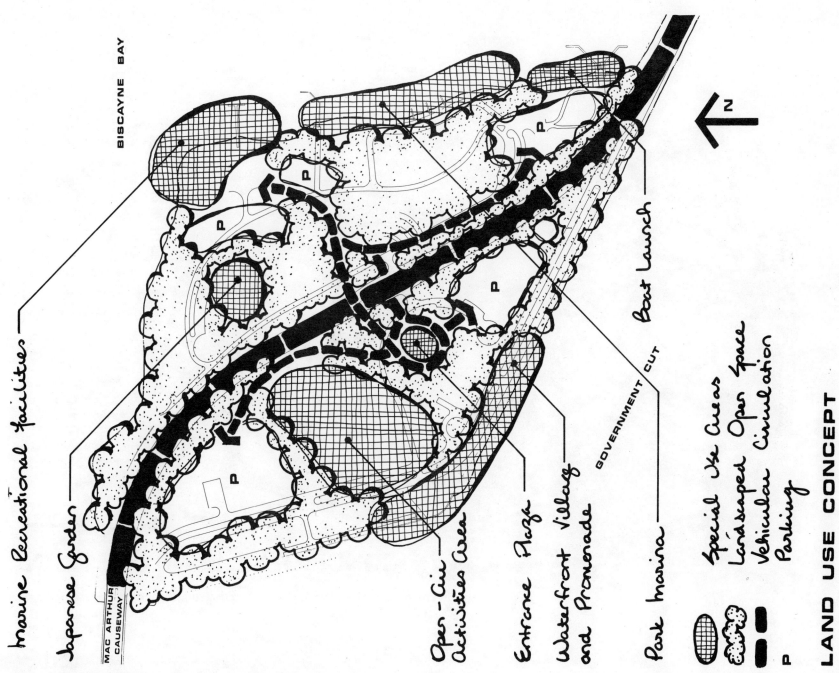

BISCAYNE BAY

Marine Recreational Facilities

Japanese Garden

MAC ARTHUR CAUSEWAY

Open-Air Activities Area

Entrance Plaza

Waterfront Village and Promenade

GOVERNMENT CUT

Boat Launch

Park Marina

Special Use Areas

Landscaped Open Space

Vehicular Circulation

P   Parking

N

LAND USE CONCEPT

Watson Island. Edward D. Stone, Jr. & Associates, P. A.

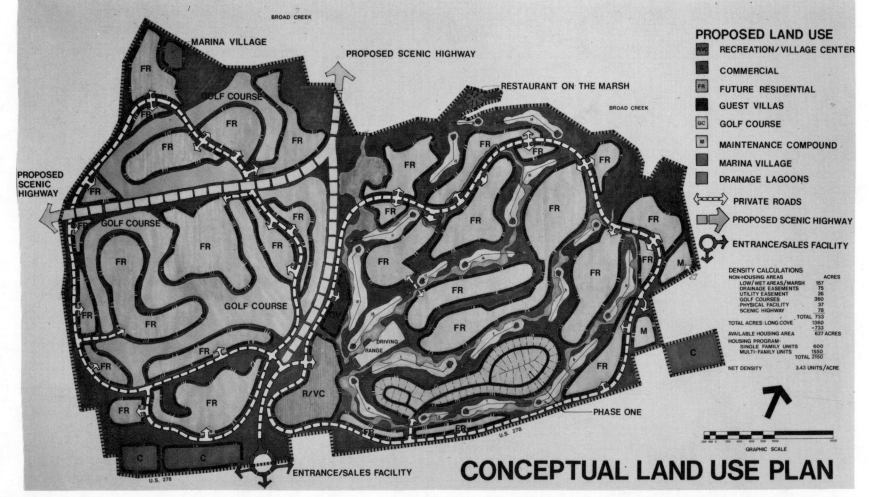

BROAD CREEK

MARINA VILLAGE

PROPOSED SCENIC HIGHWAY

RESTAURANT ON THE MARSH

BROAD CREEK

GOLF COURSE

PROPOSED
SCENIC
HIGHWAY

GOLF COURSE

GOLF COURSE

DRIVING
RANGE

R/VC

PHASE ONE

U.S. 278

ENTRANCE/SALES FACILITY

U.S. 278

PROPOSED LAND USE

RVC	RECREATION/VILLAGE CENTER
C	COMMERCIAL
FR	FUTURE RESIDENTIAL
	GUEST VILLAS
GC	GOLF COURSE
M	MAINTENANCE COMPOUND
	MARINA VILLAGE
	DRAINAGE LAGOONS
	PRIVATE ROADS
	PROPOSED SCENIC HIGHWAY
	ENTRANCE/SALES FACILITY

DENSITY CALCULATIONS

NON-HOUSING AREAS	ACRES
LOW/WET AREAS/MARSH	157
DRAINAGE EASEMENTS	75
UTILITY EASEMENT	26
GOLF COURSES	360
PHYSICAL FACILITY	37
SCENIC HIGHWAY	78
TOTAL	733
TOTAL ACRES: LONG COVE	1360
	-733
AVAILABLE HOUSING AREA	627 ACRES
HOUSING PROGRAM:	
SINGLE FAMILY UNITS	600
MULTI-FAMILY UNITS	1550
TOTAL	2150
NET DENSITY	3.43 UNITS/ACRE

GRAPHIC SCALE

CONCEPTUAL LAND USE PLAN

Conceptual Land Use Plan, Long Cove. Edward D. Stone, Jr. & Associates, P.A.

36

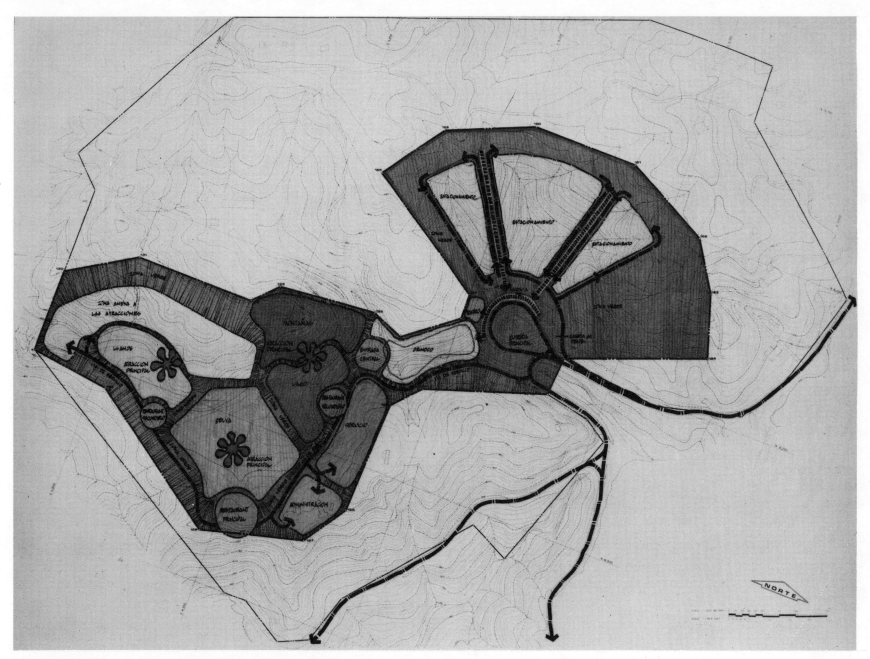

Parque de Motivos. Edward D. Stone, Jr. & Associates, P.A.

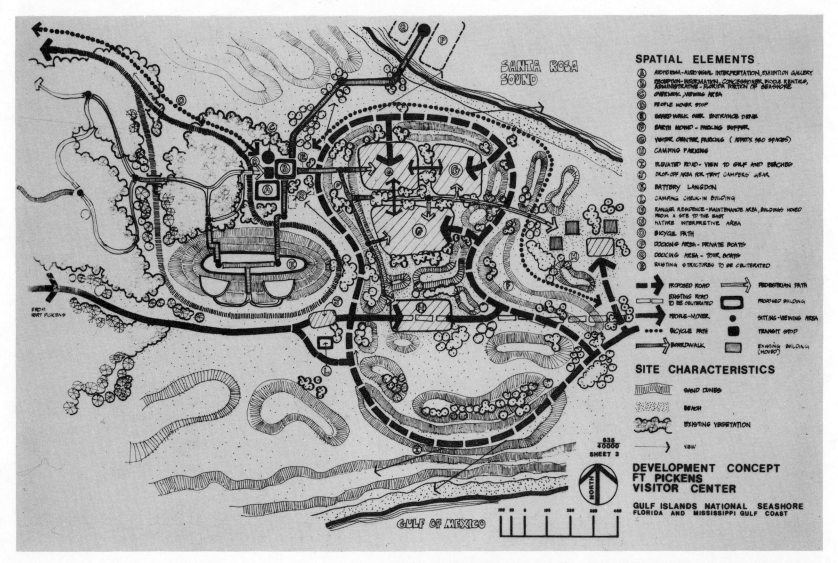

SPATIAL ELEMENTS

Ⓐ AUDITORIUM - AUDIO VISUAL INTERPRETATION, EXHIBITION GALLERY
Ⓑ RECEPTION - INFORMATION, CONCESSIONER, BICYCLE RENTALS, ADMINISTRATIVE - FLORIDA PORTION OF SEASHORE
Ⓒ OVERLOOK, VIEWING AREA
Ⓓ PEOPLE MOVER STOP
Ⓔ RAISED WALK OVER ENTRANCE DRIVE
Ⓕ EARTH MOUND - PARKING BUFFER
Ⓖ VISITOR CENTER PARKING (APPROX 350 SPACES)
Ⓗ CAMPING PARKING
Ⓘ ELEVATED ROAD - VIEW TO GULF AND BEACHES
Ⓙ DROP-OFF AREA FOR TENT CAMPERS GEAR
Ⓚ BATTERY LANGDON
Ⓛ CAMPING CHECK-IN BUILDING
Ⓜ RANGER RESIDENCE - MAINTENANCE AREA, BUILDINGS MOVED FROM A SITE TO THE EAST
Ⓝ NATURE INTERPRETIVE AREA
Ⓞ BICYCLE PATH
Ⓟ DOCKING AREA - PRIVATE BOATS
Ⓠ DOCKING AREA - TOUR BOATS
Ⓡ EXISTING STRUCTURES TO BE OBLITERATED

PROPOSED ROAD   PEDESTRIAN PATH
EXISTING ROAD TO BE OBLITERATED   PROPOSED BUILDING
PEOPLE-MOVER   SITTING-VIEWING AREA
BICYCLE PATH   TRANSIT STOP
BOARDWALK   EXISTING BUILDING (MOVED)

SITE CHARACTERISTICS

SAND DUNES
BEACH
EXISTING VEGETATION
VIEW

635
40000
SHEET 3

DEVELOPMENT CONCEPT
FT PICKENS
VISITOR CENTER

GULF ISLANDS NATIONAL SEASHORE
FLORIDA AND MISSISSIPPI GULF COAST

NORTH

SANTA ROSA SOUND

FROM FORT PICKENS

GULF OF MEXICO

Gulf Islands National Seashore. Reynolds, Smith and Hills, Architects-
Engineers-Planners, Inc., in consultation with the National Park Service.

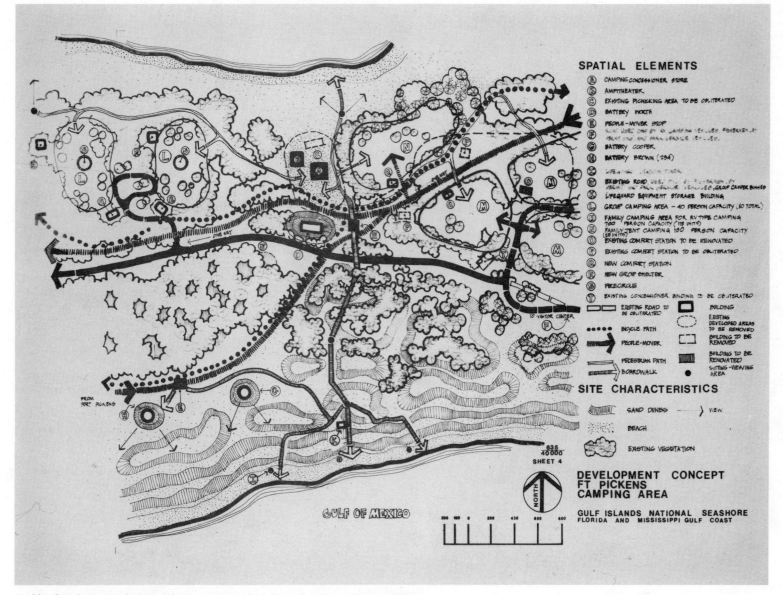

Gulf Islands National Seashore. Reynolds, Smith and Hills, Architects-
Engineers-Planners, Inc., in consultation with the National Park Service.

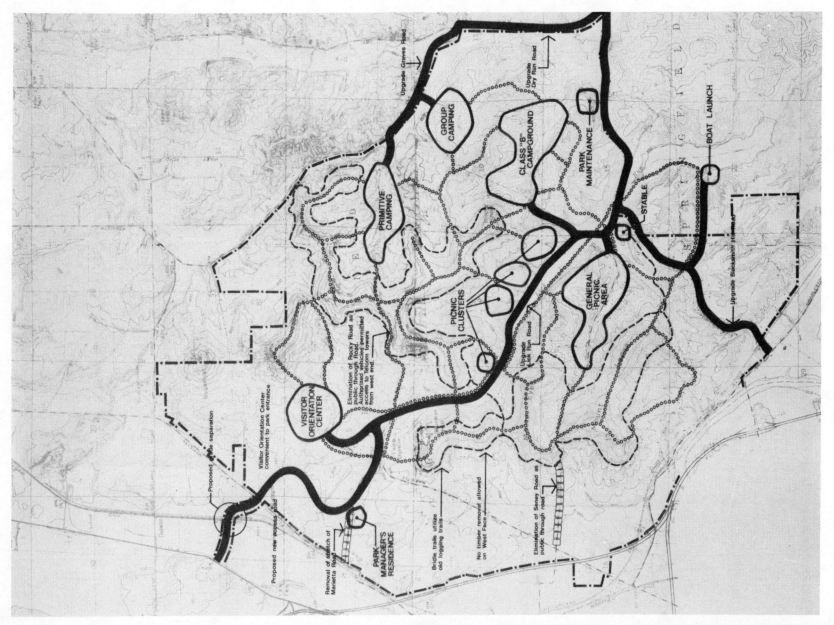

GROUP CAMPING

PRIMITIVE CAMPING

CLASS "B" CAMPGROUND

PARK MAINTENANCE

BOAT LAUNCH

STABLE

Upgrade Graves Road

Upgrade Dry Run Road

Upgrade Blacksmith Hill Road

GENERAL PICNIC AREA

PICNIC CLUSTERS

Upgrade Lick Run Road

VISITOR ORIENTATION CENTER

Elimination of Rocky Road as public through Road authorized access to Telecom towers from west end.

Visitor Orientation Center convenient to park entrance

Proposed grade separation

Proposed new access road

Removal of stretch of Marietta Road

PARK MANAGER'S RESIDENCE

Bridle trails utilize old logging trails

No timber removal allowed on West Face

Elimination of Seney Road as public through road

Plans contracted by State of Ohio, Department of Natural Resources.

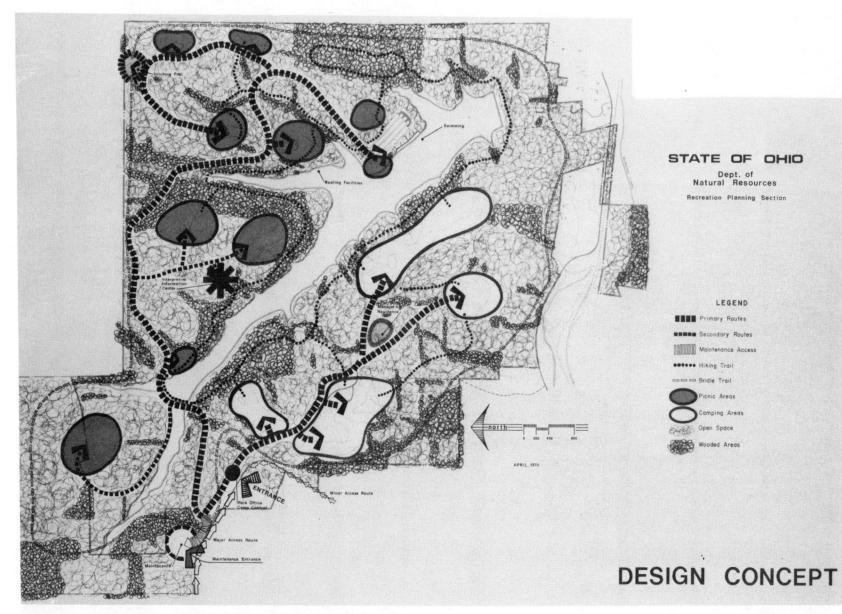

STATE OF OHIO
Dept. of
Natural Resources
Recreation Planning Section

LEGEND
▮▮▮▮ Primary Routes
▬▬▬▬ Secondary Routes
||||||||| Maintenance Access
●●●●●● Hiking Trail
▭▭▭ Bridle Trail
Picnic Areas
Camping Areas
Open Space
Wooded Areas

← north

0   200   400   800

APRIL, 1974

DESIGN CONCEPT

Hitching Post
Swimming
Boating Facilities
Interpretive Information Center
Residence
ENTRANCE
Park Office Camp Control
Minor Access Route
Major Access Route
Maintenance Entrance
Maintenance

Plans contracted by State of Ohio, Department of Natural Resources.

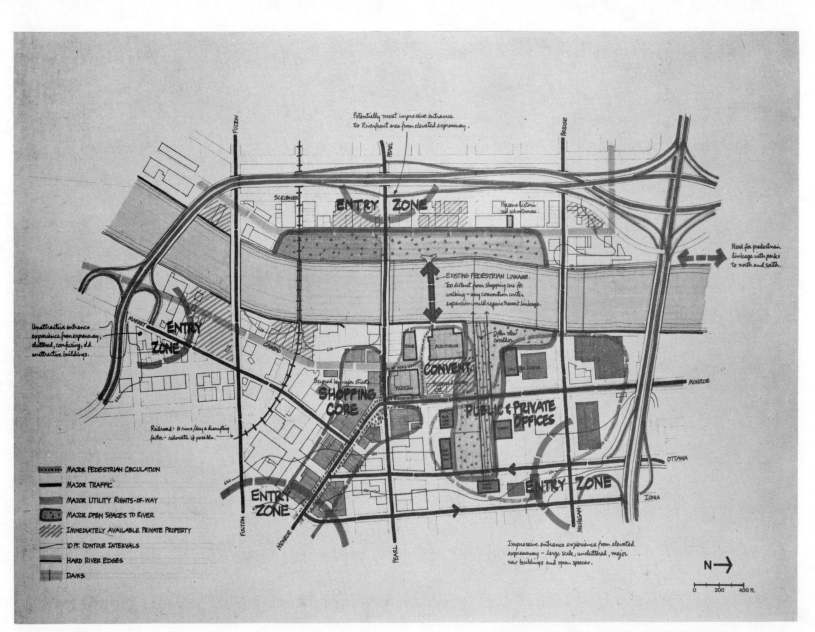

Potentially most impressive entrance
to Riverfront area from elevated expressway.

ENTRY ZONE

Preserve historic
rail schoolhouse.

Need for pedestrian
linkage with parks
to north and south.

EXISTING PEDESTRIAN LINKAGE.
Too distant from shopping core for
walking — any convention center
expansion would require transit linkage.

Open view
corridor.

Unattractive entrance
experience from expressway,
cluttered, confusing, old
unattractive buildings.

ENTRY ZONE

CONVENT.

AUDITORIUM

Severed by major streets

SHOPPING CORE

PUBLIC & PRIVATE OFFICES

MONROE

Railroad: 8 runs/day a disrupting
factor — relocate if possible.

OTTAWA

IONIA

ENTRY ZONE

ENTRY ZONE

- - - - - MAJOR PEDESTRIAN CIRCULATION
━━━━━ MAJOR TRAFFIC
▨▨▨▨ MAJOR UTILITY RIGHTS-OF-WAY
▦▦▦▦ MAJOR OPEN SPACES TO RIVER
▨▨▨▨ IMMEDIATELY AVAILABLE PRIVATE PROPERTY
〜〜〜 10 FT. CONTOUR INTERVALS
━━━━━ HARD RIVER EDGES
▥▥▥▥ DAMS

Impressive entrance experience from elevated
expressway — large scale, uncluttered, major
new buildings and open spaces.

N →

0   200   400 ft.

Site Analysis, Grand Rapids Riverfront. Johnson,
Johnson & Roy, Inc. Felt-tip marker on sepia.

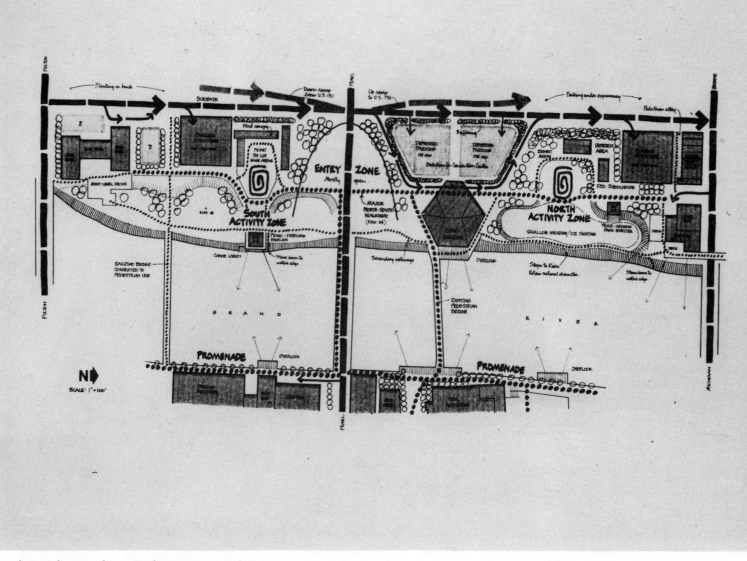

Grand Rapids Riverfront Park Concept. Johnson,
Johnson & Roy, Inc. Felt-tip marker and pencil on vellum.

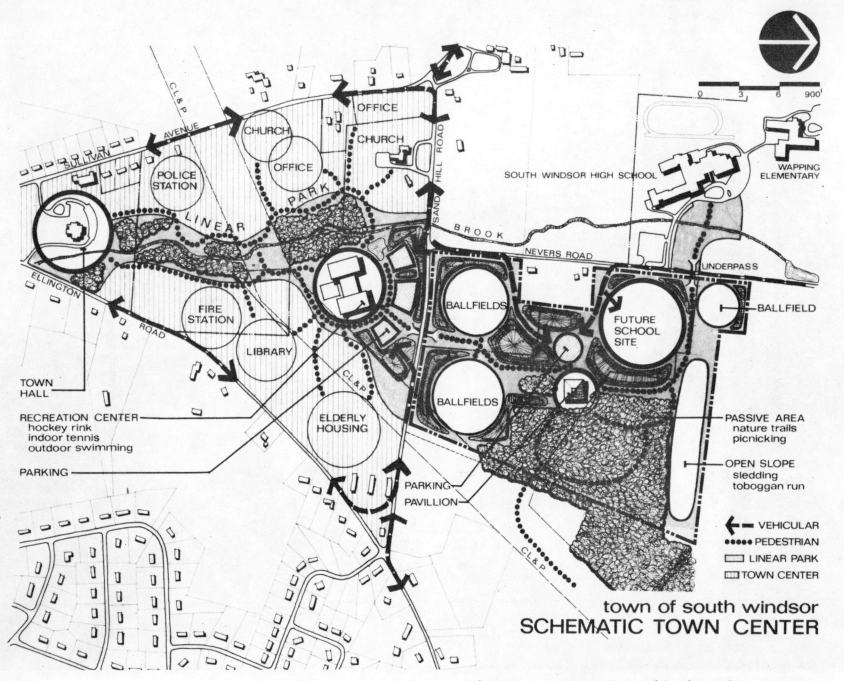

OFFICE

CHURCH

CHURCH

OFFICE

SOUTH WINDSOR HIGH SCHOOL

WAPPING
ELEMENTARY

POLICE
STATION

AVENUE

SULLIVAN

CL&P

PARK

SAND HILL ROAD

LINEAR

BROOK

NEVERS ROAD

UNDERPASS

ELLINGTON

ROAD

FIRE
STATION

BALLFIELDS

FUTURE
SCHOOL
SITE

BALLFIELD

LIBRARY

CL&P

TOWN
HALL

RECREATION CENTER
hockey rink
indoor tennis
outdoor swimming

PARKING

ELDERLY
HOUSING

BALLFIELDS

PASSIVE AREA
nature trails
picnicking

OPEN SLOPE
sledding
toboggan run

PARKING
PAVILLION

CL&P

VEHICULAR
PEDESTRIAN
LINEAR PARK
TOWN CENTER

town of south windsor
SCHEMATIC TOWN CENTER

Schematic town center, Town of South Windsor. CR3, Inc.,
by Jeffrey A. Gebrian. Client: Gregory Louis Montana, Architect.

44

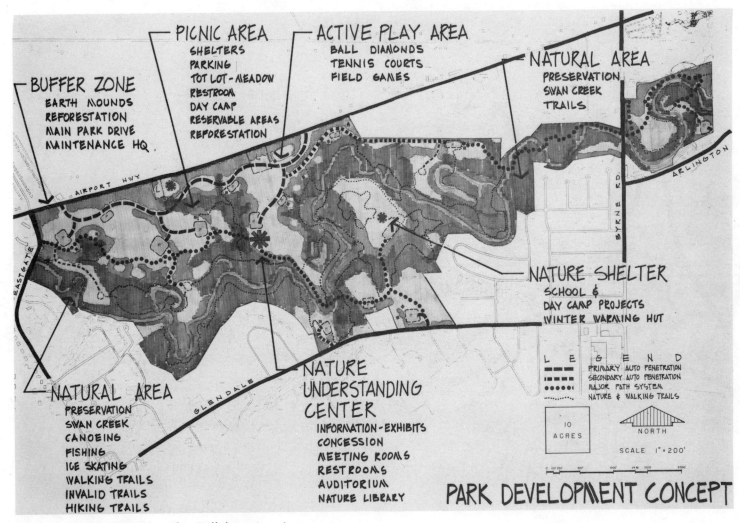

PICNIC AREA
SHELTERS
PARKING
TOT LOT - MEADOW
RESTROOM
DAY CAMP
RESERVABLE AREAS
REFORESTATION

ACTIVE PLAY AREA
BALL DIAMONDS
TENNIS COURTS
FIELD GAMES

NATURAL AREA
PRESERVATION
SWAN CREEK
TRAILS

BUFFER ZONE
EARTH MOUNDS
REFORESTATION
MAIN PARK DRIVE
MAINTENANCE HQ.

AIRPORT HWY

EASTGATE

NATURE SHELTER
SCHOOL &
DAY CAMP PROJECTS
WINTER WARMING HUT

BYRNE RD

ARLINGTON

NATURAL AREA
PRESERVATION
SWAN CREEK
CANOEING
FISHING
ICE SKATING
WALKING TRAILS
INVALID TRAILS
HIKING TRAILS

GLENDALE

NATURE
UNDERSTANDING
CENTER
INFORMATION - EXHIBITS
CONCESSION
MEETING ROOMS
RESTROOMS
AUDITORIUM
NATURE LIBRARY

L E G E N D
PRIMARY AUTO PENETRATION
SECONDARY AUTO PENETRATION
MAJOR PATH SYSTEM
NATURE & WALKING TRAILS

10
ACRES

NORTH

SCALE 1"=200'

PARK DEVELOPMENT CONCEPT

Swan Creek Metro Park. The Collaborative, Inc.

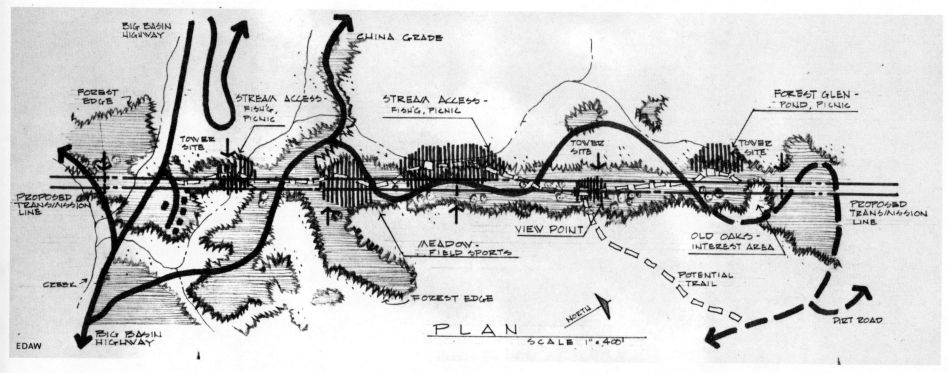

BIG BASIN
HIGHWAY

CHINA GRADE

FOREST
EDGE

STREAM ACCESS-
FISH'G,
PICNIC

STREAM ACCESS-
FISH'G, PICNIC

FOREST GLEN -
POND, PICNIC

TOWER
SITE

TOWER
SITE

TOWER
SITE

PROPOSED
TRANSMISSION
LINE

PROPOSED
TRANSMISSION
LINE

VIEW POINT

MEADOW -
FIELD SPORTS

OLD OAKS-
INTEREST AREA

CREEK

POTENTIAL
TRAIL

FOREST EDGE

NORTH

P L A N
SCALE 1"= 400'

DIRT ROAD

BIG BASIN
HIGHWAY

EDAW

Pacific Gas and Electric Co. EDAW, Inc., by Herbert Schaal.

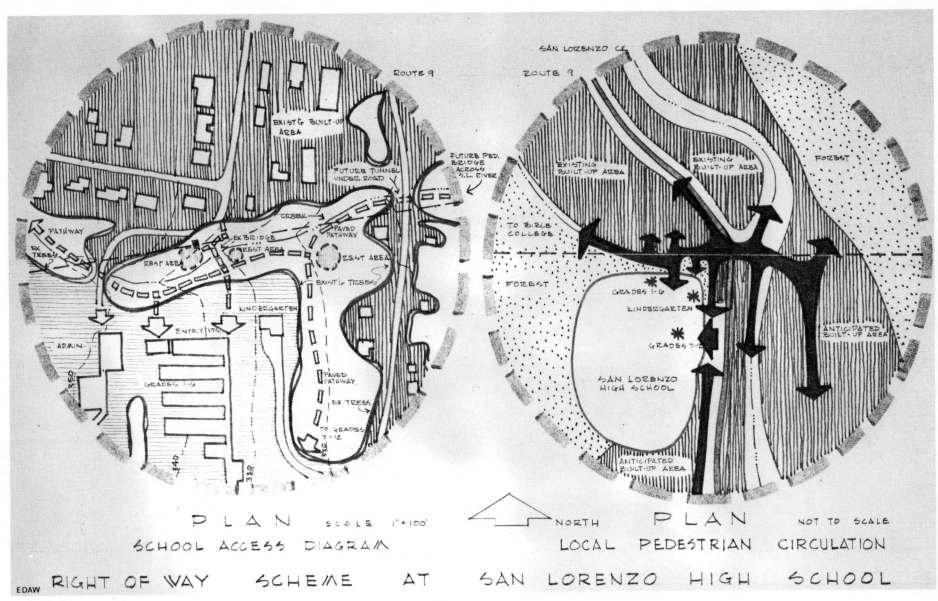

PLAN SCALE 1"=100'

SCHOOL ACCESS DIAGRAM

NORTH PLAN NOT TO SCALE

LOCAL PEDESTRIAN CIRCULATION

RIGHT OF WAY SCHEME AT SAN LORENZO HIGH SCHOOL

EDAW

Pacific Gas and Electric Co. EDAW, Inc., by Herbert Schaal.

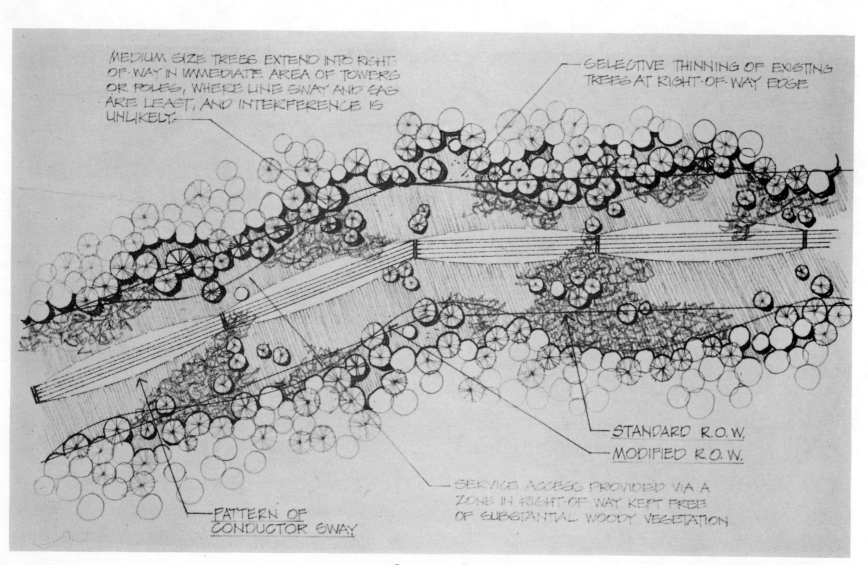

MEDIUM SIZE TREES EXTEND INTO RIGHT-OF-WAY IN IMMEDIATE AREA OF TOWERS OR POLES, WHERE LINE SWAY AND SAG ARE LEAST, AND INTERFERENCE IS UNLIKELY.

SELECTIVE THINNING OF EXISTING TREES AT RIGHT-OF-WAY EDGE

STANDARD R.O.W.
MODIFIED R.O.W.

PATTERN OF CONDUCTOR SWAY

SERVICE ACCESS PROVIDED VIA A ZONE IN RIGHT-OF-WAY KEPT FREE OF SUBSTANTIAL WOODY VEGETATION.

Consumers Power Transmission R.O.W. Study. Johnson, Johnson & Roy, Inc.

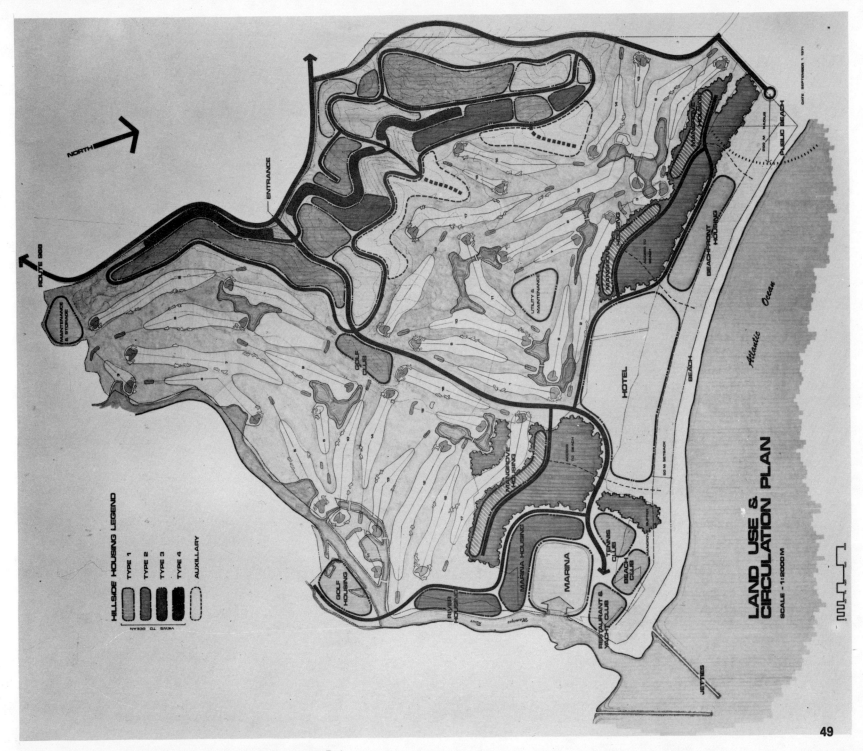

LAND USE & CIRCULATION PLAN

SCALE - 1:12000 M

HILLSIDE HOUSING LEGEND

TYPE 1
TYPE 2
TYPE 3
TYPE 4
AUXILIARY

VIEWS TO OCEAN

NORTH

ROUTE 988

ENTRANCE

MAINTENANCE & STORAGE

UTILITY & MAINTENANCE

GOLF CLUB

MANGROVE HOUSING

MANGROVE HOUSING

BEACHFRONT HOUSING

PUBLIC BEACH

Atlantic Ocean

HOTEL

BEACH

ACCESS TO BEACH

MANGROVE HOUSING

GOLF HOUSING

RIVER HOUSING

MARINA HOUSING

MARINA

RESTAURANT & YACHT CLUB

TENNIS CLUB

BEACH CLUB

JETTIES

49

Palmer Resort. Edward D. Stone, Jr. & Associates, P.A.

MASTER PLANS

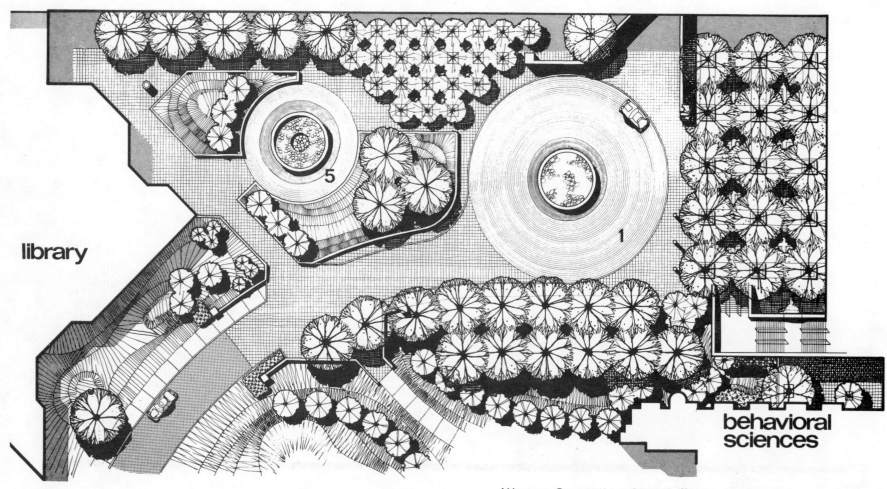

library

5

1

behavioral
sciences

Western Connecticut State College. CR3, Inc., by Kenneth Kay.

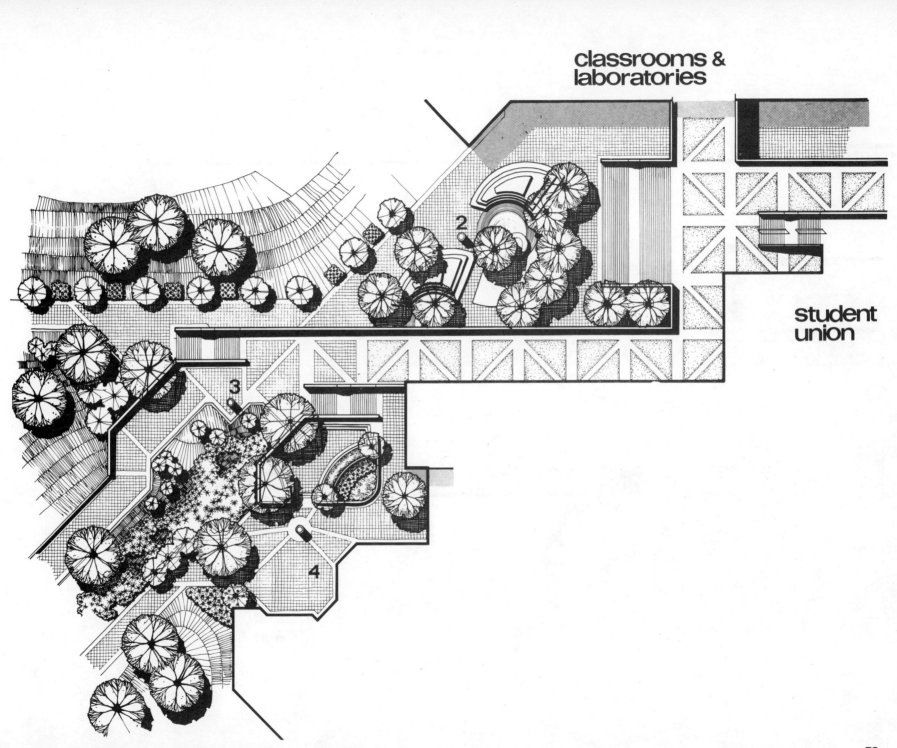

classrooms &
laboratories

student
union

Western Connecticut State College. CR3, Inc., by Kenneth Kay.

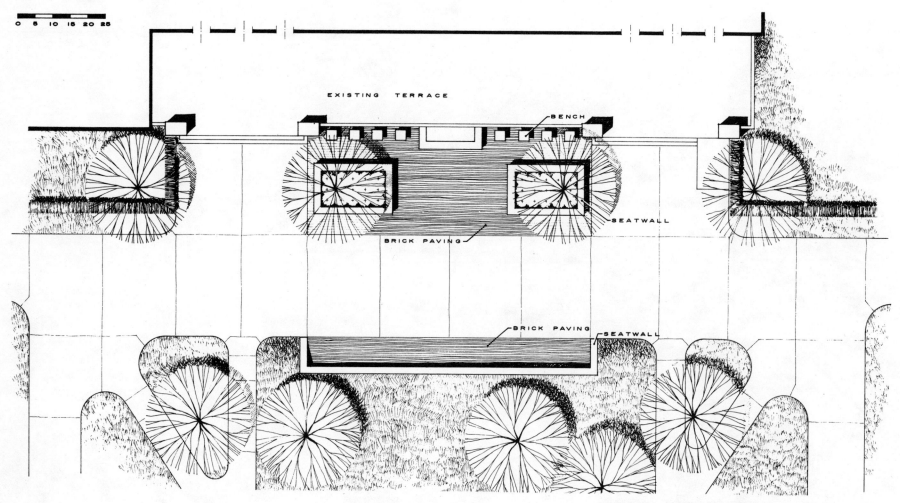

EXISTING TERRACE

BENCH

SEATWALL

BRICK PAVING

BRICK PAVING — SEATWALL

0 5 10 15 20 25

University of Illinois Office for Capital Programs.

54

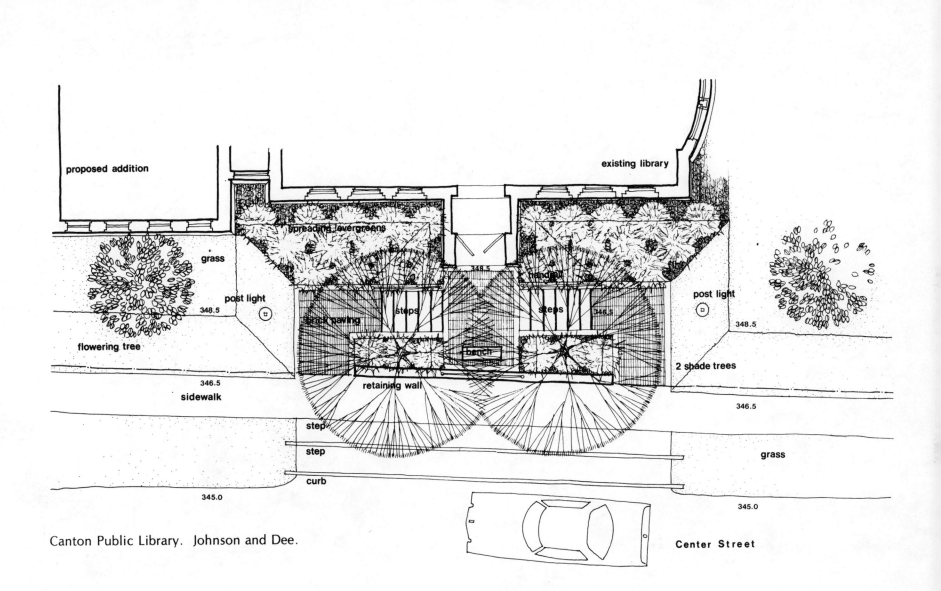

proposed addition

existing library

spreading evergreens

grass

348.5

post light

348.5

post light

flowering tree

steps

steps

handrail

346.5

2 shade trees

348.5

346.5

brick paving

bench

346.5

retaining wall

sidewalk

step

step

grass

curb

345.0

345.0

Canton Public Library.   Johnson and Dee.

Center Street

Site Plan for A. E. Bye's House. A. E. Bye & Associates; by A. E. Bye, Terry Souders, Lawrence Goldberg, Theodore Geraldi. F-lead pencil on vellum.

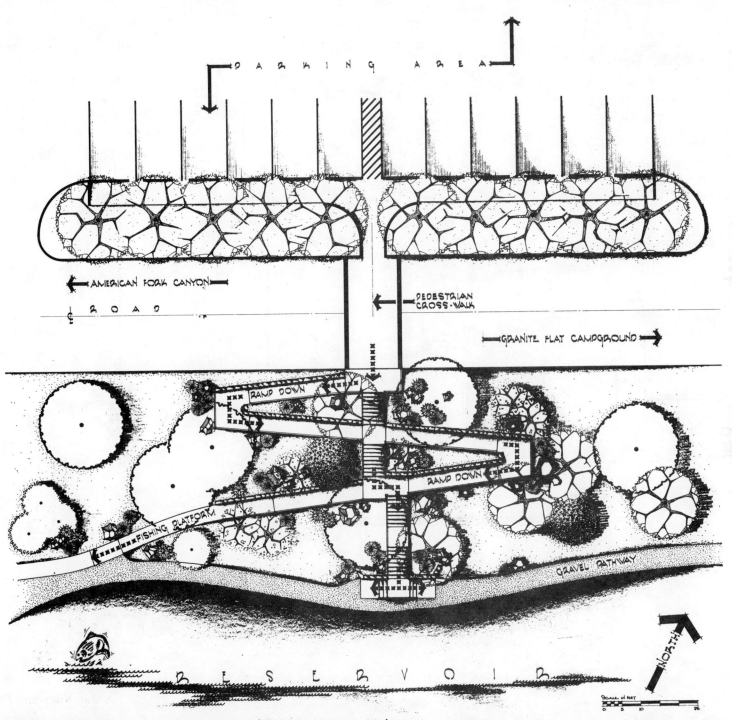

Tibble Fork Reservoir Area, Uinta National Forest. Norman Malone.

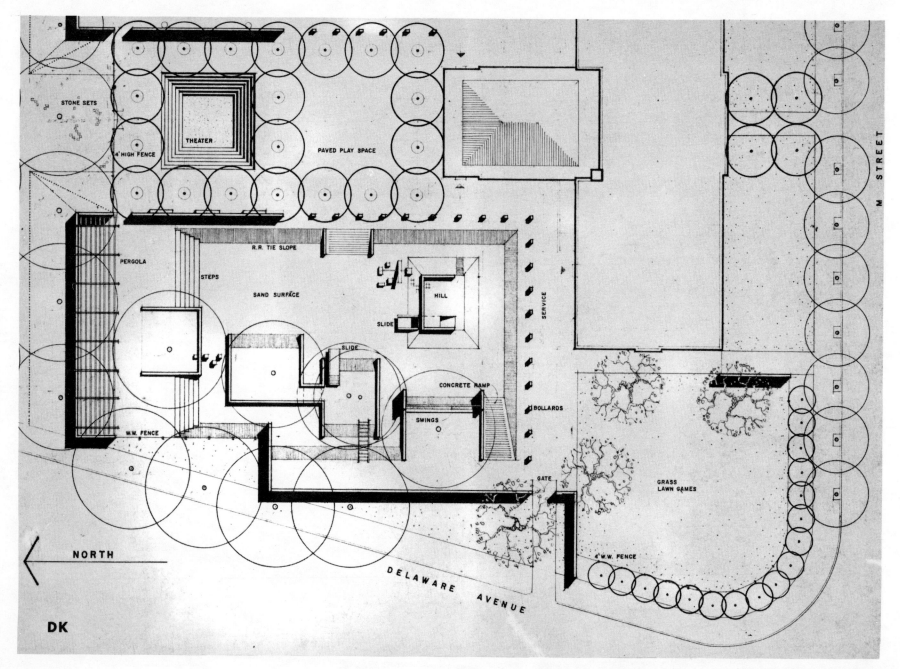

STONE SETS

4' HIGH FENCE

THEATER

PAVED PLAY SPACE

PERGOLA

R.R. TIE SLOPE

STEPS

SAND SURFACE

HILL

SLIDE

SLIDE

W.W. FENCE

CONCRETE RAMP

SWINGS

SERVICE

BOLLARDS

GATE

GRASS
LAWN GAMES

4' W.W. FENCE

NORTH

DELAWARE AVENUE

M STREET

DK

Dan Kiley and Partners.

58

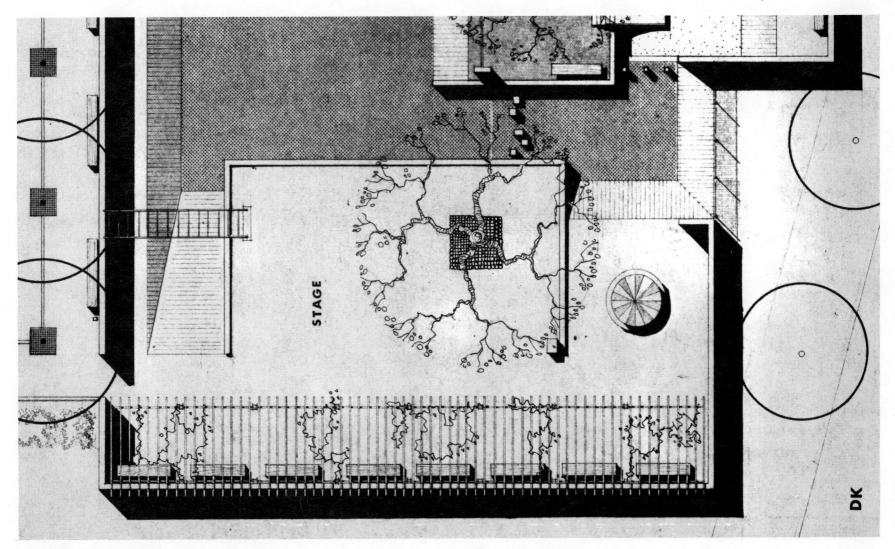

STAGE

DK

Dan Kiley and Partners.

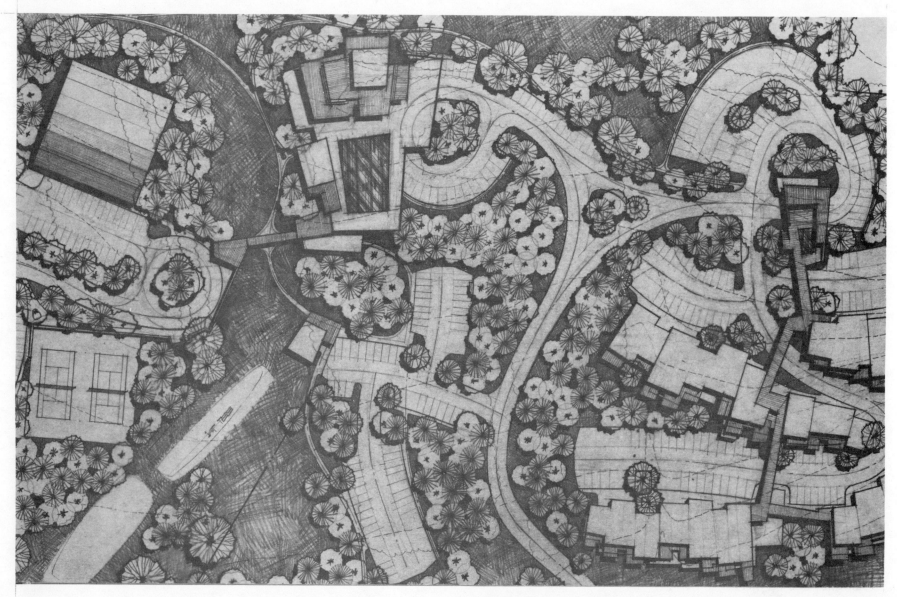

Bristol Harbour. The Reimann-Buechner Partnership by Cortland Read.

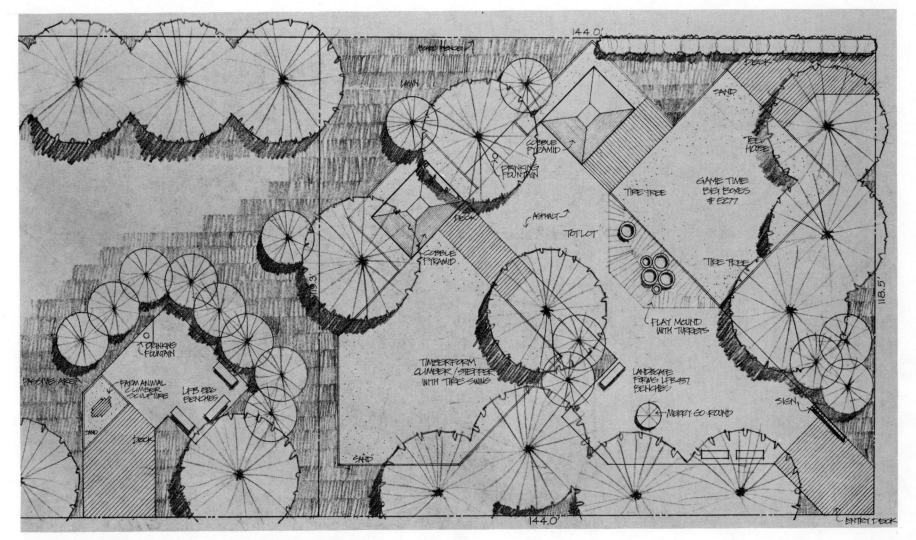

East Chicago Parks. Perkins & Will, Inc., by David Linstrum.

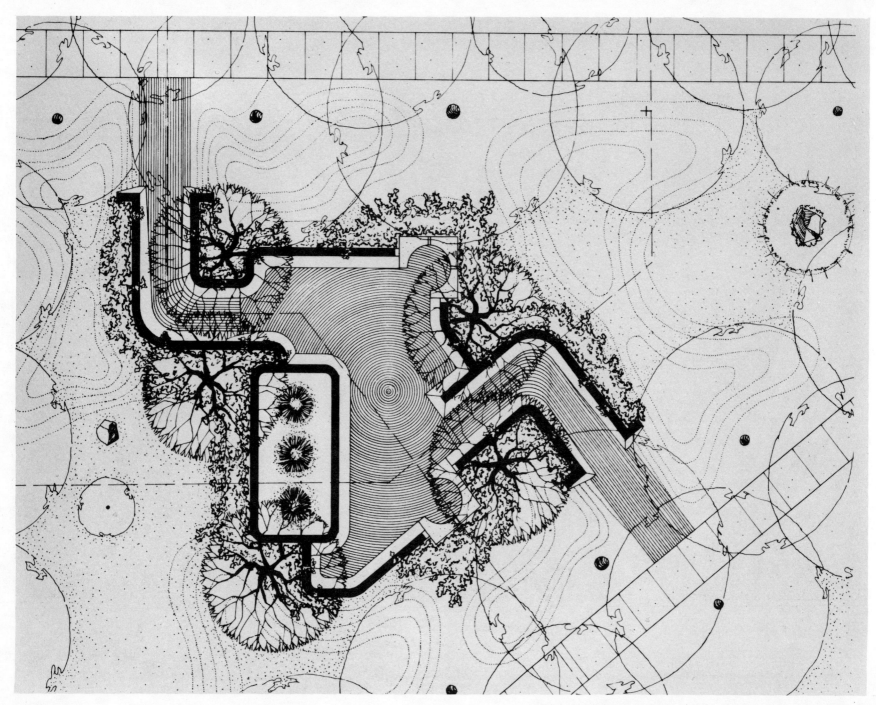

62

Dauch Memorial Park. William A. Behnke Associates.
James H. Ness, Associated Landscape Architect.

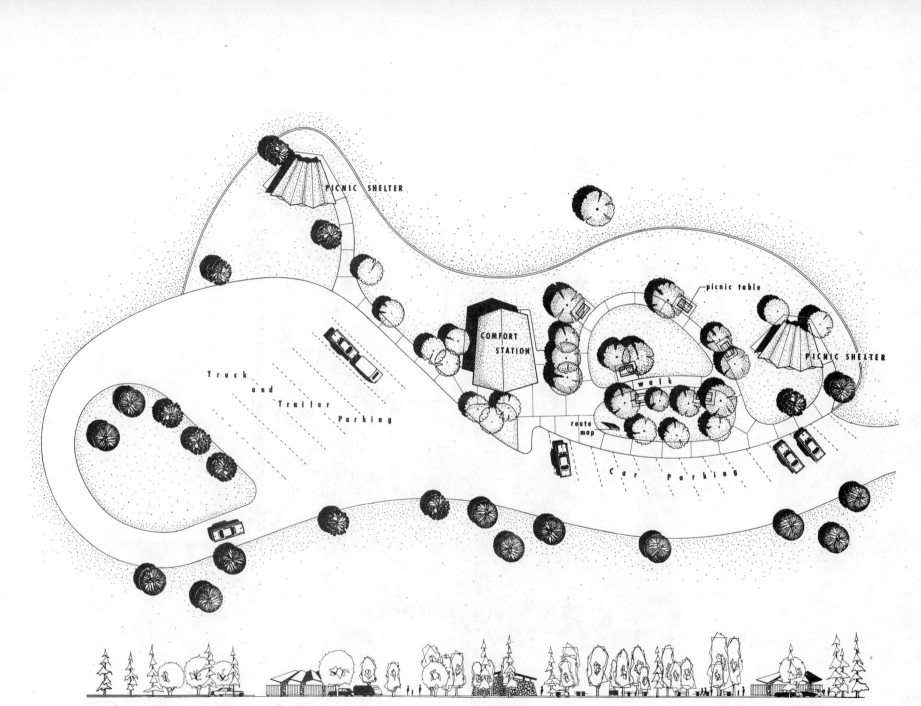

PICNIC SHELTER

Truck and Trailer Parking

COMFORT STATION

picnic table

PICNIC SHELTER

walk

route map

Car Parking

California Department of Transportation.

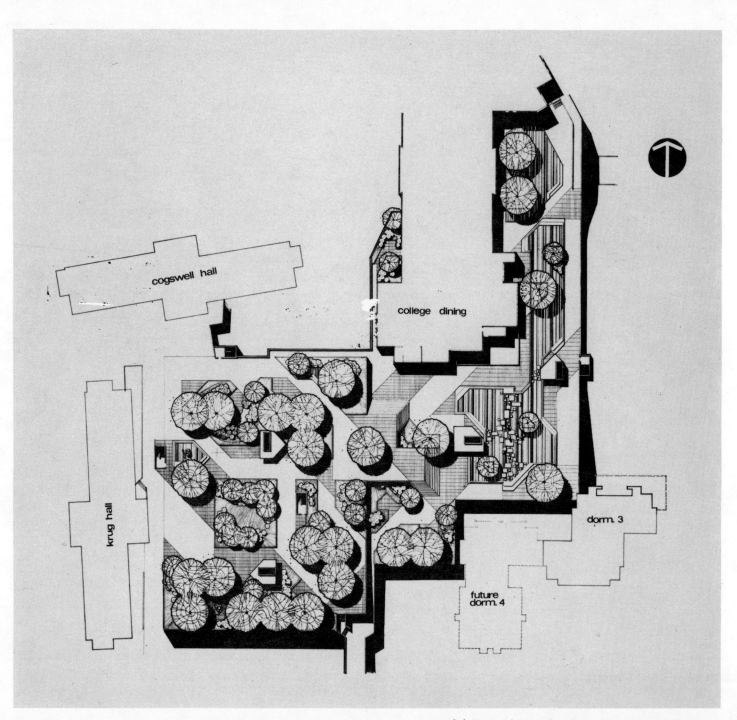

cogswell hall

college dining

krug hall

dorm. 3

future
dorm. 4

Model Secondary School for the Deaf. CR3, Inc.
Client: Hudgins, Thompson & Ball, Architects.

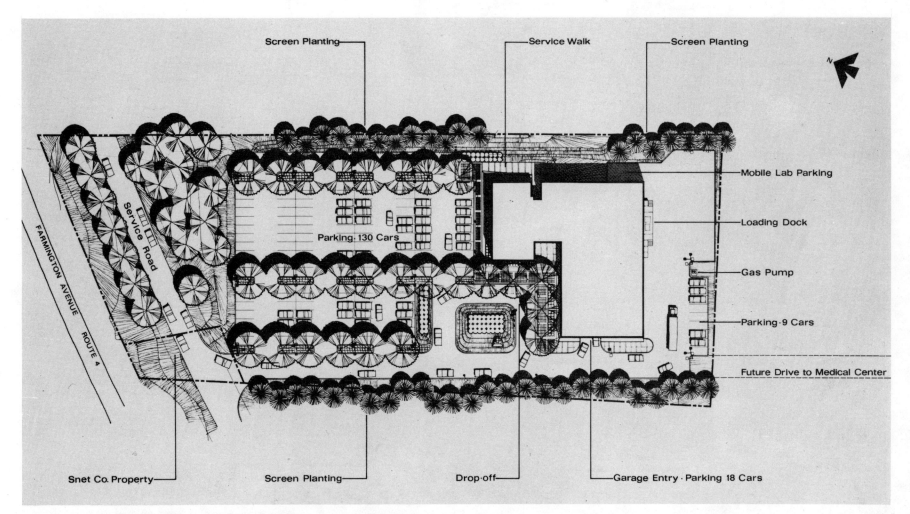

Screen Planting — Service Walk — Screen Planting

Mobile Lab Parking

Loading Dock

Gas Pump

Parking · 9 Cars

Future Drive to Medical Center

Service Road

FARMINGTON AVENUE ROUTE 4

Parking 130 Cars

Snet Co. Property — Screen Planting — Drop·off — Garage Entry · Parking 18 Cars

American Red Cross Northeast Regional Headquarters. CR3, Inc.,
by Jeffrey A. Gebrian. Client: Hirsch, Kaestle Boos, Architects.

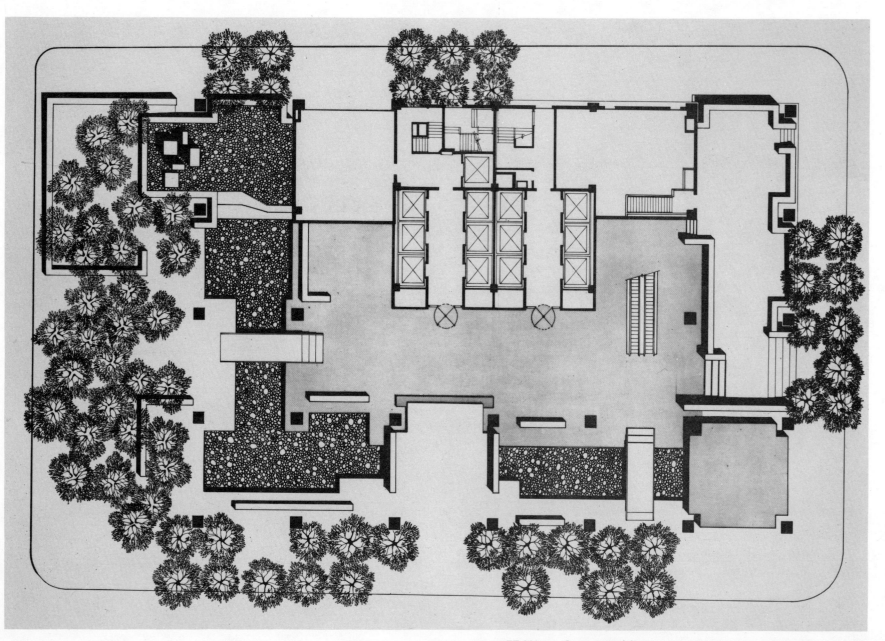

77 Water Street Building; A. E. Bye & Associates by Jane
McGuinness. Architect: Emery Roth & Sons. Ink on mylar.

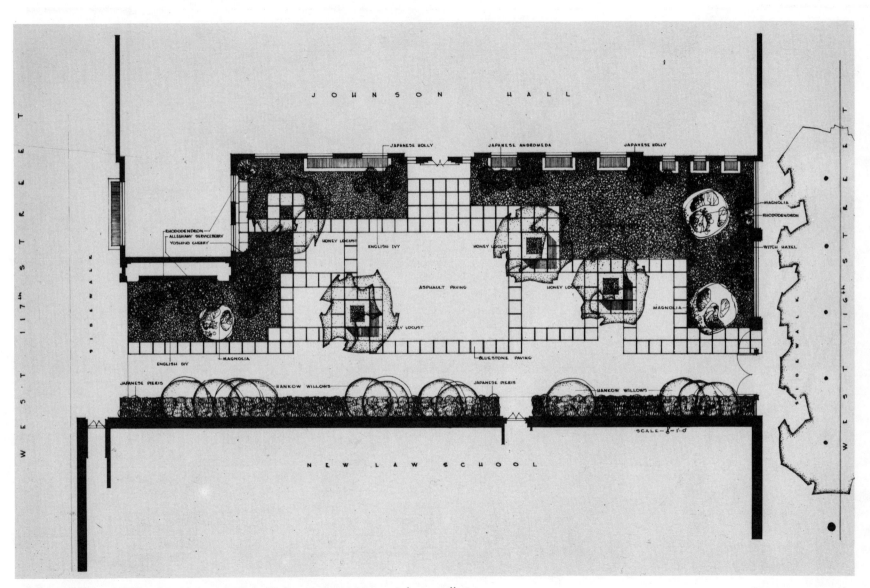

JOHNSON HALL

JAPANESE HOLLY   JAPANESE ANDROMEDA   JAPANESE HOLLY

MAGNOLIA
RHODODENDRON

RHODODENDRON
ALLEGHANY SERVICEBERRY
YOSHINO CHERRY

HONEY LOCUST   ENGLISH IVY   HONEY LOCUST

WITCH HAZEL

ASPHAULT PAVING   HONEY LOCUST

LY LOCUST

MAGNOLIA

ENGLISH IVY   MAGNOLIA   BLUESTONE PAVING

JAPANESE PIERIS   HANKOW WILLOWS   JAPANESE PIERIS   HANKOW WILLOWS

SCALE - ⅛-1'-0

NEW LAW SCHOOL

WEST 117th STREET

WEST 116th STREET

Sulzburger Plaza, Columbia University. A. E. Bye & Associates. Ink on vellum.

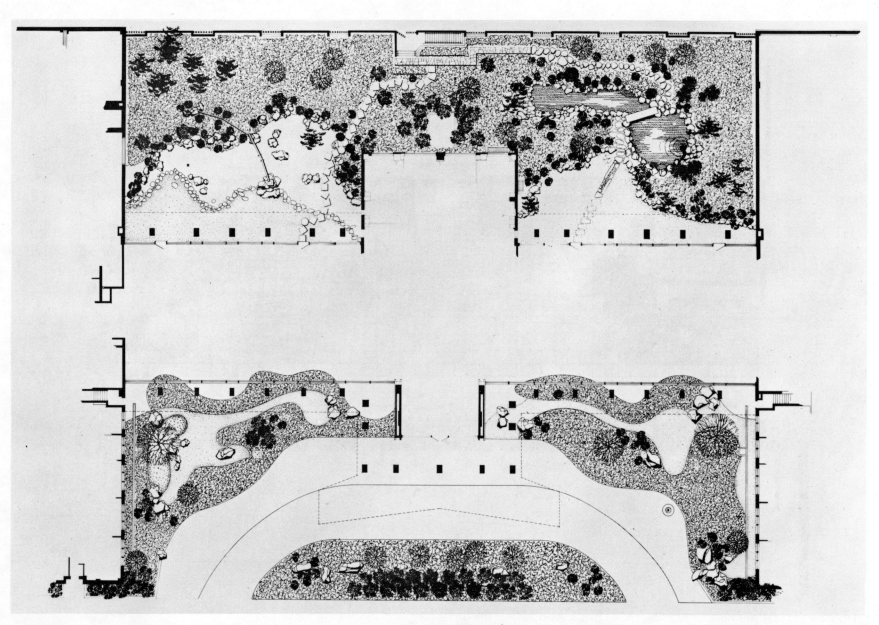

Imperial House. A. E. Bye & Associates by A. E. Bye. Ink on mylar.

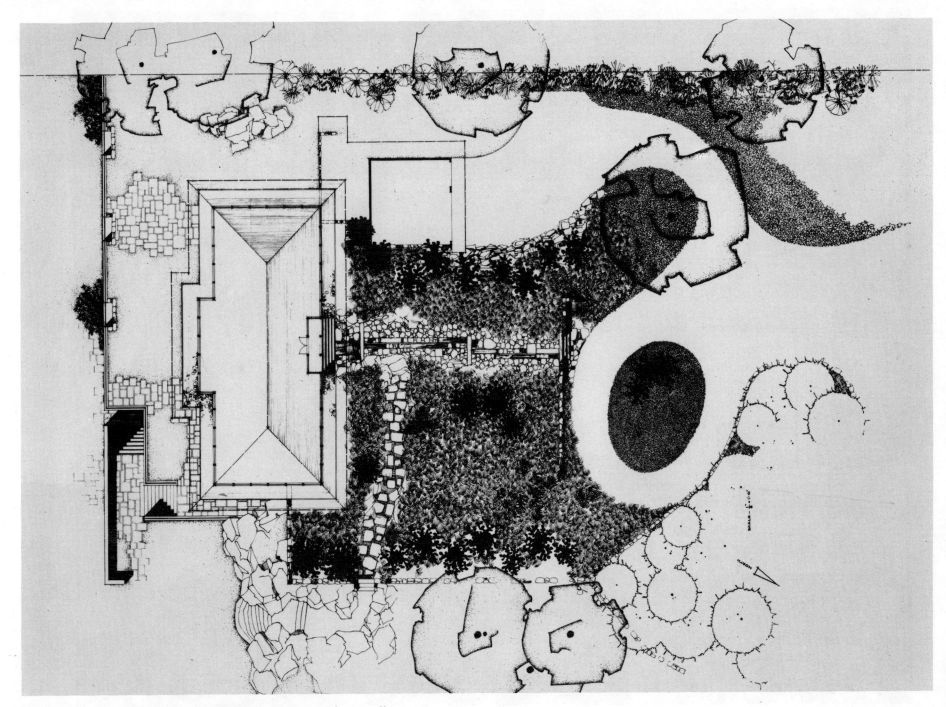

Residence. A. E. Bye & Associates by A. E. Bye. Ink on vellum.

RESIDENCE

70

Residence. A. E. Bye & Associates by Neal Bastable. Ink on mylar.

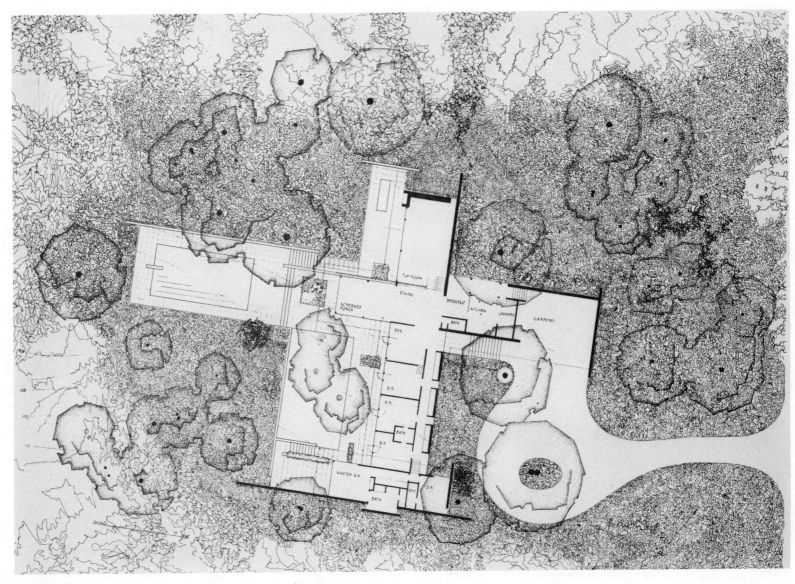

Residence. A. E. Bye & Associates. Ink on vellum.

Residence. A. E. Bye & Associates by A. E. Bye. Ink on vellum.

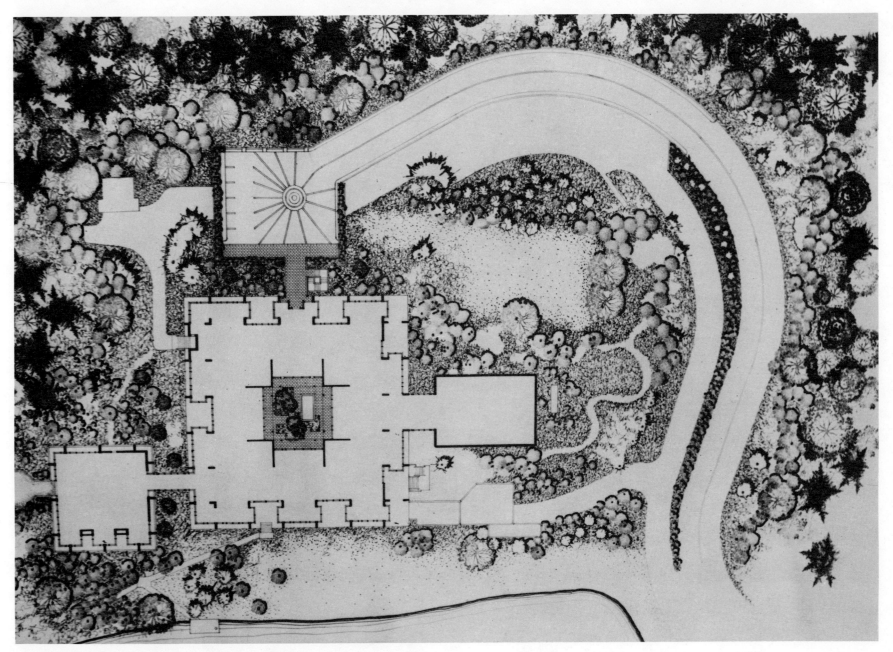

Harvey Hubbell Corporate Headquarters. A. E. Bye & Associates by
Lawrence Goldberg. Architect: Bruce Campbell Graham. Ink on vellum.

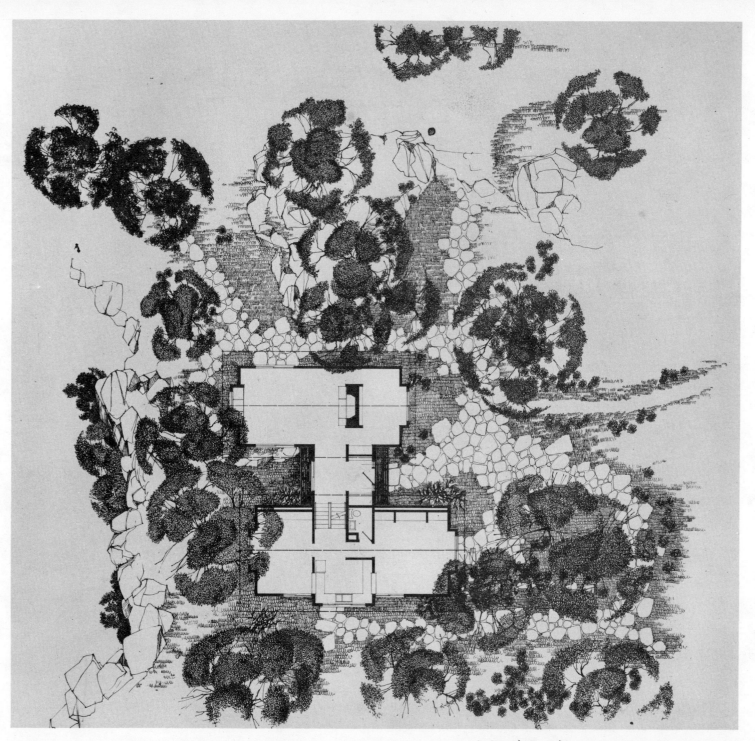

Leitzsch Residence. A. E. Bye & Associates
by James Balsley. Ink on vellum.

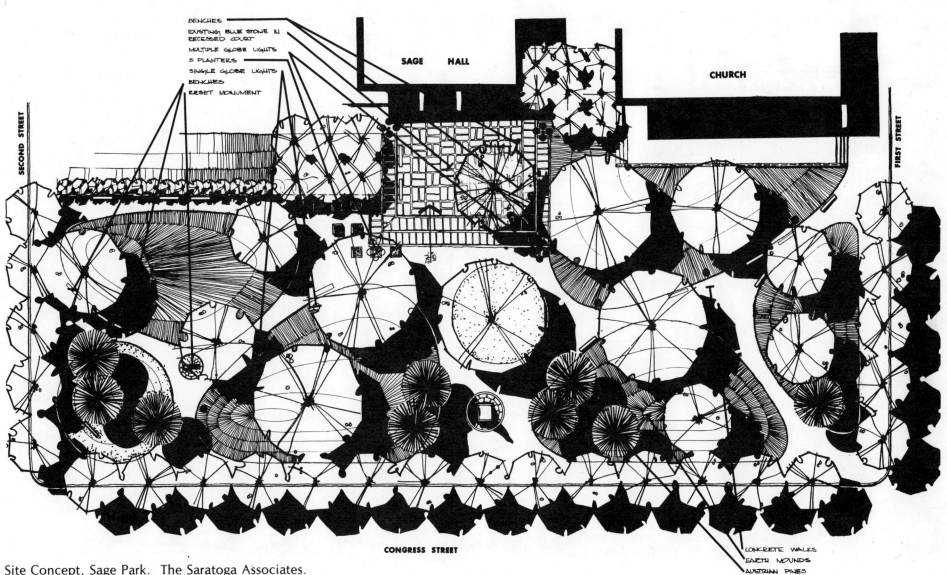

BENCHES
EXISTING BLUE STONE IN RECESSED COURT
MULTIPLE GLOBE LIGHTS
5 PLANTERS
SINGLE GLOBE LIGHTS
BENCHES
RESET MONUMENT

SAGE HALL

CHURCH

SECOND STREET

FIRST STREET

CONGRESS STREET

CONCRETE WALKS
EARTH MOUNDS
AUSTRIAN PINES

Site Concept, Sage Park. The Saratoga Associates.

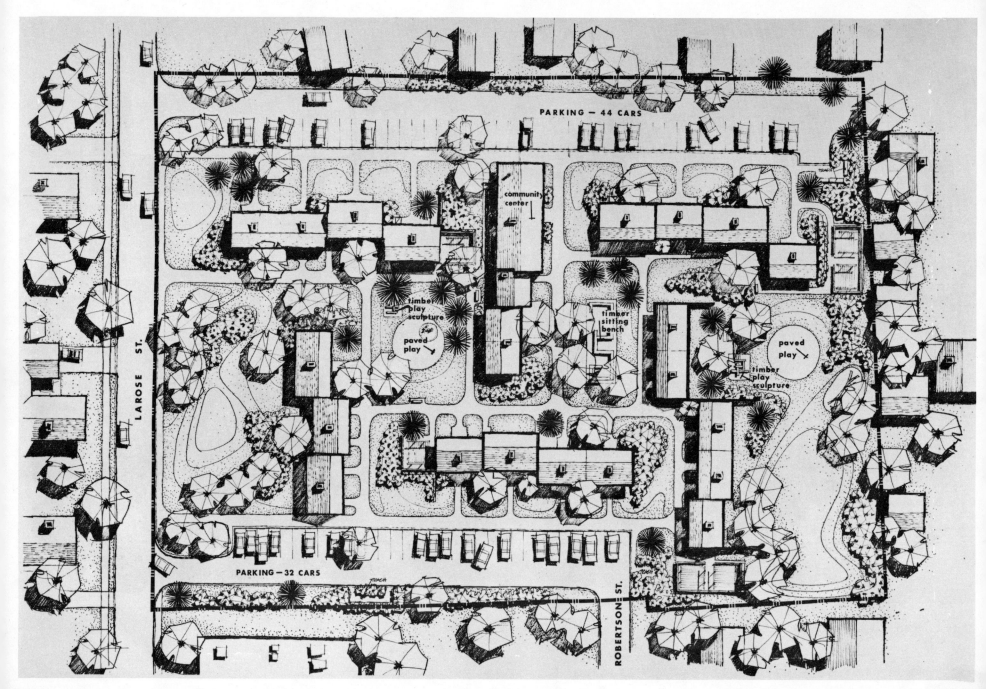

PARKING — 44 CARS

LAROSE ST.

community center

timber play sculpture

paved play

timber sitting bench

paved play

timber play sculpture

PARKING — 32 CARS

ROBERTSON ST.

Larose Gardens. The Saratoga Associates.

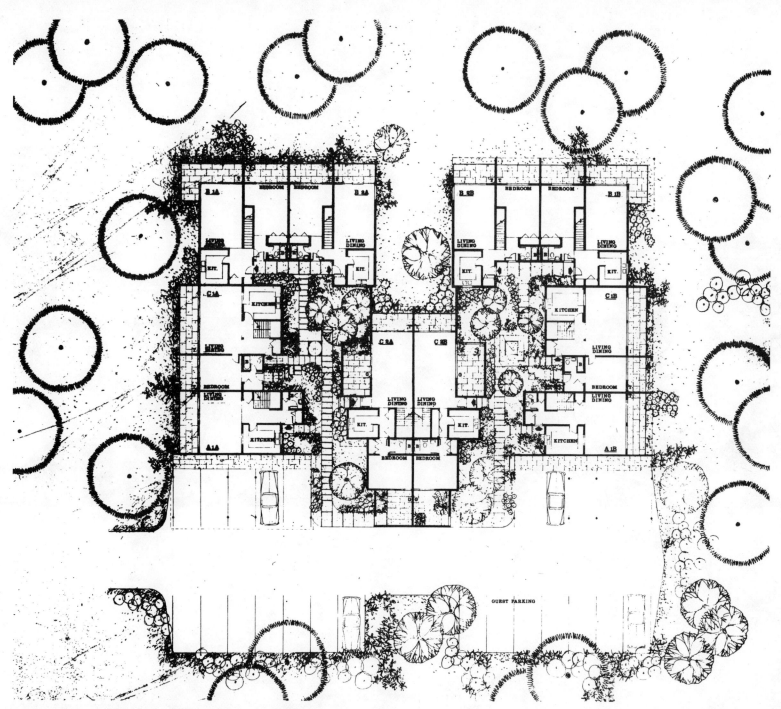

Quail Ridge Townhouse. Sasaki, Dawson, DeMay
Associates, Inc., by Philip Minervine.

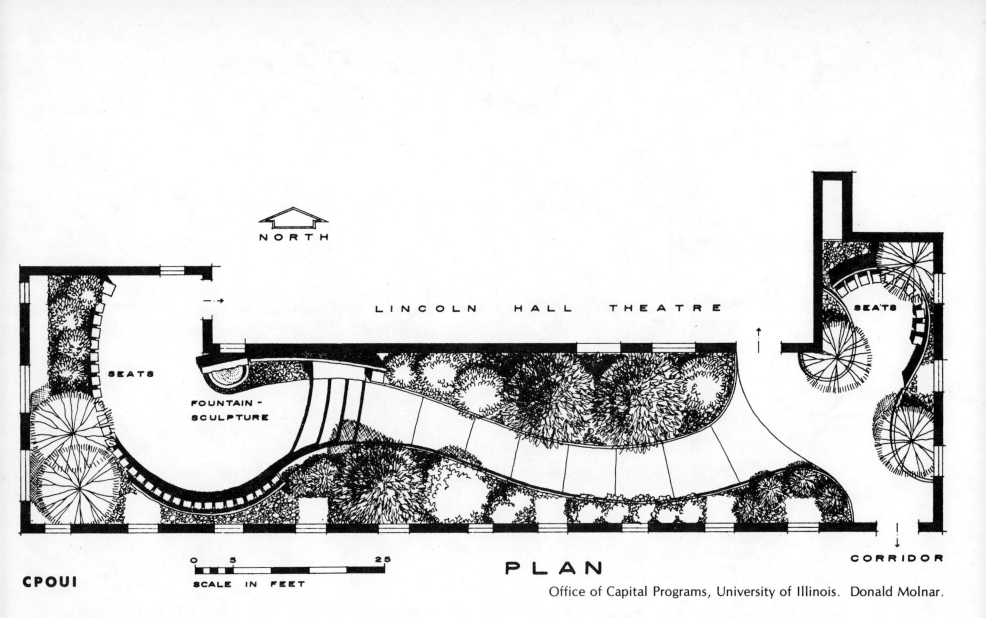

NORTH

LINCOLN HALL THEATRE

SEATS

FOUNTAIN-
SCULPTURE

SEATS

CORRIDOR

0   5   25
SCALE IN FEET

PLAN

Office of Capital Programs, University of Illinois. Donald Molnar.

CPOUI

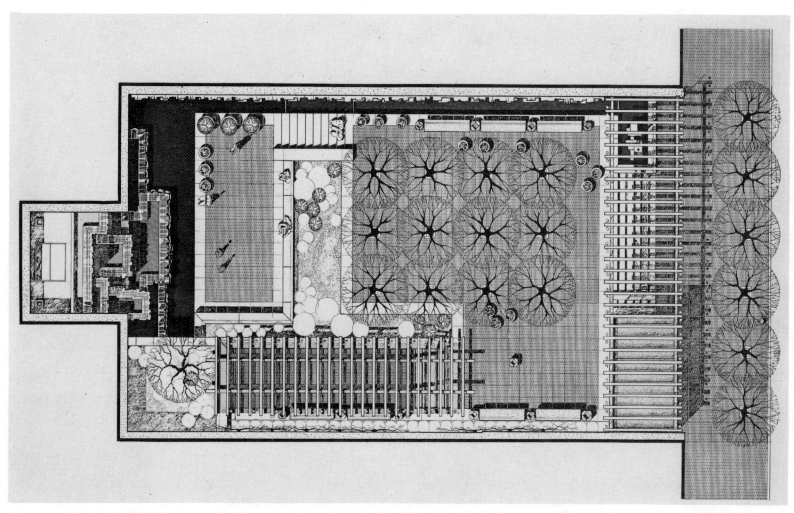

Greenacre Park. Sasaki, Dawson, DeMay Associates, Inc., by Ron Wortman.

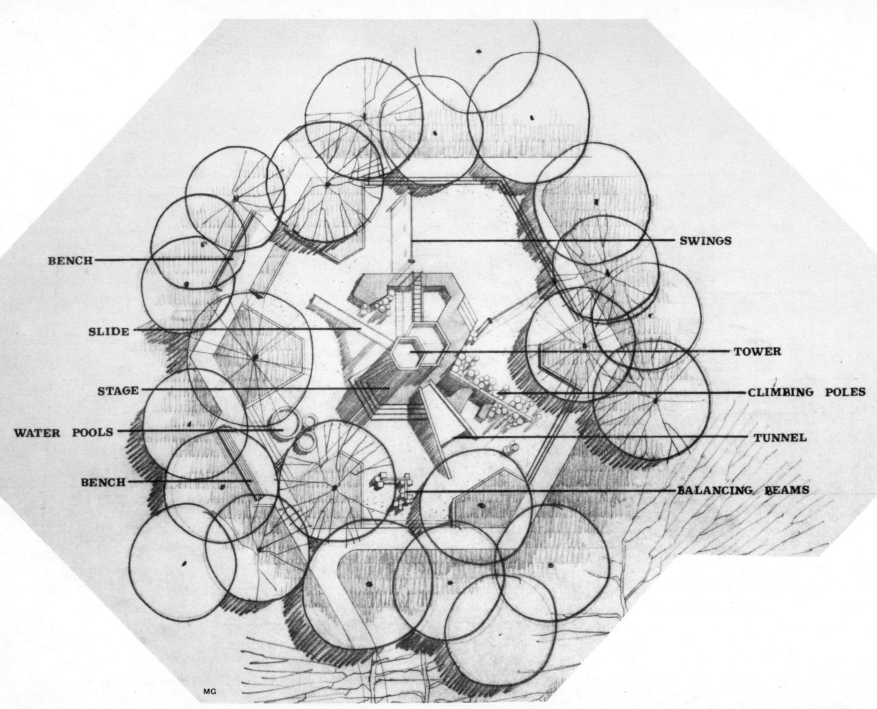

BENCH

SWINGS

SLIDE

TOWER

STAGE

CLIMBING POLES

WATER POOLS

TUNNEL

BENCH

BALANCING BEAMS

MG

Maas and Grassli.

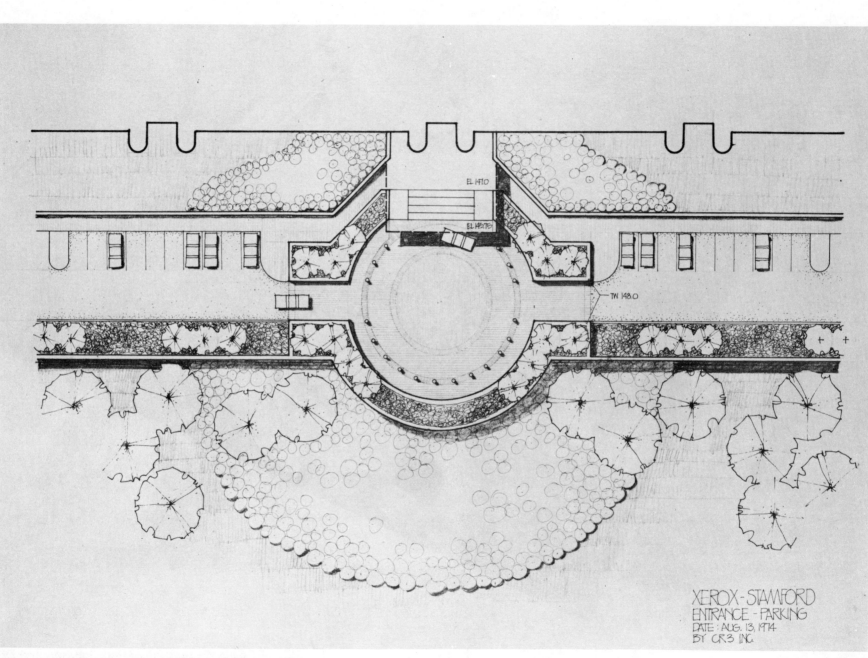

Xerox — Stamford entrance parking. CR3, Inc., by
Carl Mueller. Client: Perkins & Will, Architects.

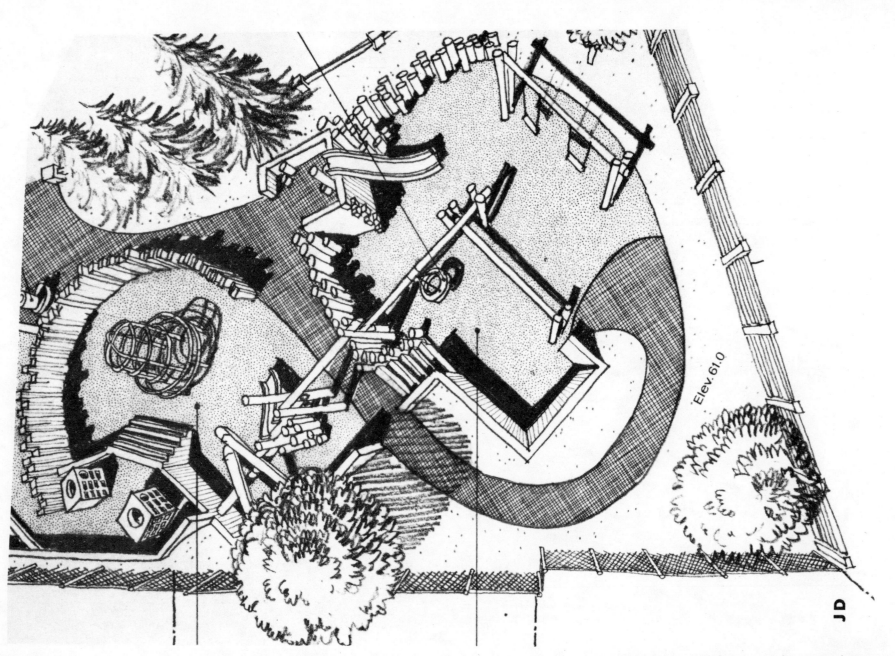

Elev. 61.0

JD

Nelton Court Play Area. Johnson and Dee.

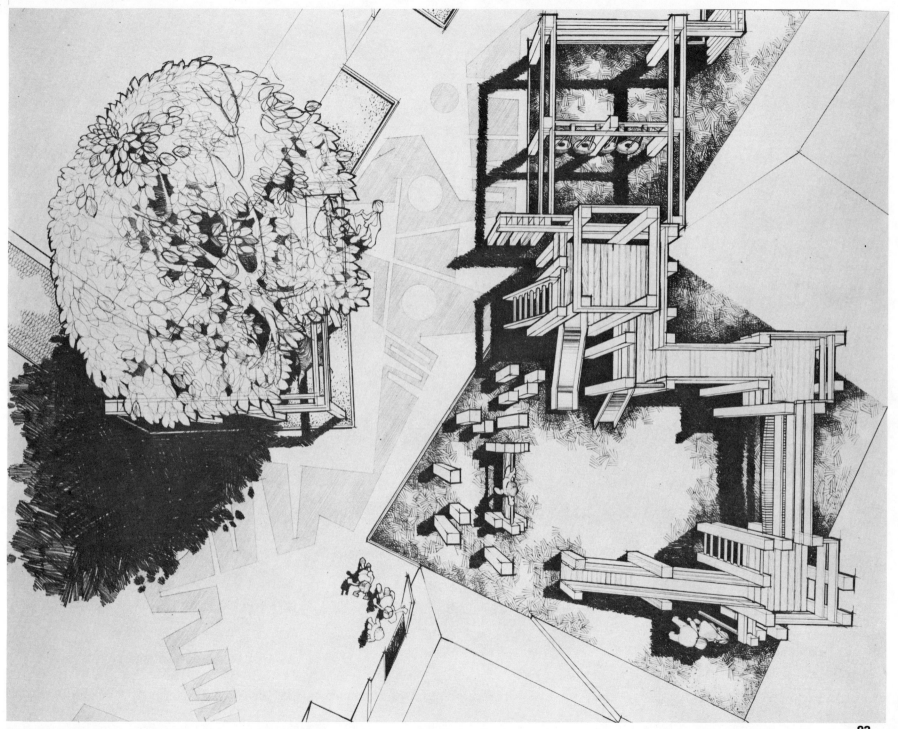

The Reimann-Buechner Partnership by Cortland Read.

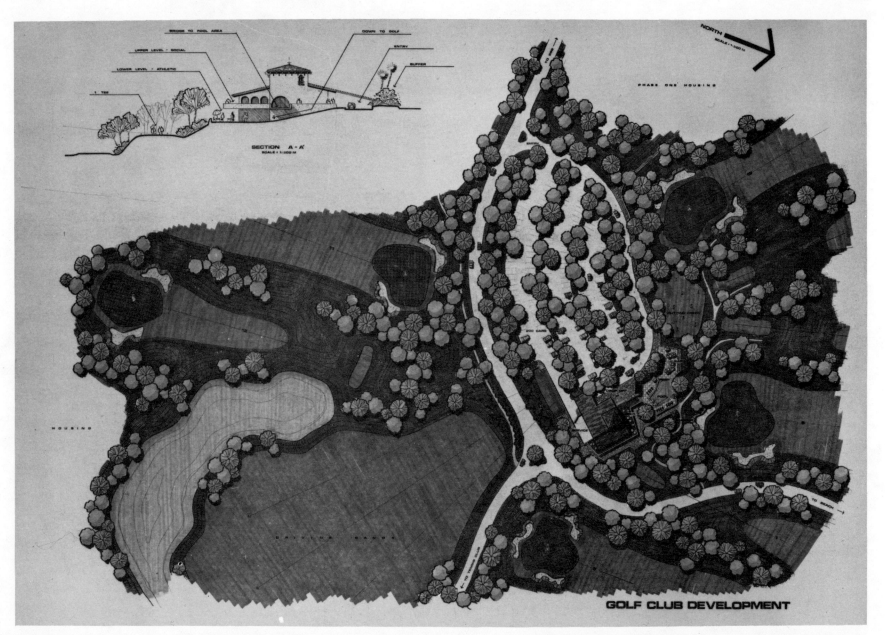

SECTION A-A'
SCALE : 1:200 M

GOLF CLUB DEVELOPMENT

Palmer Resort.   Edward D. Stone, Jr. & Associates, P. A.

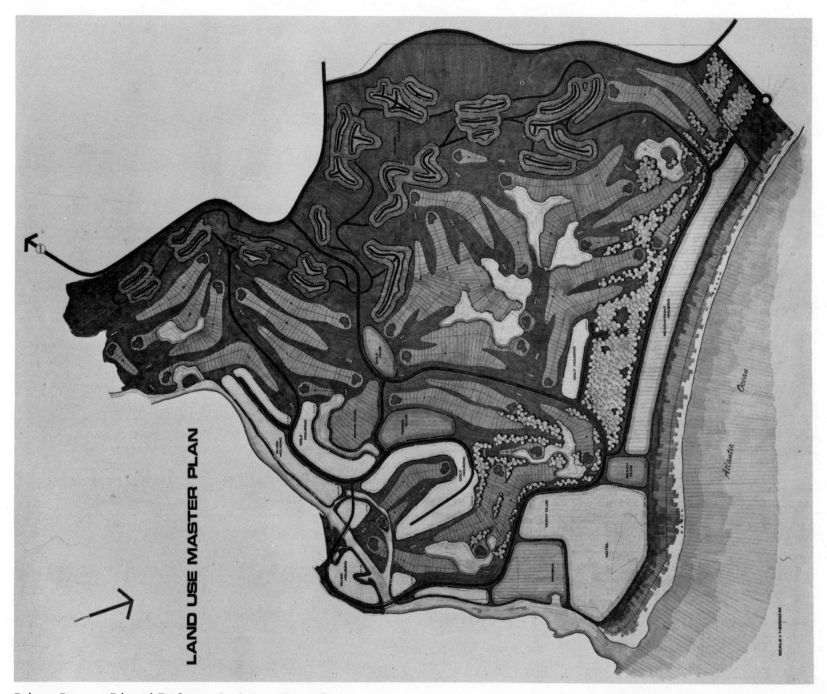

LAND USE MASTER PLAN

Palmer Resort. Edward D. Stone, Jr. & Associates, P. A.

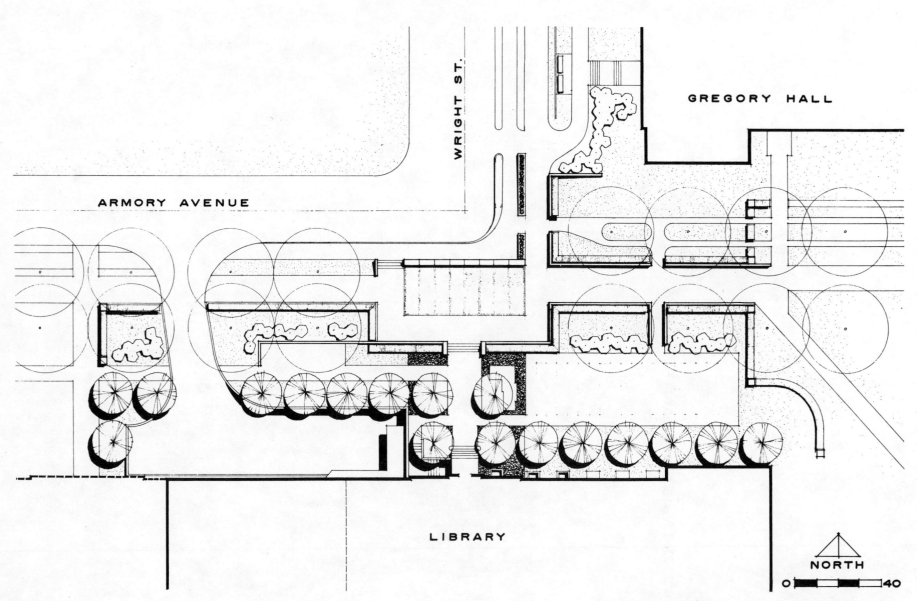

GREGORY HALL

WRIGHT ST.

ARMORY AVENUE

LIBRARY

NORTH

0 ◼◻◼◻◼ 40

University of Illinois Office for Capital Programs.

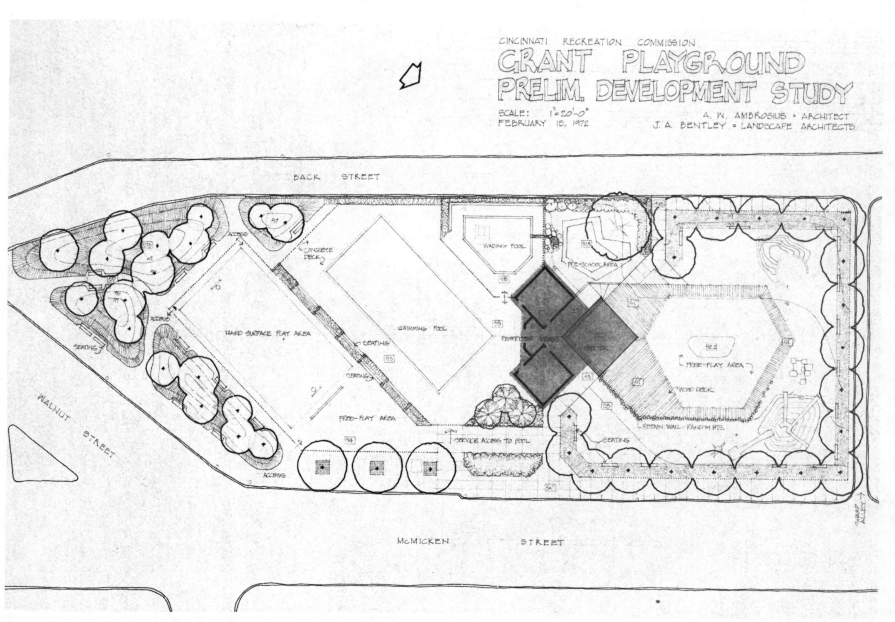

CINCINNATI RECREATION COMMISSION
GRANT PLAYGROUND
PRELIM. DEVELOPMENT STUDY
SCALE: 1"=20'-0"
FEBRUARY 15, 1972

A. W. AMBROSIUS · ARCHITECT
J. A. BENTLEY · LANDSCAPE ARCHITECTS

BACK STREET

WALNUT STREET

ACCESS

CONCRETE DECK

SEATING

HARD SURFACE PLAY AREA

SWIMMING POOL

SEATING

SEATING

FREE-PLAY AREA

ACCESS

SERVICE ACCESS TO POOL

WADING POOL

PRE-SCHOOL AREA

PERGOLA AREA

SHELTER

WOOD DECK

FREE-PLAY AREA

SEATING

RETAIN. WALL-RANDOM HTS.

SHARP ALLEY

McMICKEN STREET

Grant Playground. John A. Bentley. A. W. Ambrosius, Architect.

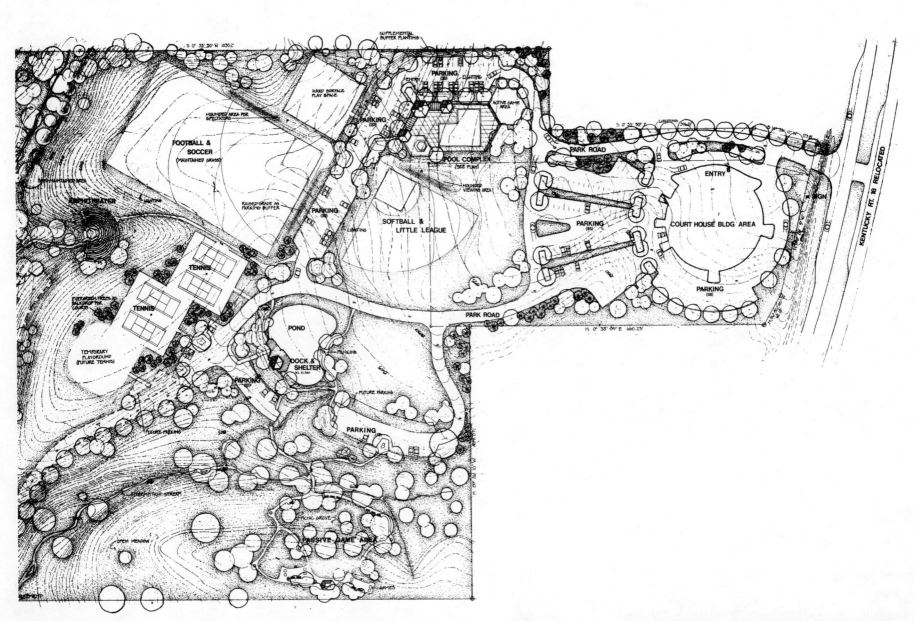

Boone Woods County Park. John A. Bentley.
Robert Ehmet Hayes & Associates, Architects.

88

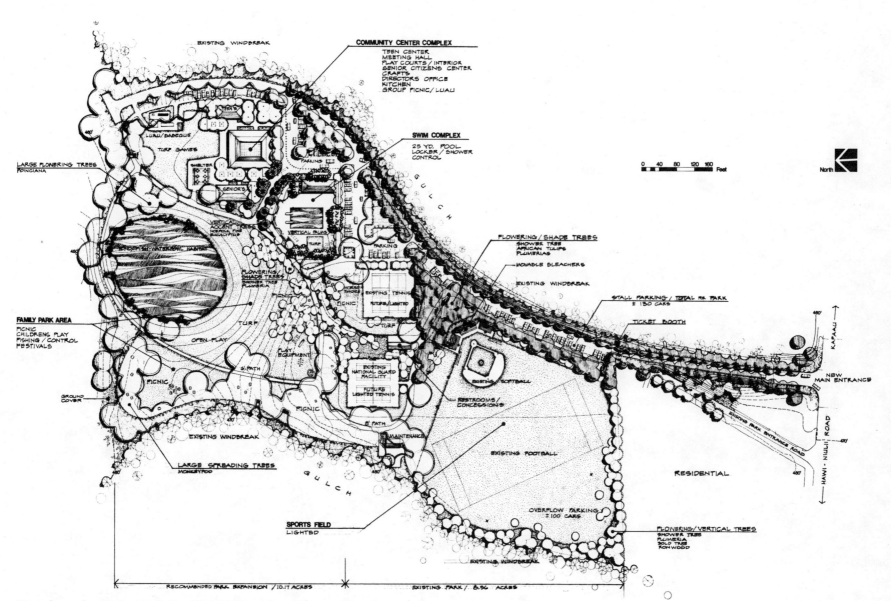

COMMUNITY CENTER COMPLEX
TEEN CENTER
MEETING HALL
PLAY COURTS / INTERIOR
SENIOR CITIZENS CENTER
CRAFTS
DIRECTORS OFFICE
KITCHEN
GROUP PICNIC / LUAU

SWIM COMPLEX
25 YD. POOL
LOCKER / SHOWER
CONTROL

EXISTING WINDBREAK

LARGE FLOWERING TREES
POINCIANA

FLOWERING / SHADE TREES
SHOWER TREE
AFRICAN TULIPS
PLUMERIAS

MOVABLE BLEACHERS

EXISTING WINDBREAK

STALL PARKING / TOTAL PK PARK
± 130 CARS

TICKET BOOTH

GULCH

VERTICAL ACCENT TREES
NORFOLK PINE
EUCALYPTUS

VERTICAL PALMS

PARKING

FLOWERING /
SHADE TREES
SHOWER TREE
PLUMERIA

PICNIC

FAMILY PARK AREA
PICNIC
CHILDRENS PLAY
FISHING / CONTROL
FESTIVALS

OPEN PLAY

TURF

PICNIC

PLAY EQUIPMENT

EXISTING TENNIS

FUTURE / LIGHTED

TURF

EXISTING
NATIONAL GUARD
FACILITY

FUTURE LIGHTED TENNIS

RESTROOMS /
CONCESSIONS

EXISTING SOFTBALL

NEW
MAIN ENTRANCE

GROUND
COVER

PICNIC

8' PATH

PICNIC

8' PATH

MAINTENANCE

EXISTING WINDBREAK

GULCH

EXISTING FOOTBALL

RESIDENTIAL

LARGE SPREADING TREES
MONKEYPOD

OVERFLOW PARKING
± 100 CARS

SPORTS FIELD
LIGHTED

FLOWERING / VERTICAL TREES
SHOWER TREE
PLUMERIA
GOLD TREE
IRONWOOD

EXISTING WINDBREAK

RECOMMENDED PARK EXPANSION / 10.17 ACRES

EXISTING PARK / 8.96 ACRES

0 40 80 120 160
Feet

North

Kamehameha Park, Hawaii. EDAW, Inc., by Ollie K. Davis.

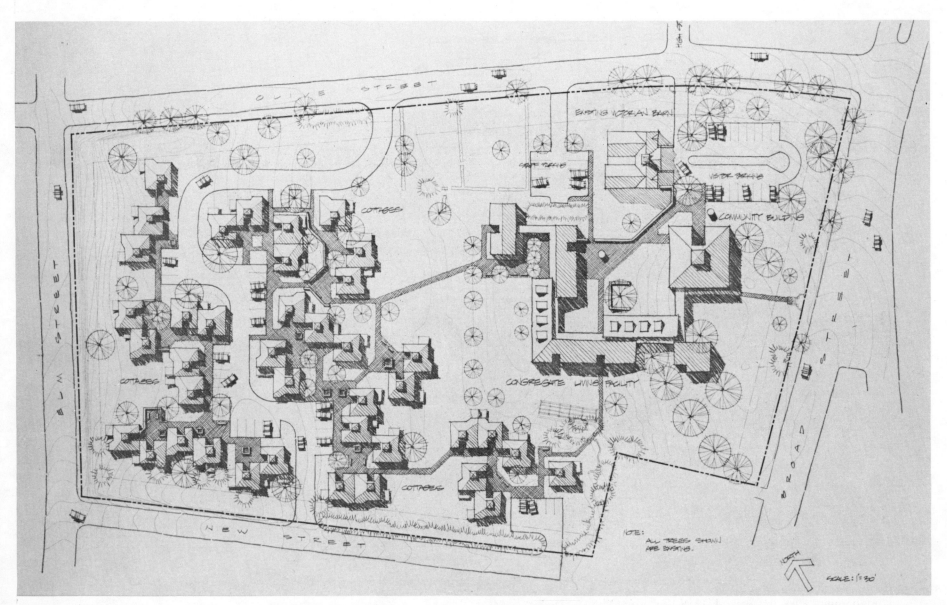

Community for the Elderly. Johnson and Dee. Jeter & Cook, Architects.

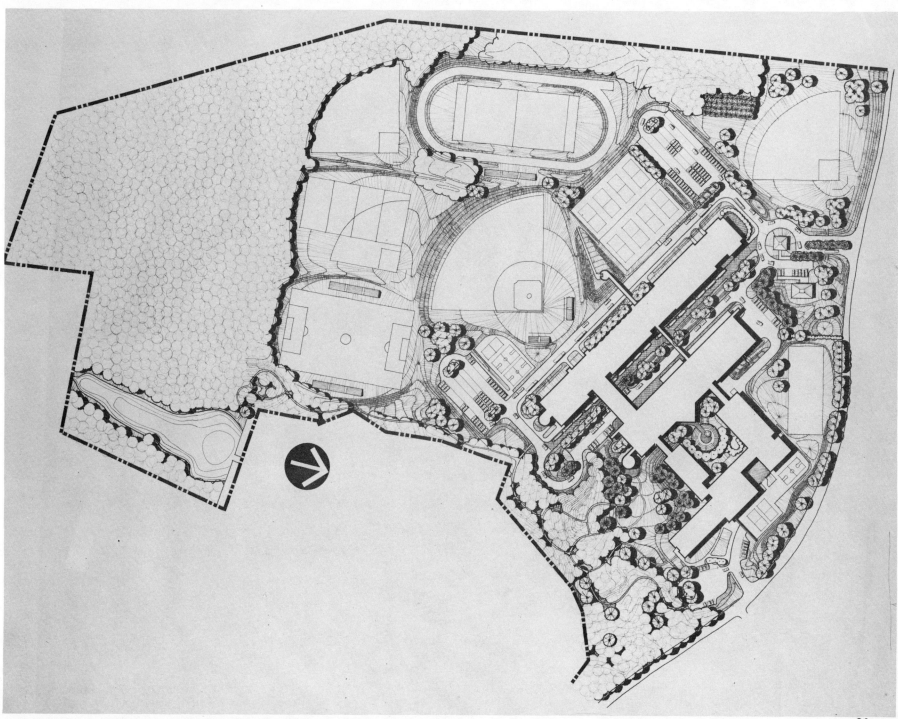

CR3, Inc., by Jeffrey A. Gebrian. Client: Jeter, Cook & Jepson, Architects.

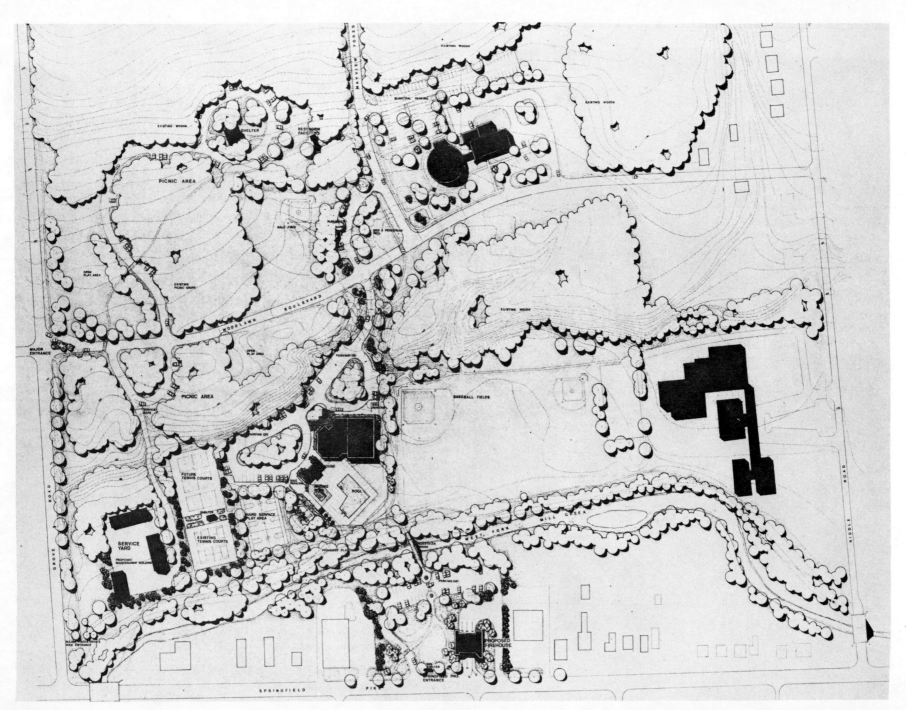

Woodlawn Municipal Park. John A. Bentley.

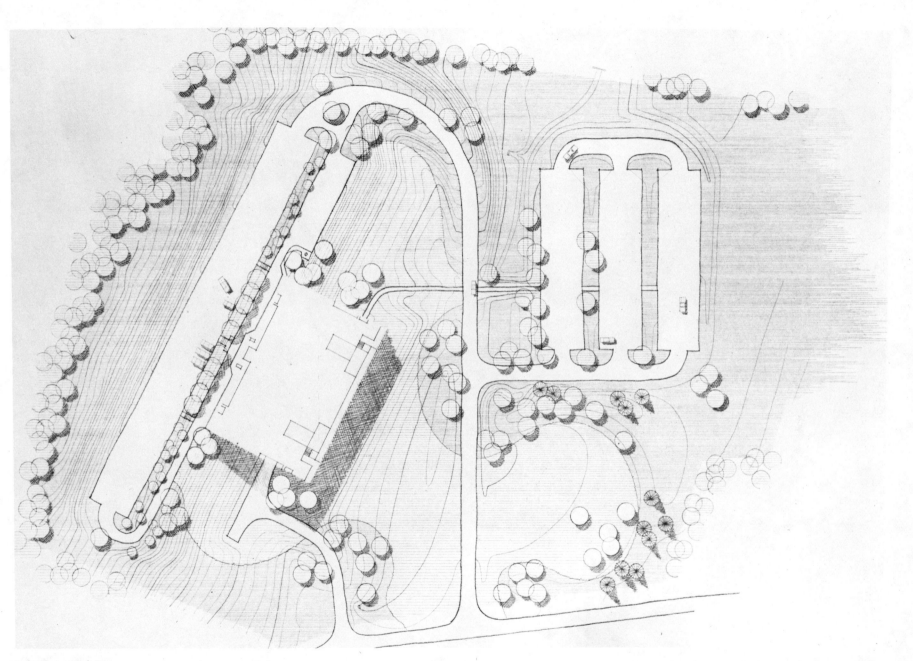

Johnson and Dee.

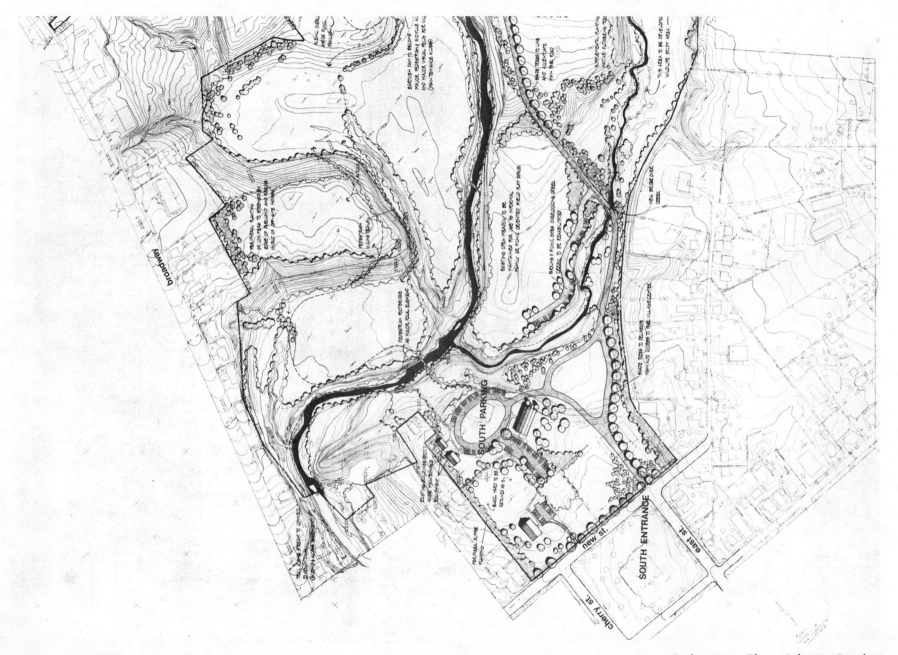

Park Master Plan. John A. Bentley.

94

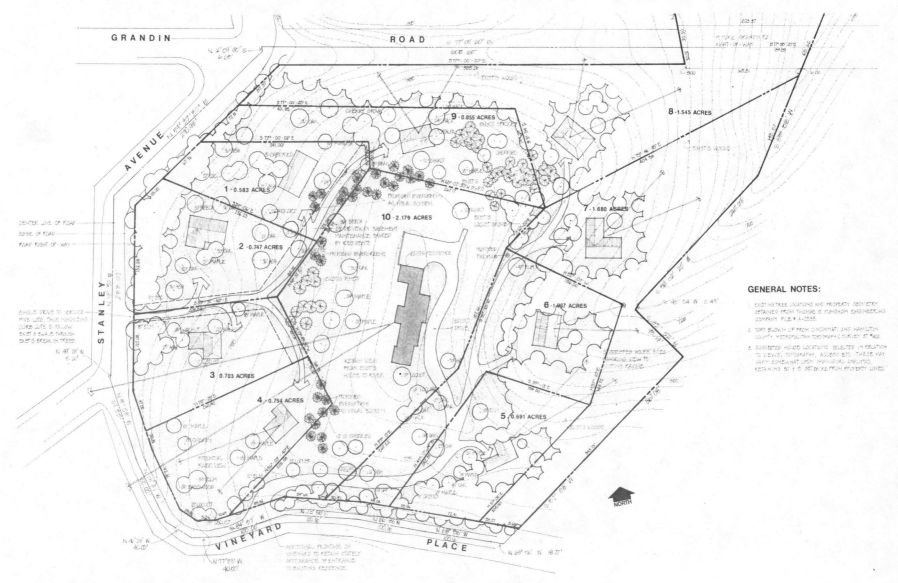

Vineyard Hills. John A. Bentley.

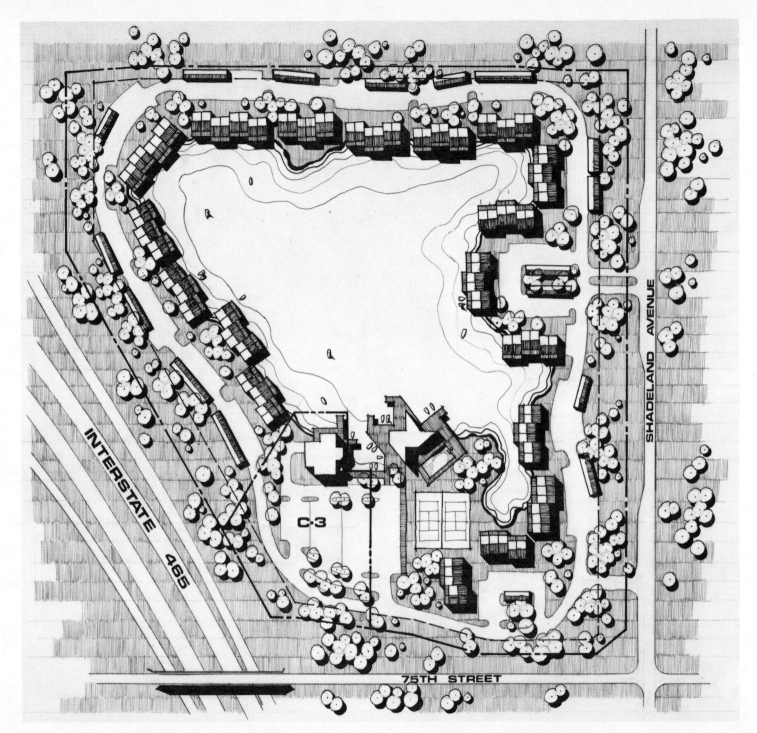

INTERSTATE 465

SHADELAND AVENUE

C-3

75TH STREET

Browning, Day, Pollak Associates, Inc.

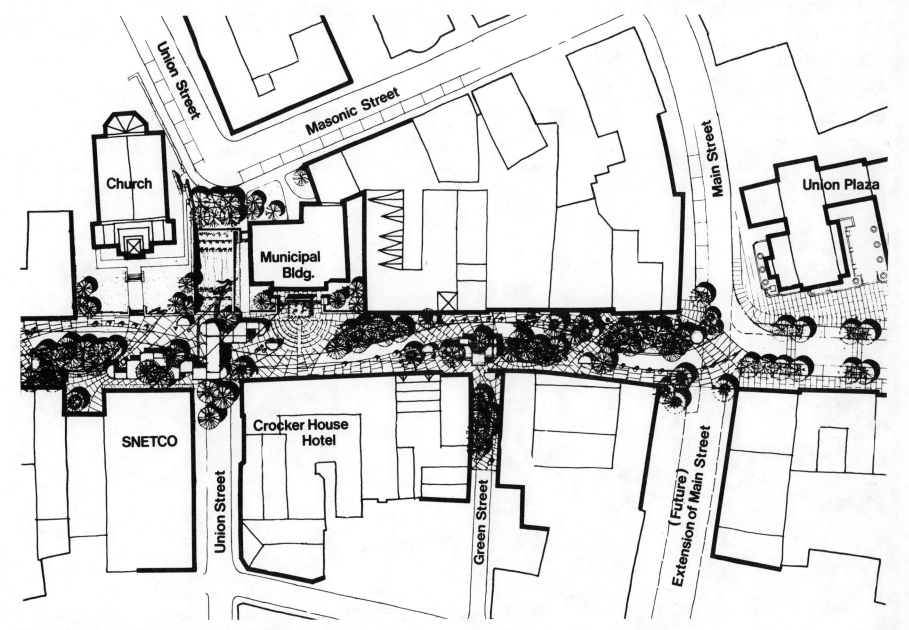

State Street Semi-Mall. Johnson and Dee.

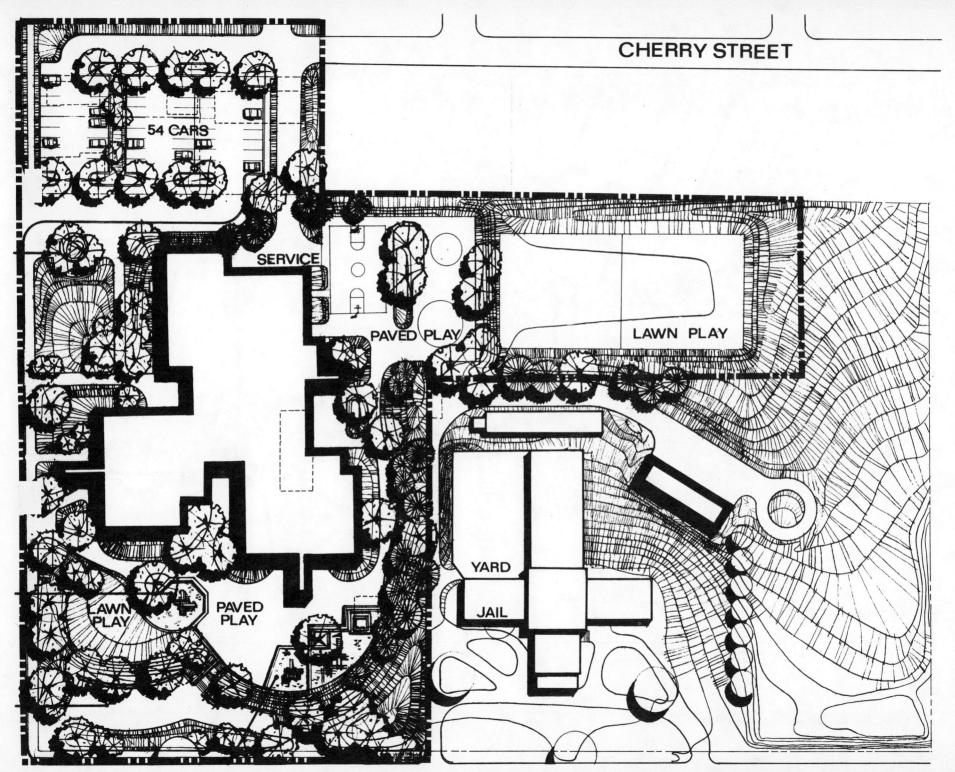

CHERRY STREET

54 CARS

SERVICE

PAVED PLAY

LAWN PLAY

LAWN PLAY

PAVED PLAY

YARD

JAIL

East Side Community School. CR3, Inc., by Robert Wordell.

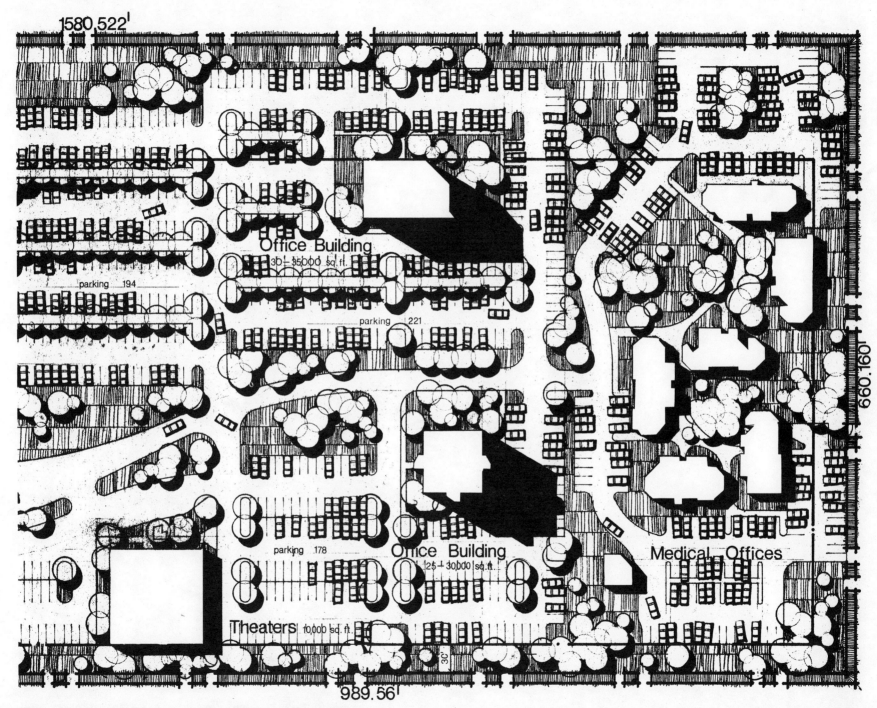

1580,522'

Office Building
30 - 35,000 sq. ft.

parking 194

parking 221

Office Building
25 - 30,000 sq. ft.

parking 178

Theaters 10,000 sq. ft.

30'

Medical Offices

660.160'

989.56'

Fidelity Center. Browning, Day, Pollak Associates, Inc.

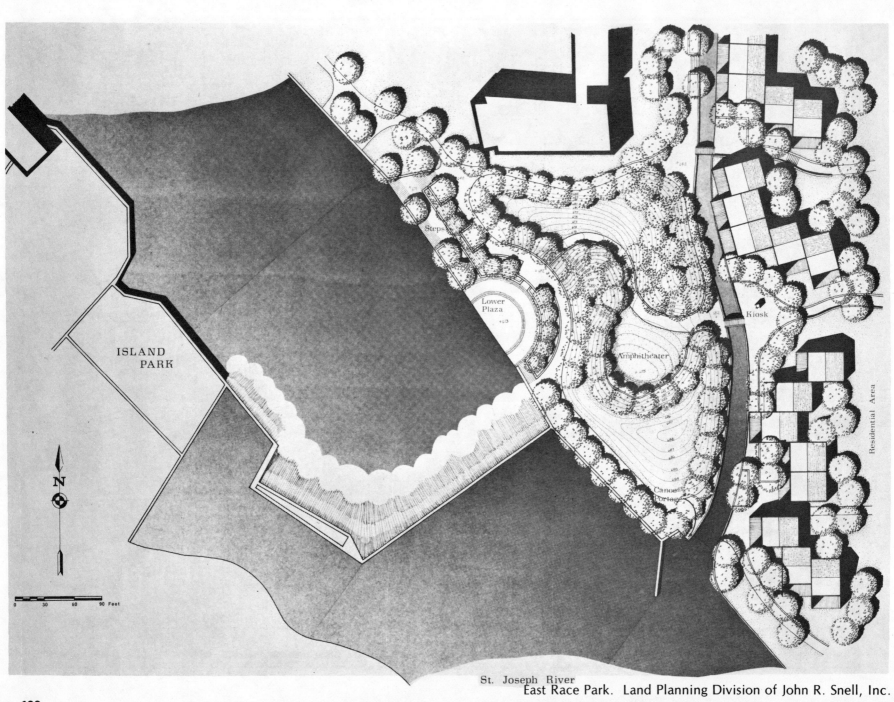

ISLAND PARK

N

0   30   60   90 Feet

Steps

Lower Plaza

Amphitheater

Kiosk

Canoe Portage

Residential Area

St. Joseph River

East Race Park. Land Planning Division of John R. Snell, Inc.

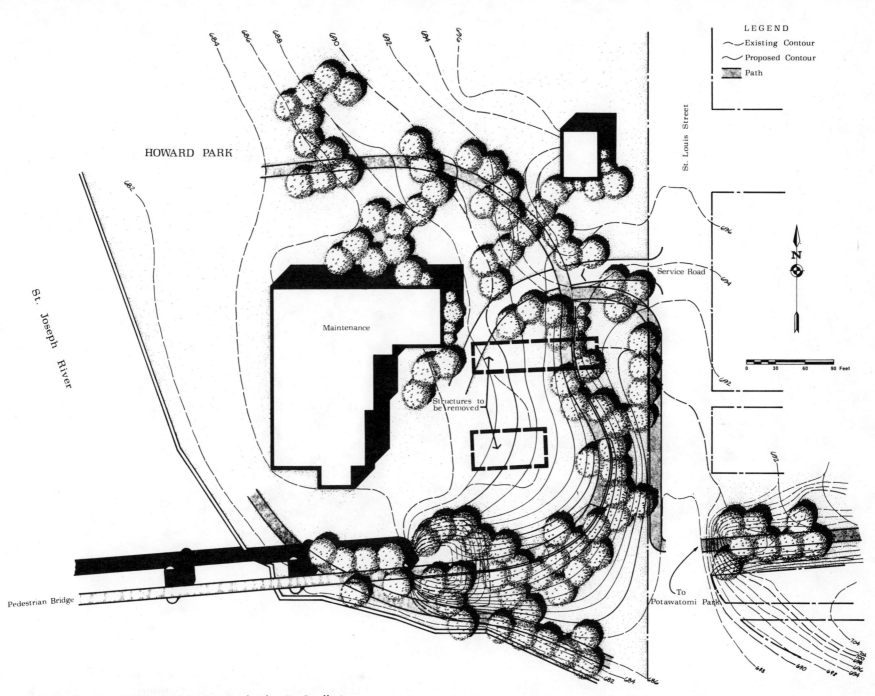

HOWARD PARK

LEGEND
Existing Contour
Proposed Contour
Path

St. Louis Street

St. Joseph River

Maintenance

Service Road

Structures to be removed

N

0   30   60   90 Feet

Pedestrian Bridge

To Potawatomi Park

Howard Park. Land Planning Division of John R. Snell, Inc.

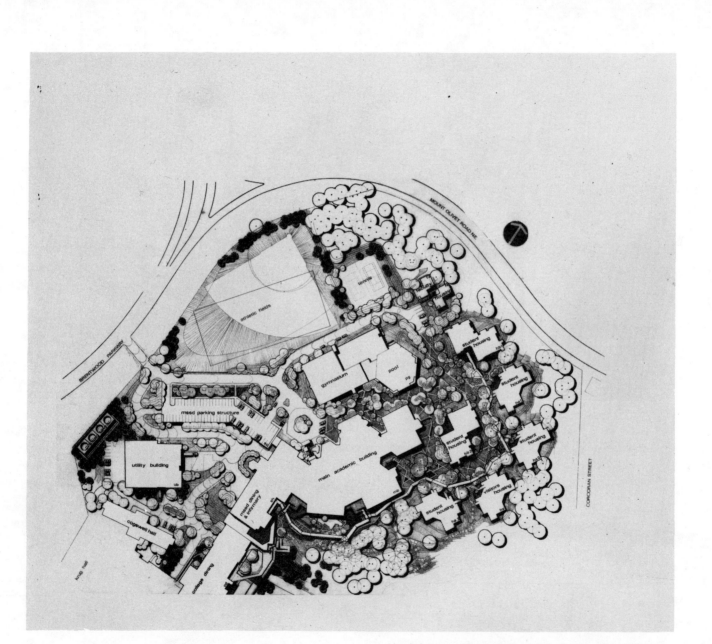

Model Secondary School for the Deaf. CR3, Inc.
Client: Hudgins, Thompson, & Ball, Architects.

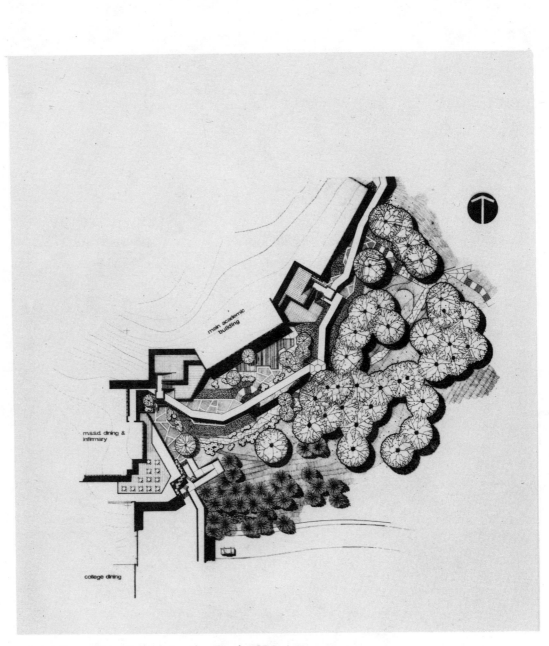

Model Secondary School for the Deaf. CR3, Inc.
Client: Hudgins, Thompson, & Ball, Architects.

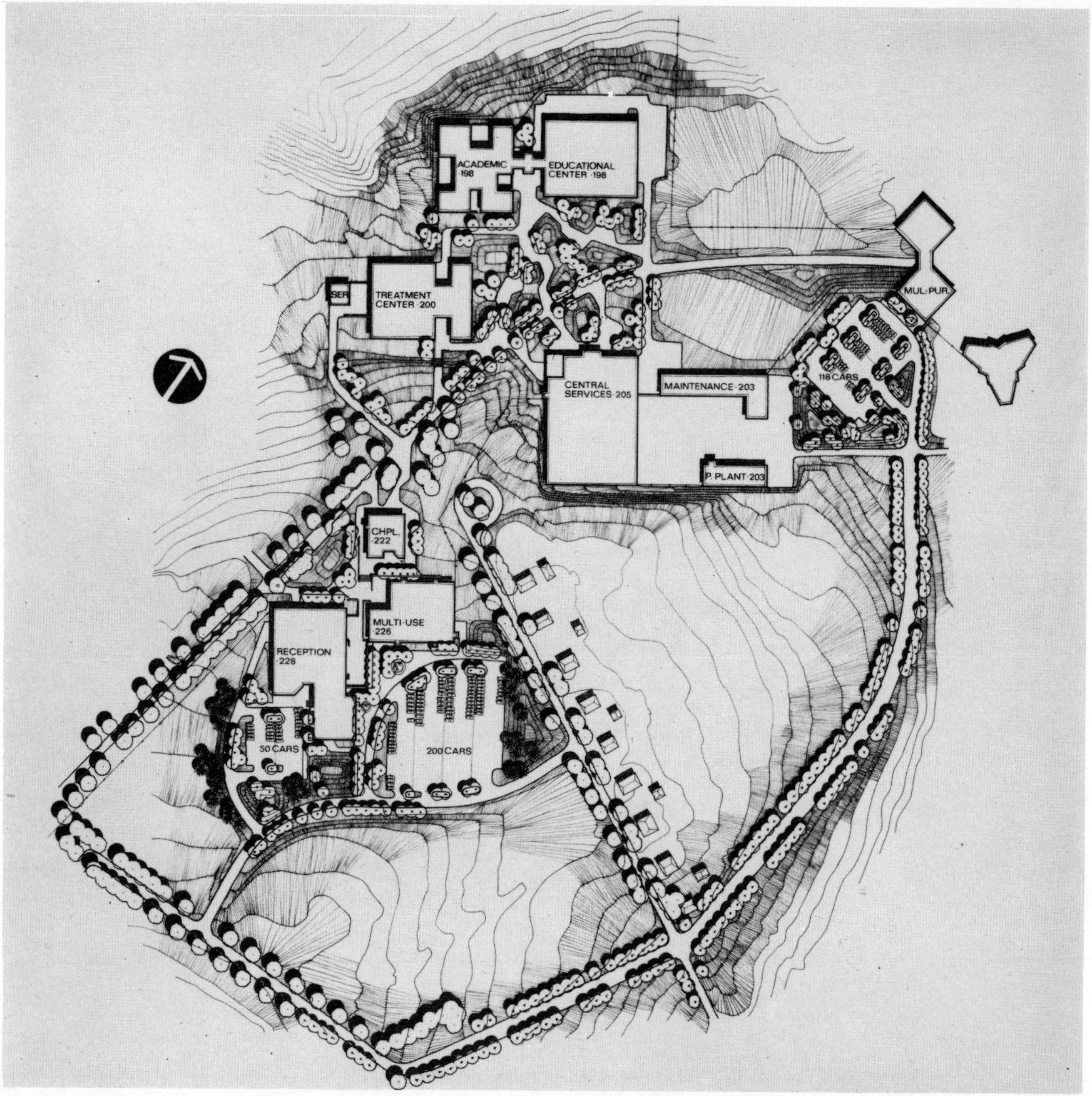
ACADEMIC ·198
EDUCATIONAL CENTER ·198
SER
TREATMENT CENTER ·200
MUL·PUR.
CENTRAL SERVICES·205
MAINTENANCE·203
118 CARS
P. PLANT·203
CHPL. ·222
MULTI-USE ·226
RECEPTION ·228
50 CARS
200 CARS

Cheshire Corrections Community. CR3, Inc., by Jeffrey A. Gebrian. Client: Close, Jensen, Miller.

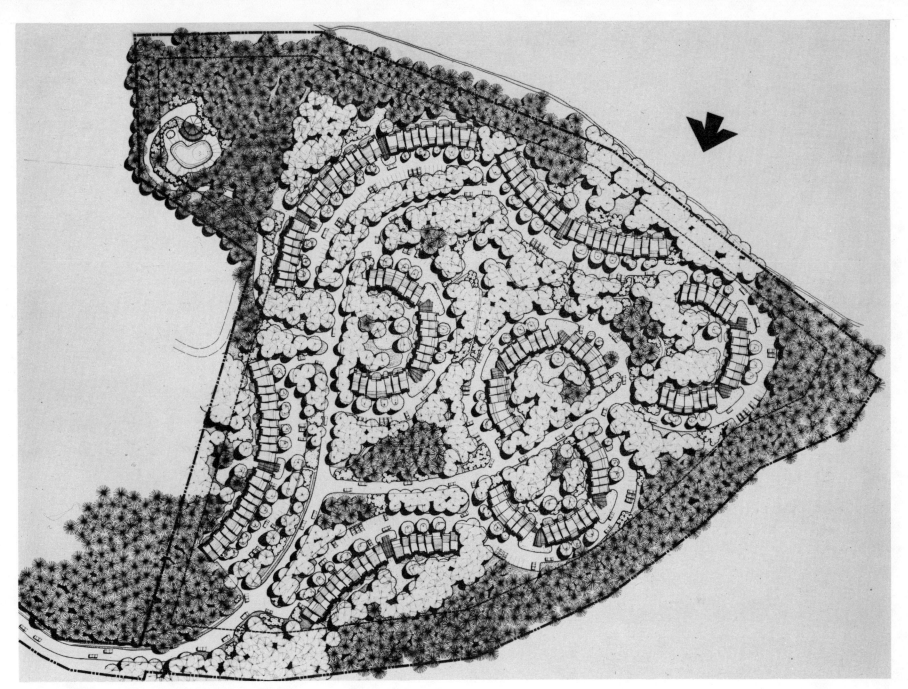

Tunxis Village. CR3, Inc., by Jeffrey A. Gebrian.
Client: Hirsch, Kaestle Boos, Architects.

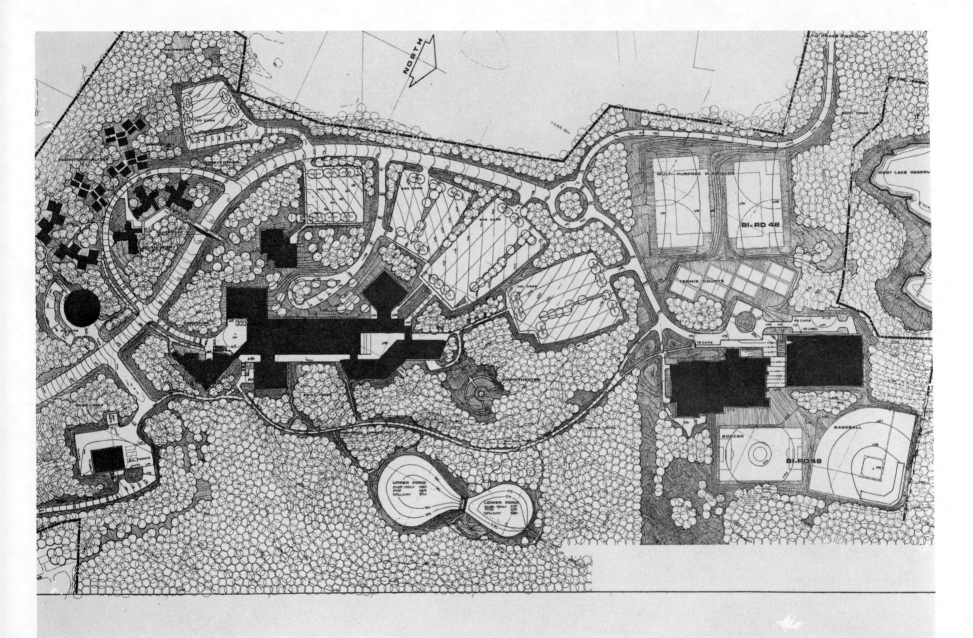

Western Connecticut State College. CR3, Inc., by Jeffrey A. Gebrian.
Coordinating Architect: Russell, Gibson, von Dohlen.

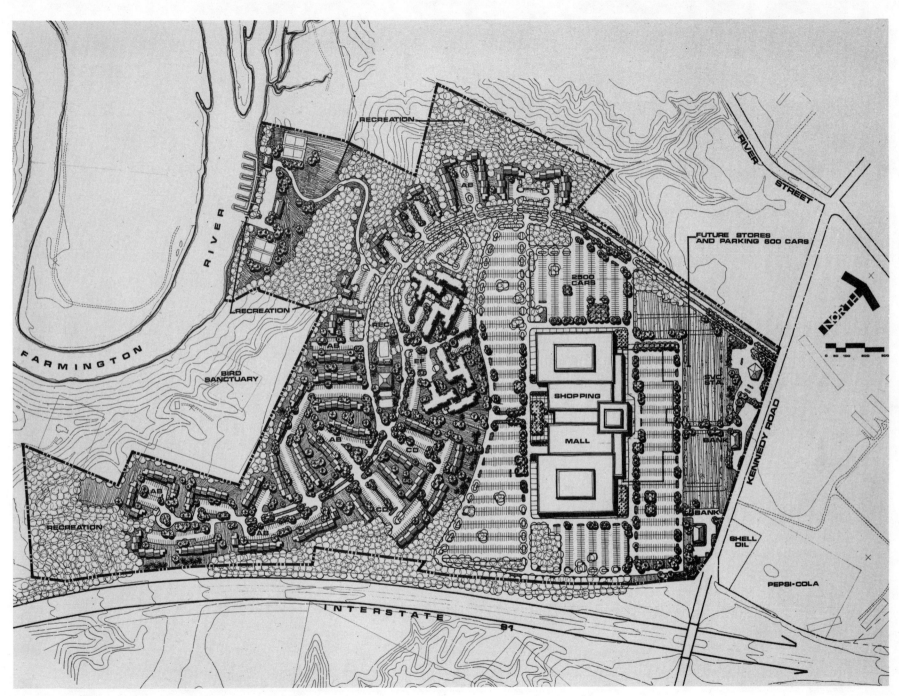

Windsor Plaza. CR3, Inc., by Jeffrey A. Gebrian.
Client: Phillip J. DiCorcia, Architect.

Milwaukee War Memorial. Johnson, Johnson & Roy, Inc.
Pencil, ink, black "zip-a-tone" and "zip-a-tone" screens.

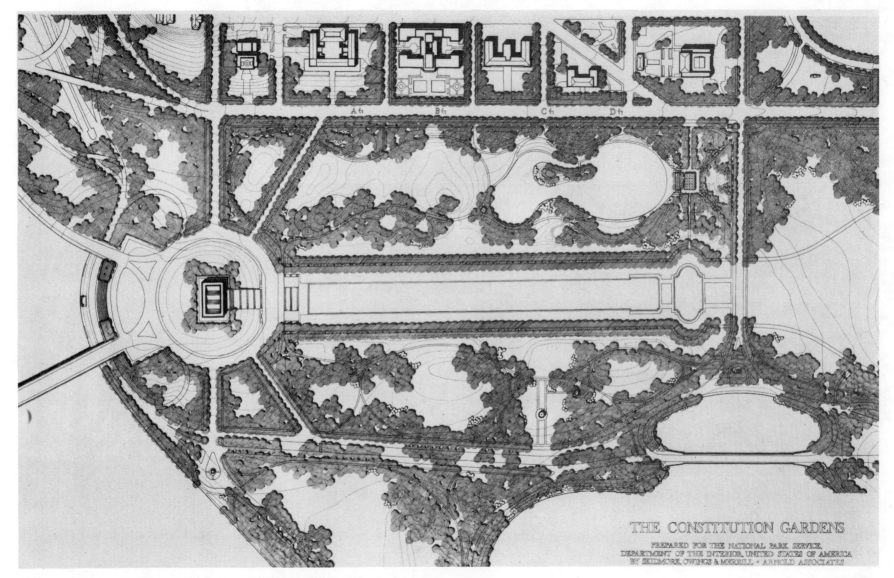

The Constitution Gardens.   Skidmore, Owings and Merrill.   Arnold Associates.

THE CONSTITUTION GARDENS

PREPARED FOR THE NATIONAL PARK SERVICE,
DEPARTMENT OF THE INTERIOR, UNITED STATES OF AMERICA
BY SKIDMORE, OWINGS & MERRILL · ARNOLD ASSOCIATES.

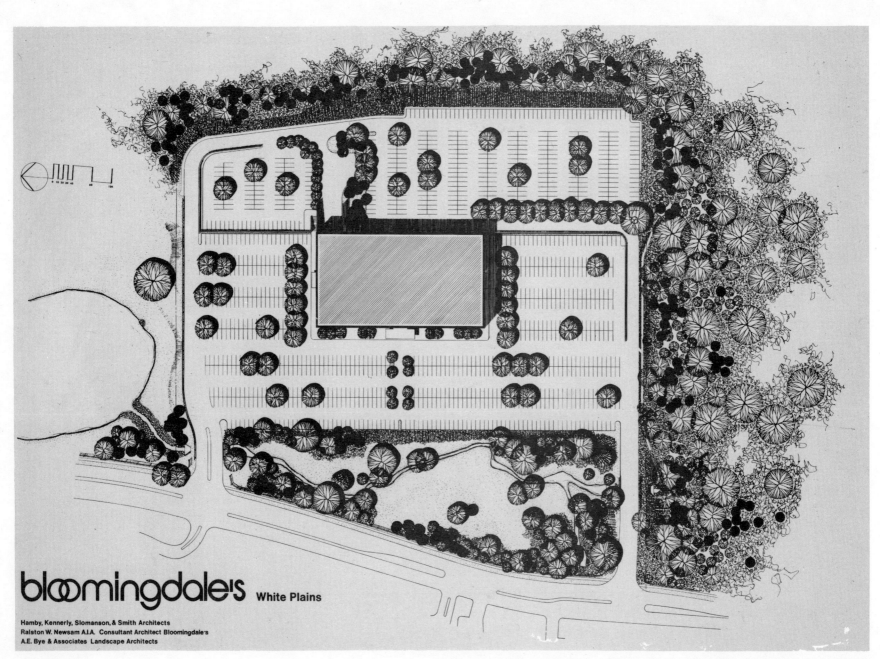

bloomingdale's White Plains

Hamby, Kennerly, Slomanson, & Smith Architects
Ralston W. Newsam A.I.A. Consultant Architect Bloomingdale's
A.E. Bye & Associates Landscape Architects

Bloomingdale's. A. E. Bye & Associates. Kennerly, Slomanson and Smith, Architects. Ralston W. Newsom, A.I.A., Consultant Architect.

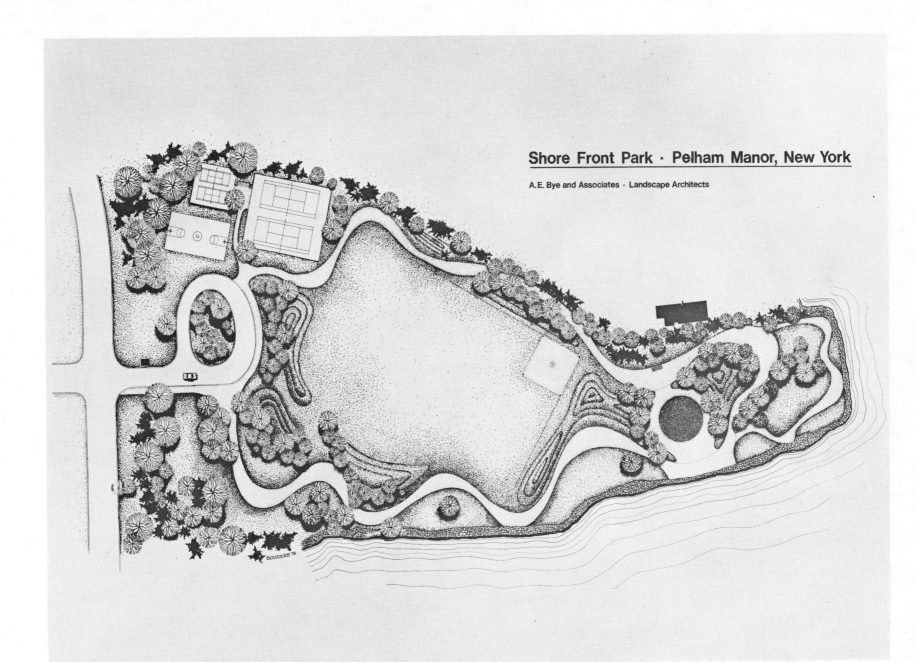

Shore Front Park · Pelham Manor, New York

A. E. Bye and Associates · Landscape Architects

Shore Front Park.   A. E. Bye & Associates.

Jupiter Trails. Edward D. Stone, Jr. & Associates, P. A.

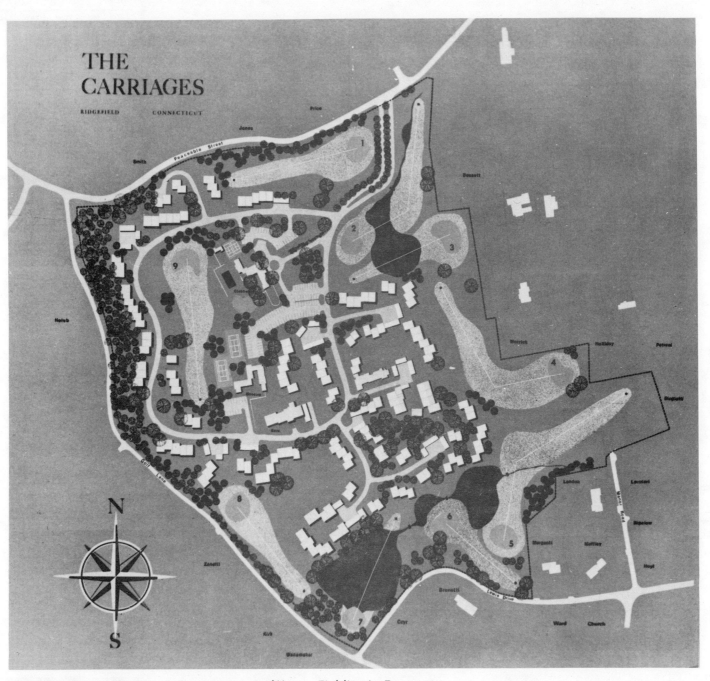

The Carriages. A. E. Bye & Associates. Architect: Fielding L. Bowman.

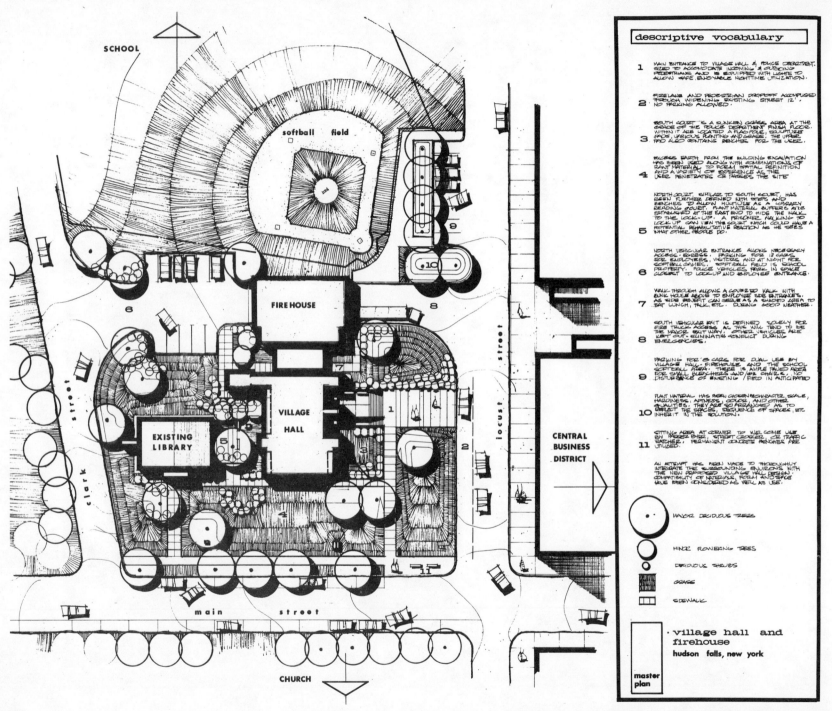

Village Hall and Firehouse. The Saratoga Associates.

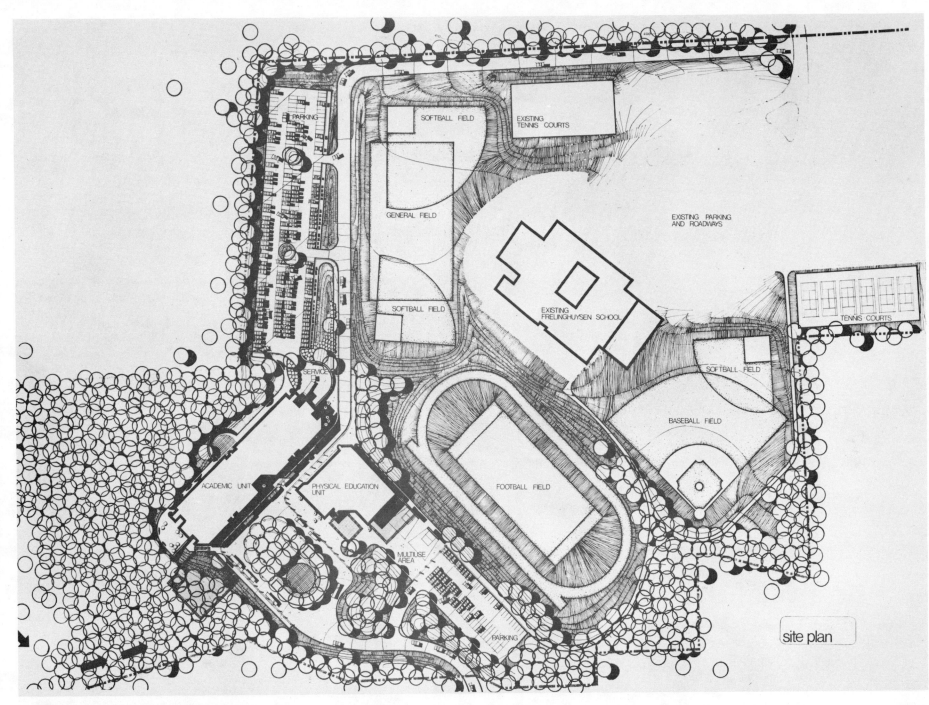

EL PARKING

SOFTBALL FIELD

EXISTING
TENNIS COURTS

GENERAL FIELD

EXISTING PARKING
AND ROADWAYS

SOFTBALL FIELD

EXISTING
FRELINGHUYSEN SCHOOL

TENNIS COURTS

SERVICE

SOFTBALL FIELD

BASEBALL FIELD

ACADEMIC UNIT

PHYSICAL EDUCATION
UNIT

FOOTBALL FIELD

MULTIUSE
AREA

PARKING

site plan

Site Plan. The Saratoga Associates.

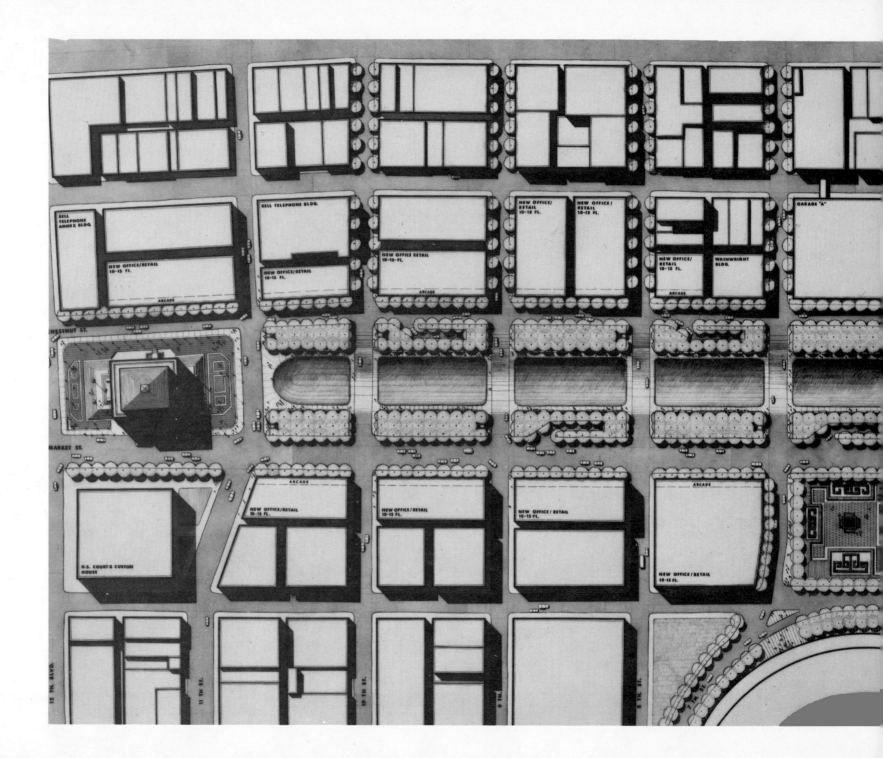

BELL
TELEPHONE
ANNEX BLDG.

NEW OFFICE/RETAIL
10-15 FL.

ARCADE

BELL TELEPHONE BLDG.

NEW OFFICE/RETAIL
10-15 FL.

NEW OFFICE RETAIL
10-15 FL.

ARCADE

NEW OFFICE/
RETAIL
10-15 FL.

NEW OFFICE/
RETAIL
10-15 FL.

NEW OFFICE/
RETAIL
10-15 FL.

WAINWRIGHT
BLDG.

ARCADE

GARAGE "A"

CHESTNUT ST.

MARKET ST.

U.S. COURT & CUSTOM
HOUSE

ARCADE

NEW OFFICE/RETAIL
10-15 FL.

NEW OFFICE/RETAIL
10-15 FL.

NEW OFFICE/RETAIL
10-15 FL.

ARCADE

NEW OFFICE/RETAIL
10-15 FL.

12 TH. BLVD.

11 TH ST.

10 TH. ST.

9 TH. ST.

8 TH. ST.

7 TH. ST.

116

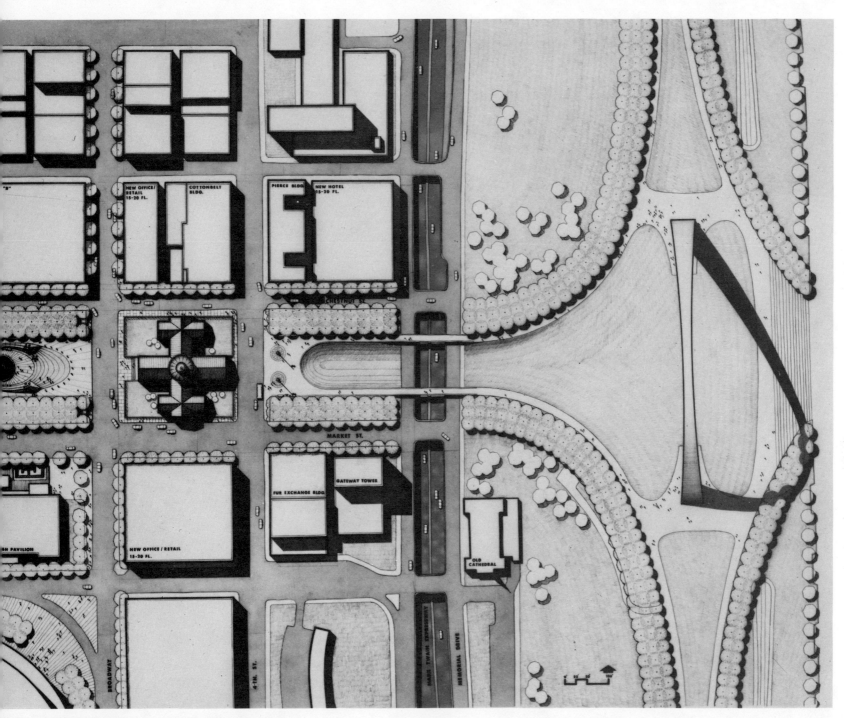

Labels visible in illustration:

NEW OFFICE/RETAIL 15-20 FL. COTTONBELT BLDG. PIERCE BLDG. NEW HOTEL 15-20 FL.

CHESTNUT ST.

MARKET ST.

FUR EXCHANGE BLDG. GATEWAY TOWER

NEW OFFICE/RETAIL 15-20 FL.

SH PAVILION

OLD CATHEDRAL

BROADWAY 4TH. ST. MARK TWAIN EXPRESSWAY MEMORIAL DRIVE

t. Louis Mall. Sasaki, Dawson, DeMay
ssociates, Inc. Hutchins Photography, Inc.

117

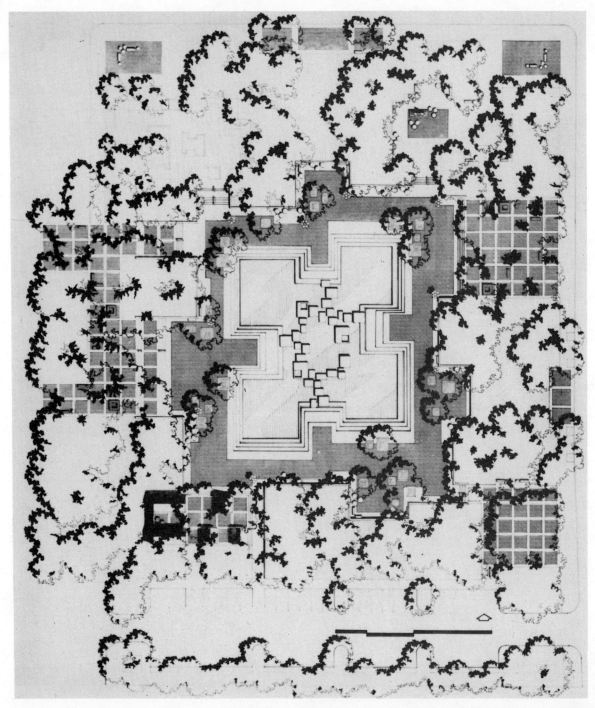

Freimann Square. Browning, Day, Pollak Associates, Inc.

PARKING

WAR MEMORIAL
AND FLAGS

PARKING

WATER JET

TO
FUTURE DEVELOPMENT

PLEASANT VIEW DRIVE

WASHINGTON BLVD

SECTION EAST WEST

SECTION NORTH SOUTH

NORTH

North Ogden Triangle. Maas and Grassli.

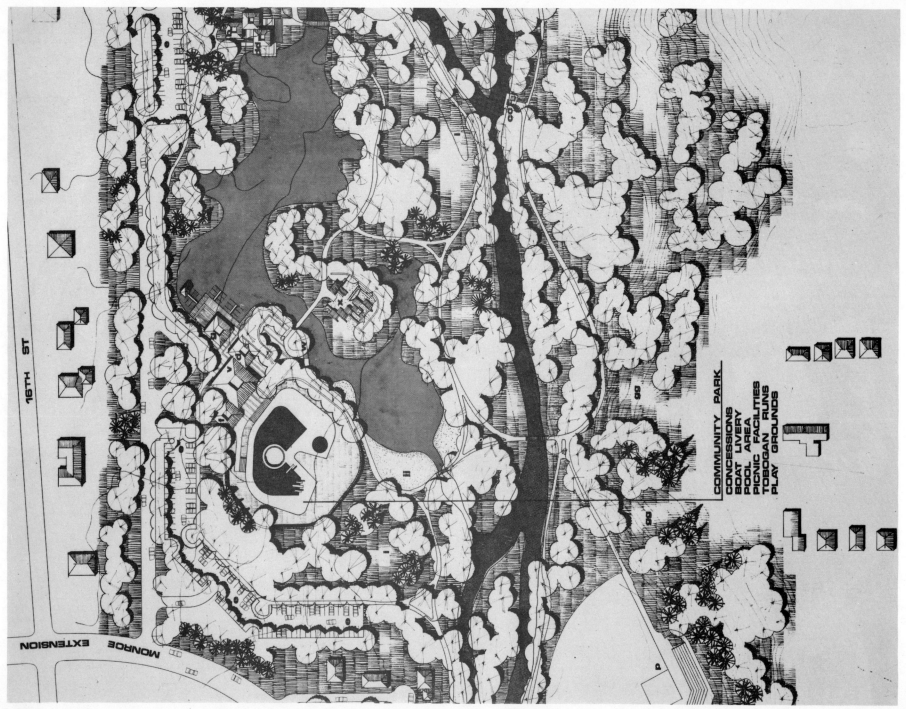

COMMUNITY PARK
CONCESSIONS
BOAT LIVERY
POOL AREA
PICNIC FACILITIES
TOBOGAN RUNS
PLAY GROUNDS

16TH ST

MONROE EXTENSION

120

Ogden River Parkway. Maas and Grassli.

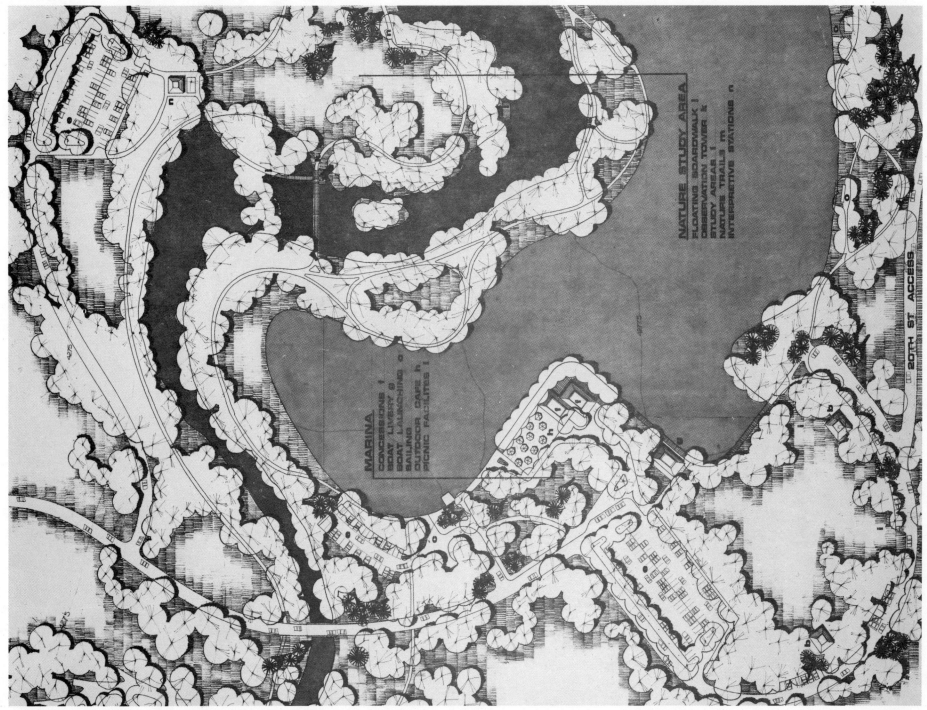

NATURE STUDY AREA

FLOATING BOARDWALK j
OBSERVATION TOWER k
STUDY AREAS l
NATURE TRAILS m
INTERPRETIVE STATIONS n

MARINA

CONCESSIONS f
BOAT LIVERY g
BOAT LAUNCHING o
SAILING
OUTDOOR CAFE h
PICNIC FACILITIES i

20TH ST ACCESS

Ogden River Parkway. Maas and Grassli.

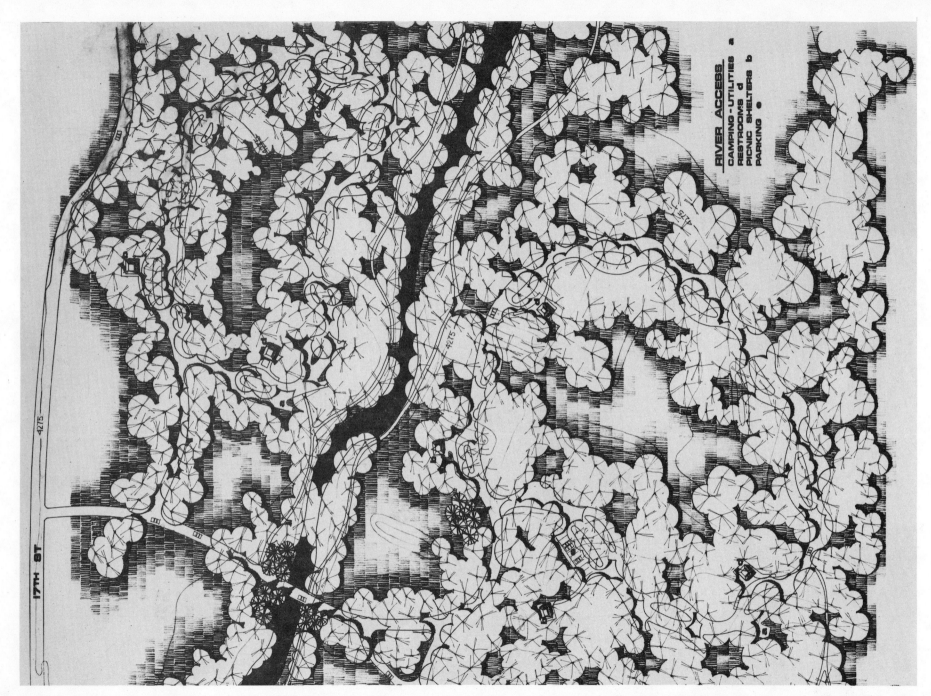

Ogden River Parkway. Maas and Grassli.

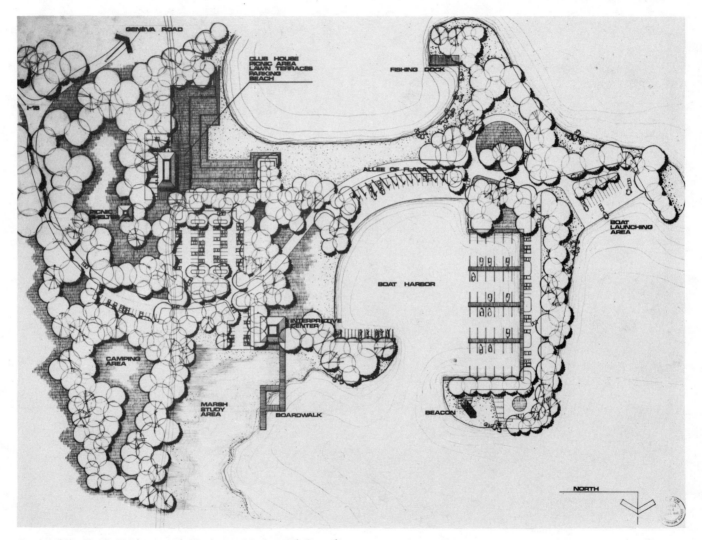

Orem City Boat Harbor and Marina. Maas and Grassli.

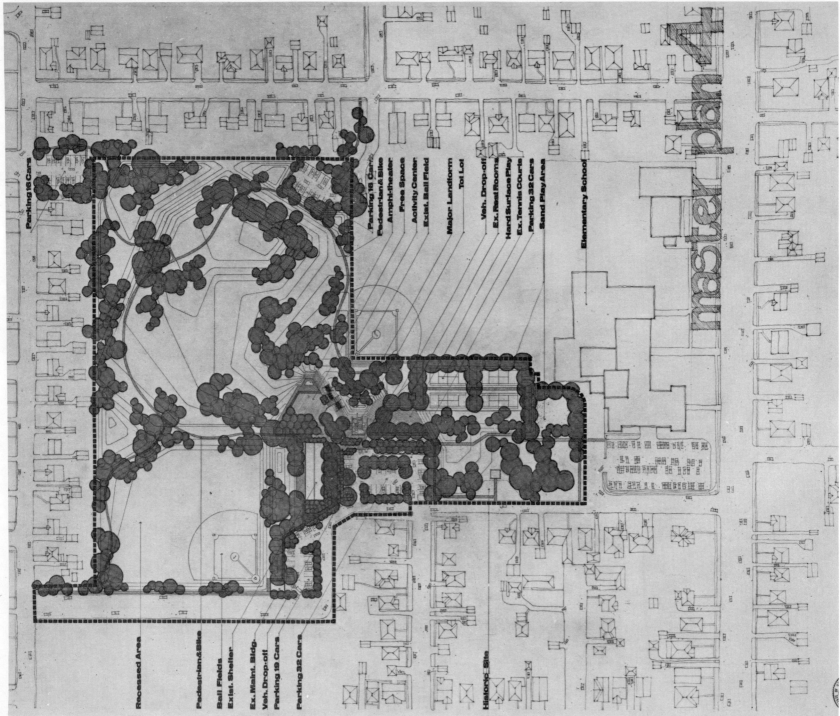

Parking 16 Cars
Pedestrian & Bike
Amphitheater
Free Space
Activity Center
Exist. Ball Field
Major Landform
Tot Lot
Veh. Drop-off
Ex. Rest Rooms
Hard Surface Play
Ex. Tennis Courts
Parking 32 Cars
Sand Play Area
Elementary School

Recessed Area
Pedestrian & Bike
Ball Fields
Exist. Shelter
Ex. Maint. Bldg.
Veh. Drop-off
Parking 19 Cars
Parking 32 Cars

Historic Site

124

Maas and Grassli.

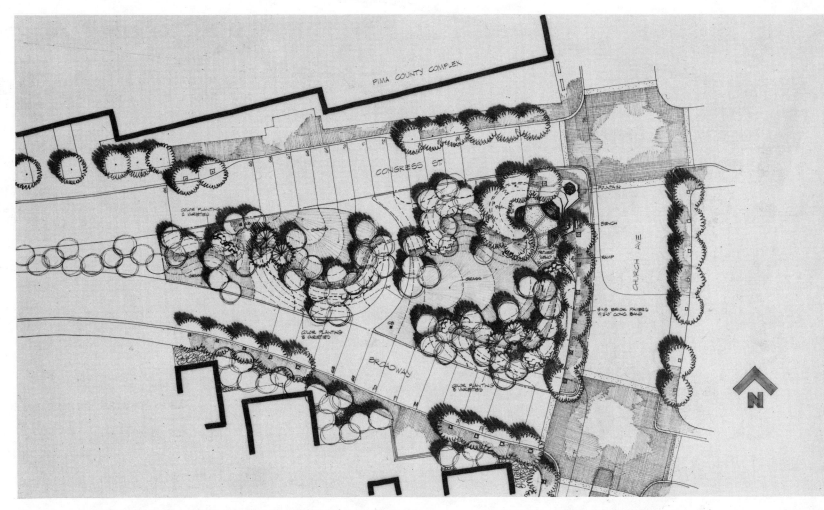

Congress and Church Street Park. EDAW, Inc., by John L. Stevenson.

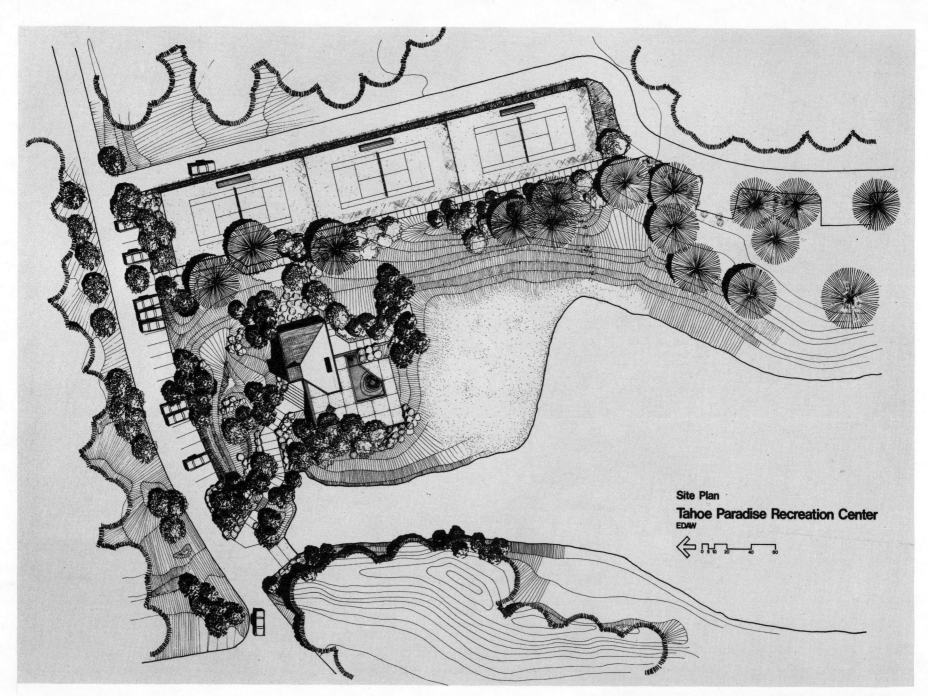

Site Plan
Tahoe Paradise Recreation Center
EDAW

0 5 10   20   40   60

Landscape Design Guide for the Citizens of Pueblo.
EDAW, Inc., by Daniel A. Sudquist.

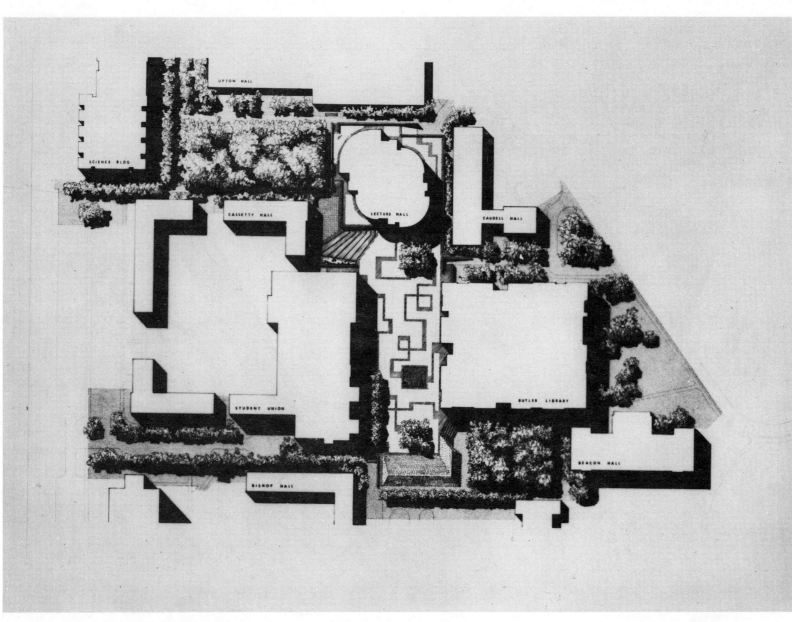

Academic Core, State University College.
A. E. Bye & Associates. Ink on vellum.

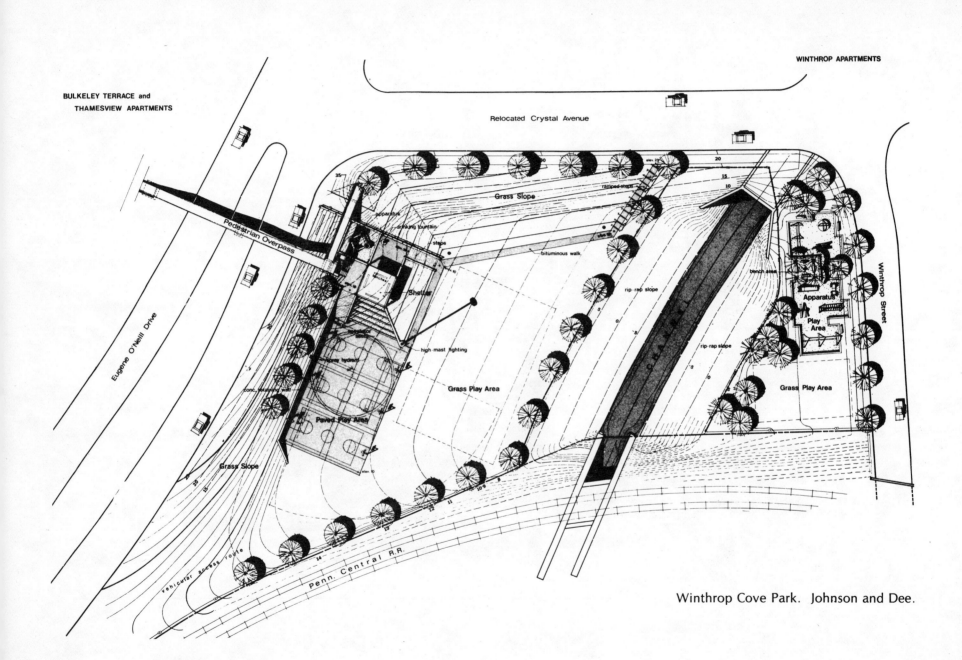

WINTHROP APARTMENTS

BULKELEY TERRACE and
THAMESVIEW APARTMENTS

Relocated Crystal Avenue

Grass Slope

ramped steps

Pedestrian Overpass

apparatus

drinking fountain

steps

bituminous walk

Shelter

rip-rap slope

Eugene O'Neill Drive

high-mast lighting

Apparatus

Play
Area

benches

fire hydrant

Grass Play Area

rip-rap slope

conc. retaining wall

Grass Play Area

Paved Play Area

Winthrop Street

Grass Slope

elev. 10

vehicular access route

Penn Central R.R.

Winthrop Cove Park. Johnson and Dee.

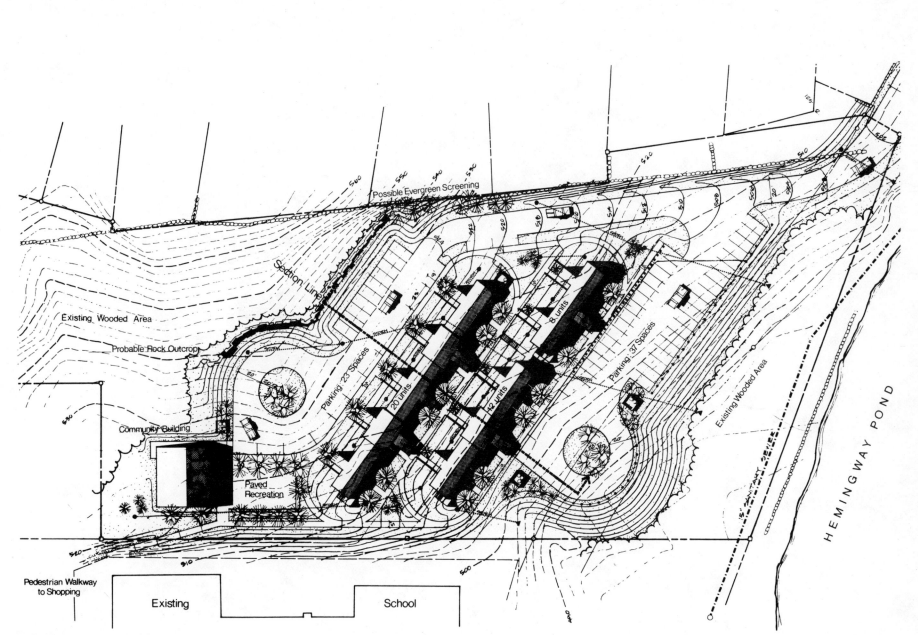

Possible Evergreen Screening

Section Line

Existing Wooded Area

Probable Rock Outcrop

Parking 23 Spaces

20 units

Community Building

Paved Recreation

Pedestrian Walkway to Shopping

Existing

School

8 units

Parking 37 Spaces

Existing Wooded Area

HEMINGWAY POND

Elderly Housing. Johnson and Dee.

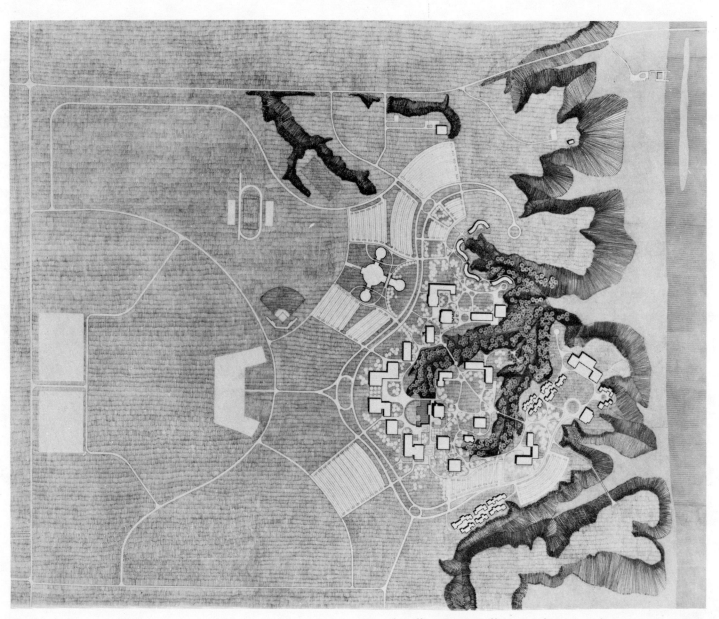

Grand Valley State College. Johnson, Johnson & Roy, Inc.

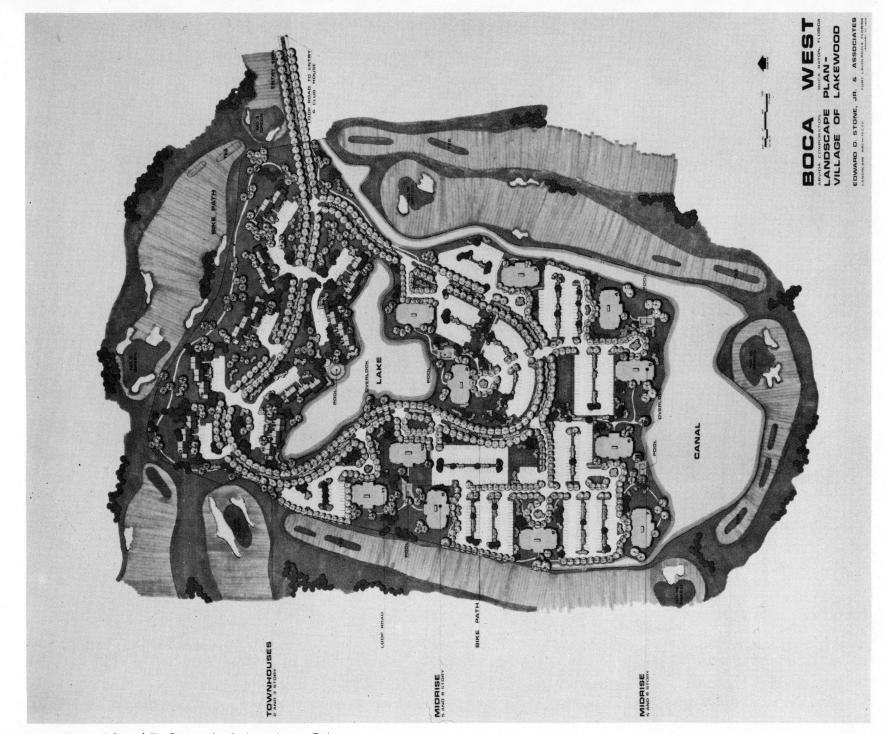

Boca West. Edward D. Stone, Jr. & Associates, P.A.

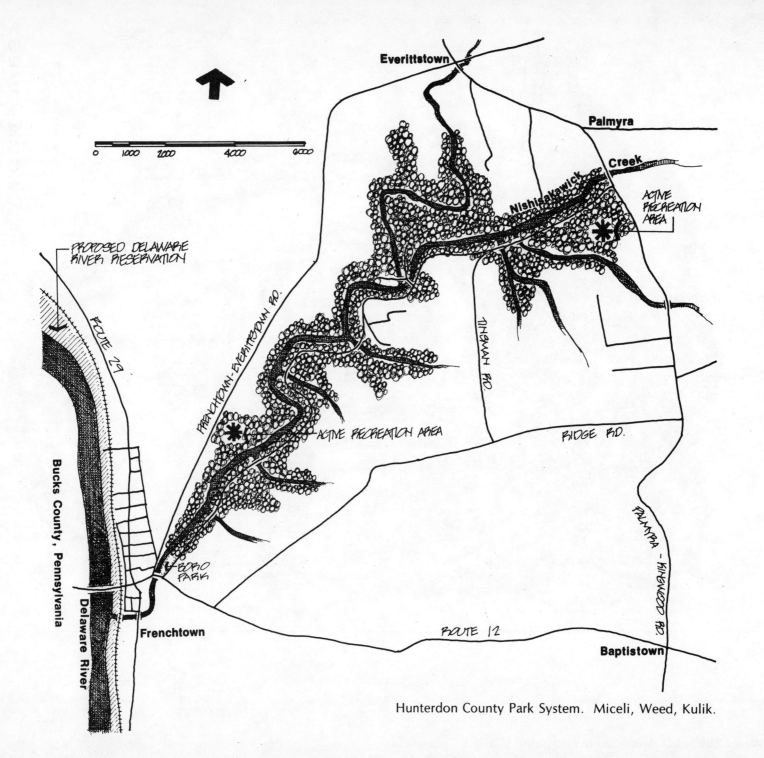

Everittstown

Palmyra

Creek

Nishisakawick

ACTIVE
RECREATION
AREA

PROPOSED DELAWARE
RIVER RESERVATION

ROUTE 29

FRENCHTOWN-EVERITTSTOWN RD.

TINBMAH RD.

ACTIVE RECREATION AREA

BIDGE RD.

Bucks County, Pennsylvania

Delaware River

4-BORO
PARK

PALMYRA-KINGWOOD RD.

ROUTE 12

Frenchtown

Baptistown

Hunterdon County Park System. Miceli, Weed, Kulik.

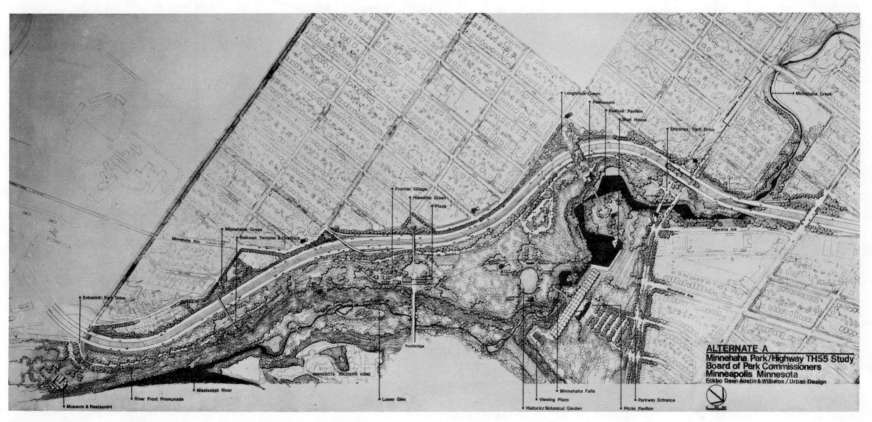

Minnehaha Park. EDAW, Inc., by Charles M. McCulloch.

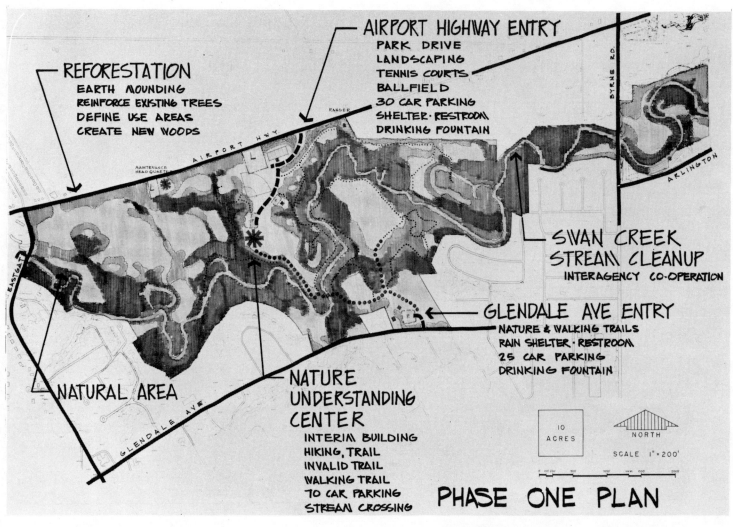

REFORESTATION
EARTH MOUNDING
REINFORCE EXISTING TREES
DEFINE USE AREAS
CREATE NEW WOODS

AIRPORT HIGHWAY ENTRY
PARK DRIVE
LANDSCAPING
TENNIS COURTS
BALLFIELD
30 CAR PARKING
SHELTER·RESTROOM
DRINKING FOUNTAIN

SWAN CREEK STREAM CLEANUP
INTERAGENCY CO·OPERATION

GLENDALE AVE ENTRY
NATURE & WALKING TRAILS
RAIN SHELTER·RESTROOM
25 CAR PARKING
DRINKING FOUNTAIN

NATURAL AREA

NATURE UNDERSTANDING CENTER
INTERIM BUILDING
HIKING TRAIL
INVALID TRAIL
WALKING TRAIL
70 CAR PARKING
STREAM CROSSING

10 ACRES

NORTH

SCALE 1"=200'

PHASE ONE PLAN

Swan Creek Metro Park. The Collaborative, Inc.

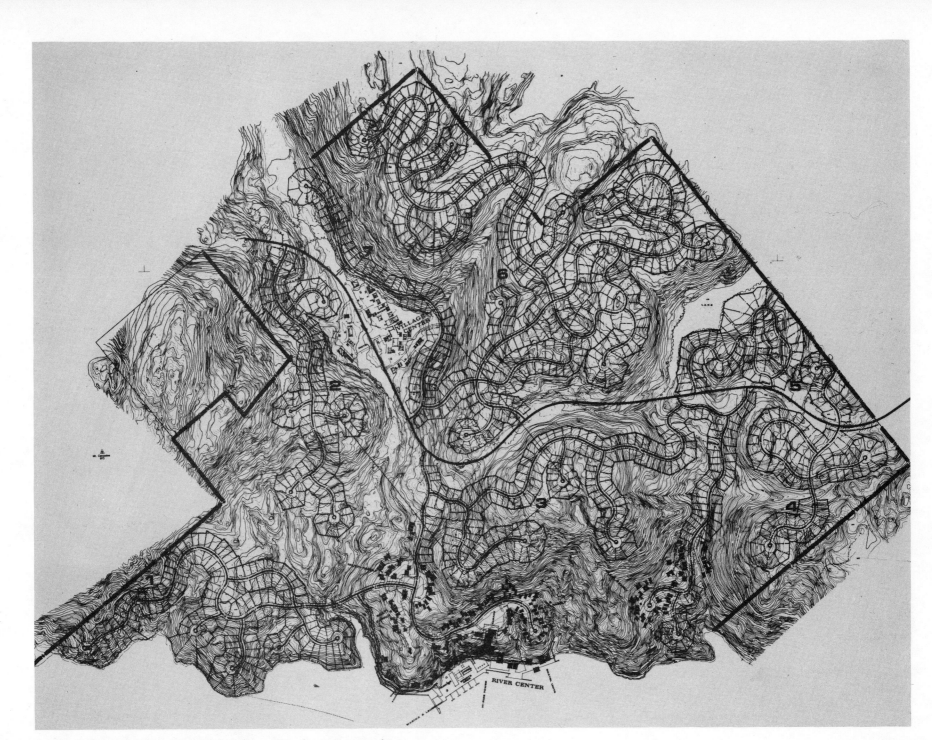

Conner Planned Community. Reimann-Buechner Partnership.

LOW DENSITY HOUSING

MEDIUM DENSITY HOUSING

MIDDLEFIELD

OLD POWDER HILL ROAD

ROUTE 147

RAIL-ROAD

MILLER RD.

COMMERCIAL CENTER
MEDIUM DENSITY HOUSING
CLUB RECREATION
CLUBHOUSE
EXISTING GOLF COURSE

ROUTE 157

DURHAM

SCHOOL

MIDDLEFIELD
DURHAM

COMMUNITY RECREATION

MEDIUM DENSITY HOUSING

LOW DENSITY HOUSING

POWER TRANSMISSION LINE

ROUTE 66

300   1000   2000

MEDIUM DENSITY HOUSING

Lyman Farms. CR3, Inc., by Jeffrey A.
Gebrian. Client: William McHugh, Architect.

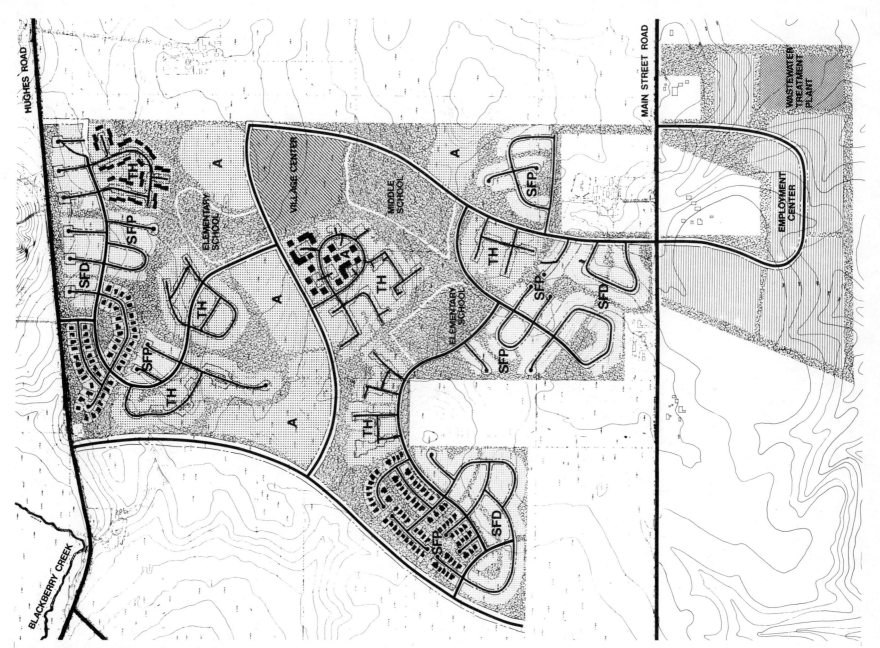

West Valley Land Plan. Perkins & Will, Inc.

FREEHAND PLANS

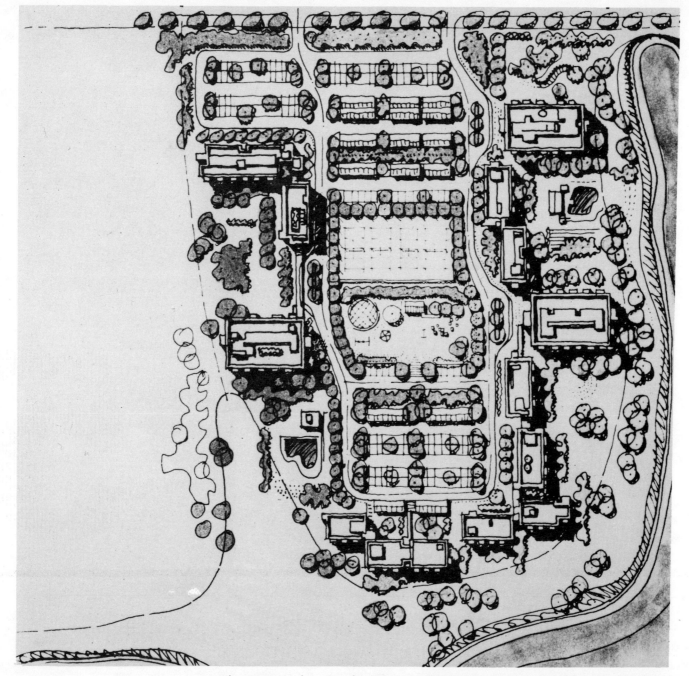

The Hammocks. Sasaki, Dawson, DeMay Associates, Inc., by Frank James.

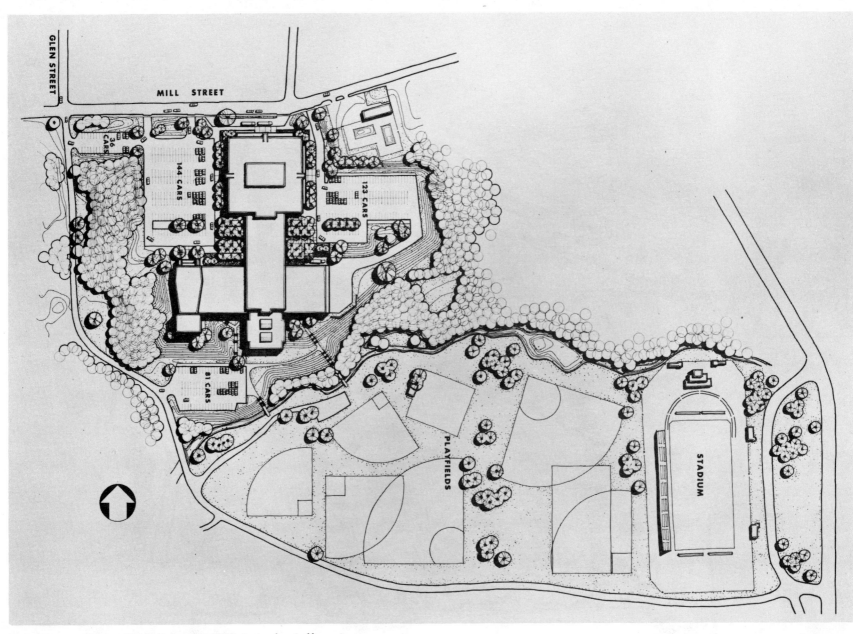

New Britain Senior High School. CR3, Inc., by Jeffrey A.
Gebrian. Client: Hirsch, Kaestle Boos, Architects.

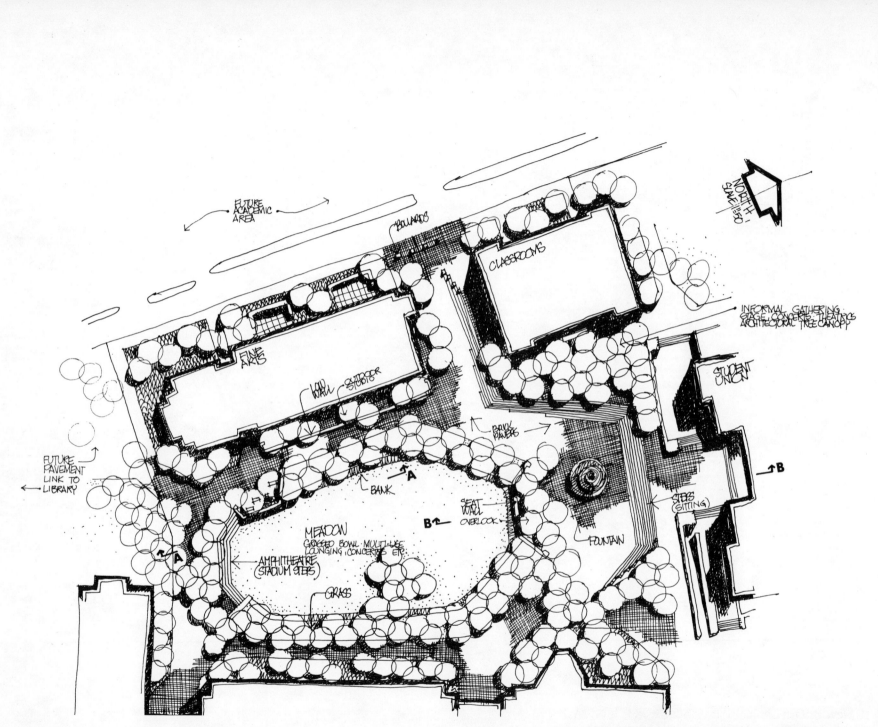

FUTURE
ACADEMIC
AREA

NORTH
SCALE 1"=50'

BOLLARDS

CLASSROOMS

INFORMAL GATHERING
STAGE CONCERTS THEATRICS
ARCHITECTURAL TREE CANOPY

FINE
ARTS

LOW
WALL

OUTDOOR
STUDIOS

STUDENT
UNION

FUTURE
PAVEMENT
LINK TO
LIBRARY

BRICK
PAVERS

↑A

↑B

BANK

SEAT
WALL
OVERLOOK

STEPS
(SITTING)

B↑

FOUNTAIN

↑A

MEADOW
GRASSED BOWL MULTI-USE
LOUNGING CONCERTS ETC

AMPHITHEATRE
(STADIUM STEPS)

GRASS

142

Student Center Mall. Miceli, Weed, Kulik.

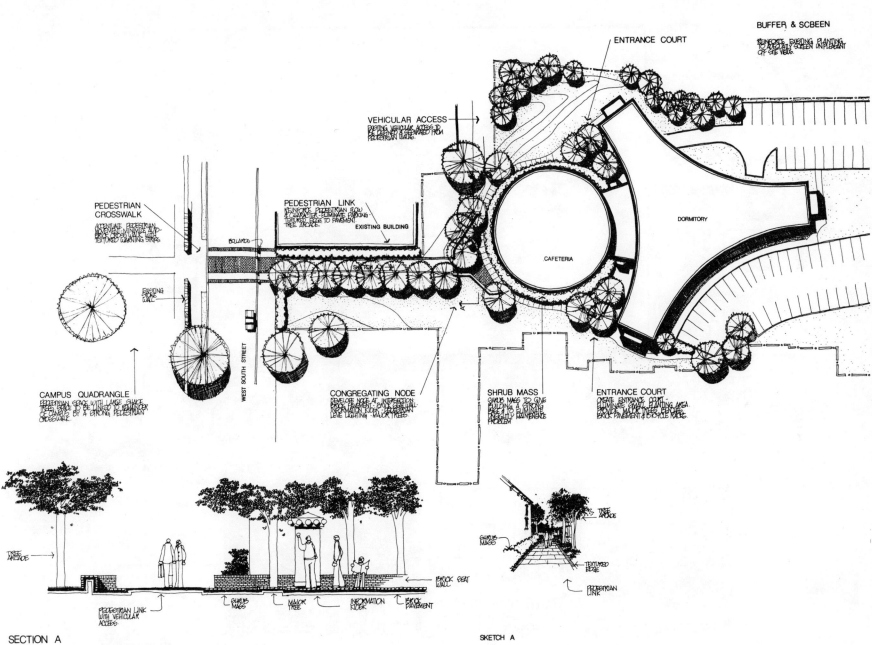

BUFFER & SCREEN
REINFORCE EXISTING PLANTING TO ADEQUATELY SCREEN UNPLEASANT OFF SITE VIEWS.

ENTRANCE COURT

VEHICULAR ACCESS
EXISTING VEHICULAR ACCESS TO BE DEEMPHASIZED & SEPARATED FROM PEDESTRIAN USAGE.

PEDESTRIAN LINK
REINFORCE PEDESTRIAN FLOW & CHARACTER. ELIMINATE PARKING. TEXTURED EDGE TO PAVEMENT. TREE ARCADE.

EXISTING BUILDING

DORMITORY

CAFETERIA

PEDESTRIAN CROSSWALK
ACCENTUATE PEDESTRIAN MOVEMENT. MINIMIZE AUTO. BRICK CROSS WALK. TEXTURED WARNING STRIP.

BOLLARDS

EXISTING WALL

WEST SOUTH STREET

CAMPUS QUADRANGLE
PEDESTRIAN SPACE WITH LARGE SHADE TREES. SPACE TO BE LINKED TO ENTRANCE & CAMPUS BY A STRONG PEDESTRIAN CROSSWALK.

CONGREGATING NODE
DEVELOP NODE AT INTERSECTION. BRICK PAVEMENT. BRICK SEAT WALL. INFORMATION KIOSK. PEDESTRIAN LEVEL LIGHTING. MAJOR TREES.

SHRUB MASS
SHRUB MASS TO GIVE BUILDING A STRONG BASE & TO ELIMINATE DENSITY/MAINTENANCE PROBLEM.

ENTRANCE COURT
CREATE ENTRANCE COURT. ELIMINATE SMALL PLANTING AREA. PROVIDE MAJOR TREES. PROVIDE BRICK PAVEMENT & BICYCLE RACKS.

TREE ARCADE

SHRUB MASS

TEXTURED EDGE

PEDESTRIAN LINK

TREE ARCADE

BRICK SEAT WALL

PEDESTRIAN LINK WITH VEHICULAR ACCESS

SHRUB MASS

MAJOR TREE

INFORMATION KIOSK

BRICK PAVEMENT

SECTION A

SKETCH A

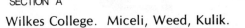
Wilkes College. Miceli, Weed, Kulik.

143

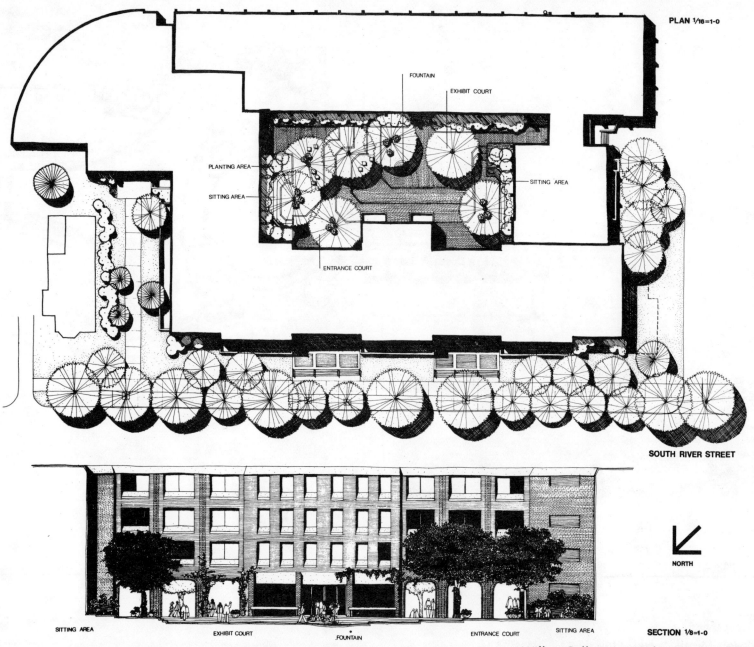

PLAN 1/16=1-0

FOUNTAIN

EXHIBIT COURT

PLANTING AREA

SITTING AREA

SITTING AREA

ENTRANCE COURT

SOUTH RIVER STREET

NORTH

SITTING AREA   EXHIBIT COURT   FOUNTAIN   ENTRANCE COURT   SITTING AREA

SECTION 1/8=1-0

Wilkes College. Miceli, Weed, Kulik.

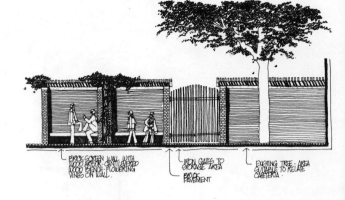

SERVICE ENTRY

SOUTH FRANKLIN STREET

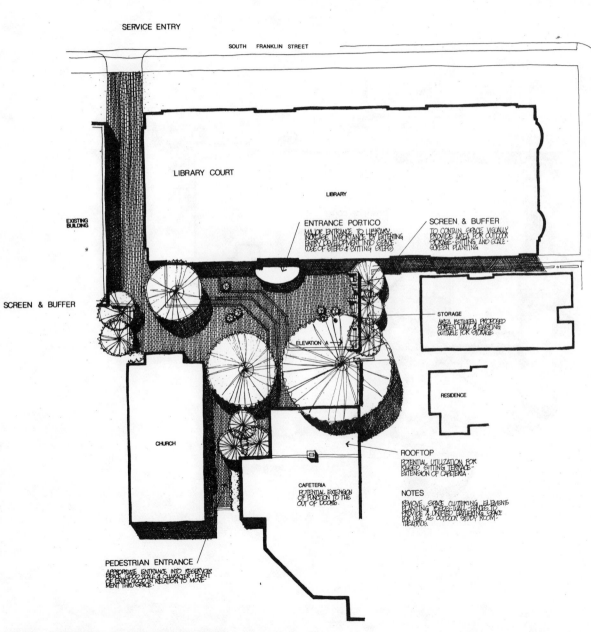

LIBRARY COURT

LIBRARY

EXISTING BUILDING

ENTRANCE PORTICO
MAJOR ENTRANCE TO LIBRARY.
INCREASE IMPORTANCE BY EXTENDING
ENTRY DEVELOPMENT INTO SPACE.
USE OF STEPS & SITTING STEPS.

SCREEN & BUFFER
TO CONTAIN SPACE VISUALLY.
PROVIDE AREA FOR OUTDOOR
STORAGE, SITTING, AND SCALE.
SCREEN PLANTING.

SCREEN & BUFFER

STORAGE
AREA BETWEEN PROPOSED
SCREEN WALL & EXISTING
SUITABLE FOR STORAGE.

ELEVATION A

RESIDENCE

ROOFTOP
POTENTIAL UTILIZATION FOR
RAISED SITTING TERRACE -
EXTENSION OF CAFETERIA.

CHURCH

CAFETERIA
POTENTIAL EXTENSION
OF FUNCTION TO THE
OUT OF DOORS.

NOTES
REMOVE SPACE CLUTTERING ELEMENTS
PLANTING & SCREEN WALL
PROVIDE & UNIFIED GATHERING SPACE
FOR USE AS OUTDOOR STUDY ROOM -
THEATRICS.

PEDESTRIAN ENTRANCE
APPROPRIATE ENTRANCE INTO SPACE. VISUALLY
DEPENDING SCALE & CHARACTER. ELEMENT
DEVELOPMENT IN RELATION TO MOVE-
MENT THROUGH SPACE.

ELEVATION A

BRICK GARDEN WALL WITH
WOOD ARBOR - CANTILEVERED
WOOD BENCH. FLOWERING
VINES ON WALL.

IRON GATES TO
STORAGE AREA
BRICK
PAVEMENT

EXISTING TREE - AREA
SUITABLE TO RELATE
CAFETERIA.

Wilkes College. Miceli, Weed, Kulik.

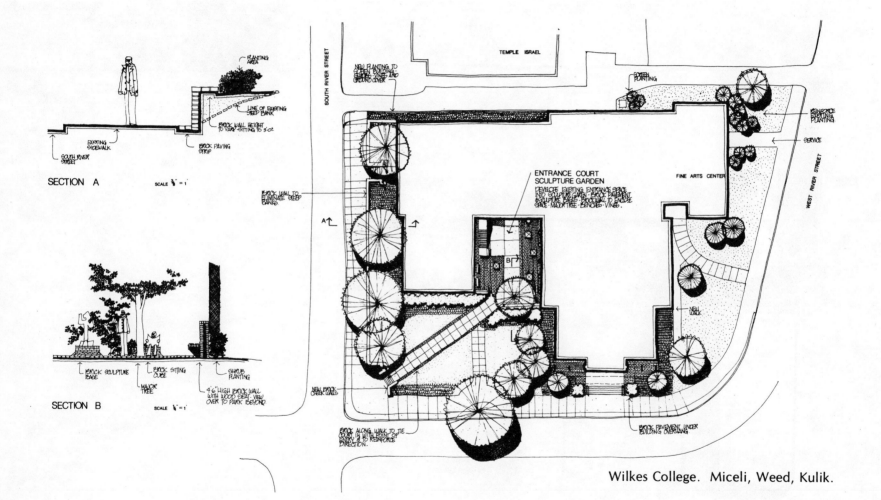

SECTION A

SCALE ¾" = 1'

PLANTING AREA

LINE OF EXISTING STEEP BANK

BRICK WALL HEIGHT TO VARY SITTING TO 3'-0"

BRICK PAVING STRIP

EXISTING SIDEWALK

SOUTH RIVER STREET

SECTION B

SCALE ⅛" = 1'

BRICK SCULPTURE BASE

BRICK CURVE

MAJOR TREE

BRICK SITTING

SHRUB PLANTING

4'6" HIGH BRICK WALL WITH WOOD SEAT. VIEW OVER TO PARK BEYOND.

SOUTH RIVER STREET

TEMPLE ISRAEL

NEW PLANTING TO COVER EXISTING BUILDING WINES AND GROUND COVER

SCREEN PLANTING

REINFORCE EXISTING PLANTING

SERVICE

BRICK WALL TO ELIMINATE STEEP BANK

ENTRANCE COURT SCULPTURE GARDEN

DEVELOPE EXISTING ENTRANCE SPACE INTO SCULPTURE GARDEN. BRICK PAVEMENT. SCULPTURE BASE. BRICK WALL TO ENCLOSE SPACE. MAJOR TREE. BENCHES. VINES.

FINE ARTS CENTER

WEST RIVER STREET

A

B

NEW WALK

NEW BRICK CHEEK WALLS

BRICK ALONG WALK TO TIE ENTRY IN WITH FRONT OF DIRECTION.

BRICK PAVEMENT UNDER BUILDING OVERHANG.

Wilkes College. Miceli, Weed, Kulik.

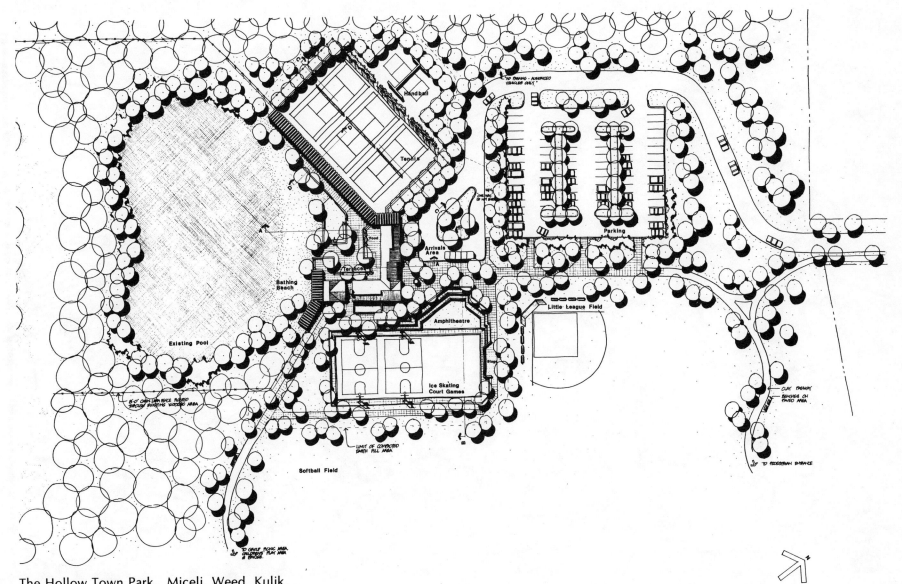

The Hollow Town Park. Miceli, Weed, Kulik.

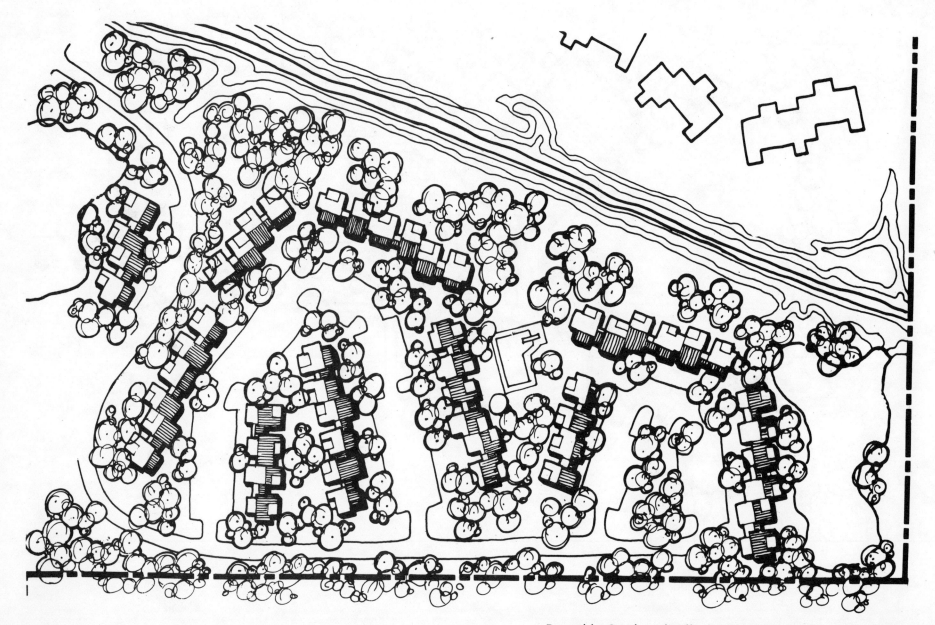

Reynolds, Smith and Hills, by David Linstrum. Ink on mylar.

Reynolds, Smith and Hills, by David Linstrum. Ink on mylar.

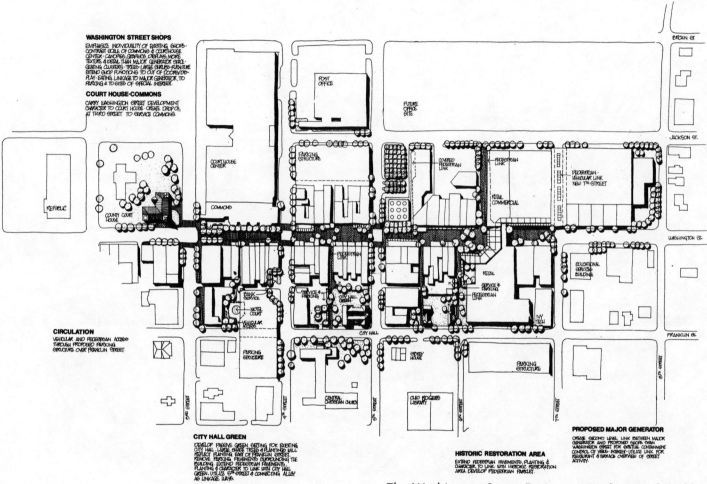

WASHINGTON STREET SHOPS
EMPHASIZE INDIVIDUALITY OF EXISTING SHOPS·
CONTRAST SCALE OF COMMONS & COURTHOUSE
CENTER · CANOPIES, GRAPHICS, DISPLAYS, MORE
TEXTURE & DETAIL THAN MAJOR GENERATOR SPACE·
SEATING CLUSTERS · TREES · LARGE SHRUBS · FURNITURE
EXTEND SHOP FUNCTIONS TO OUT OF DOORS/DIS-
PLAY · EATING. LINKAGE TO MAJOR GENERATOR, TO
PARKING & TO SITES OF SPECIAL INTEREST.

COURT HOUSE-COMMONS
CARRY WASHINGTON STREET DEVELOPMENT
CHARACTER TO COURT HOUSE · CREATE DROP OF,
AT THIRD STREET TO SERVICE COMMONS.

CIRCULATION
VEHICULAR AND PEDESTRIAN ACCESS
THROUGH PROPOSED PARKING
STRUCTURE OVER FRANKLIN STREET

CITY HALL GREEN
DEVELOP PASSIVE GREEN SETTING FOR EXISTING
CITY HALL · LARGE SHADE TREES & PLANTING WILL
REFLECT PLANTING EAST OF FRANKLIN STREET·
REMOVE PARKING. PAVEMENTS SURROUNDING THE
BUILDING · EXTEND PEDESTRIAN PAVEMENTS ·
PLANTING & CHARACTER TO LINK WITH CITY HALL
GREEN · UTILIZE 5TH STREET & CONNECTING ALLEY
AS LINKAGE WAYS.

HISTORIC RESTORATION AREA
EXTEND PEDESTRIAN PAVEMENTS, PLANTING &
CHARACTER TO LINK WITH HISTORIC RESTORATION
AREA · DEVELOP PEDESTRIAN FAMILY.

PROPOSED MAJOR GENERATOR
CREATE SECOND LEVEL LINK BETWEEN MAJOR
GENERATOR AND PROPOSED SHOPS. SPAN
WASHINGTON STREET FOR SPATIAL CONTAINMENT.
CONTROL OF VIEWS · INTEREST · UTILIZE LINK FOR
RESTAURANT & TERRACE OVERVIEW OF STREET
ACTIVITY.

The Washington Street Project. Miceli, Weed, Kulik.

150

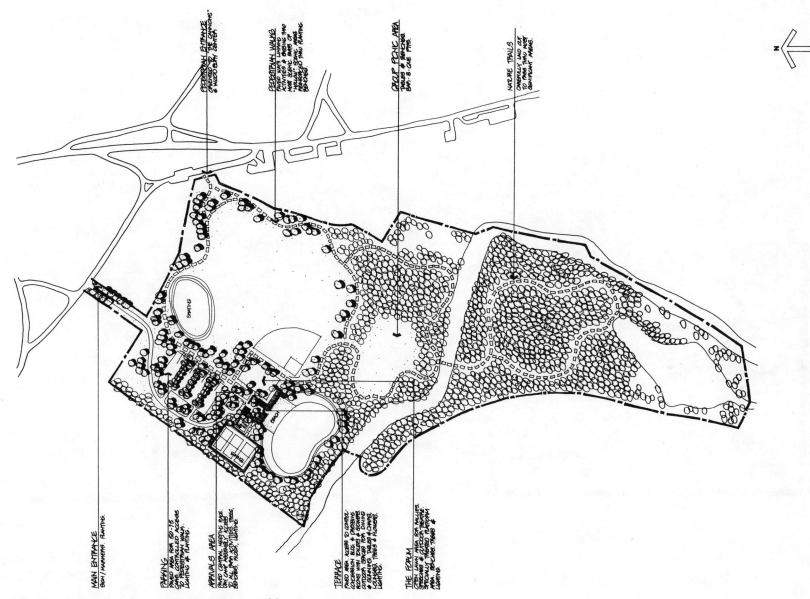

PEDESTRIAN ENTRANCE
ORIENTED TO "THE CANNONS" & W.S.O. COMM. CENTER

PEDESTRIAN WALKS
PAVED WAYS LINKING ACTIVITIES & PASSING THRU MAJOR SCENIC AREAS "HARD WALK" SPINE, HARDENED TURF PLANTING BENCHES

GROUP PICNIC AREA
TABLES & BENCHES BAR-B-QUE PITS

NATURE TRAILS
UNDERLY LAND CUT TO PASS THRU MOST SIGNIFICANT AREAS

N

SKATING

CREEK

MAIN ENTRANCE
SIGN/MARKERS PLANTING

PARKING
PAVED AREA FOR 150-175 CARS CONTROLLED ACCESS TO PEDESTRIAN WALK LIGHTING & PLANTING

ARRIVALS AREA
PAVED CENTRAL MEETING PLACE ON-CALL ASSEMBLY AREAS TO ALL PARK ACTIVITIES TREES, BENCHES, KIOSK, LIGHTING

TERRACE
PAVED AREA KIOSKS TO CONTROL CONCESSION BLDG. & DRESSING ROOMS WITH TOILETS & SHOWERS OUTDOOR SPACES FOR DINING & SUNNING TABLES & CHAIRS LOUNGES, TREES & FLOWERS LIGHTING

THE FORUM
OPEN LAWN AREA FOR RALLIES OPENING & OUTDOOR THEATRE SPECIALLY TREATED TURF/TURF AREA, BENCHES, TREES & LIGHTING

The Hollow Town Park. Miceli, Weed, Kulik.

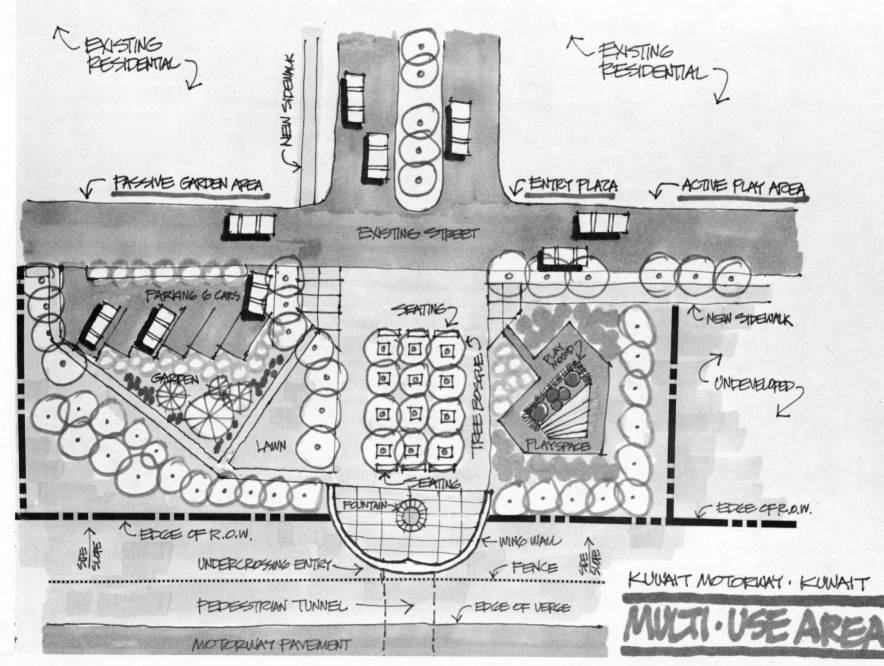

EXISTING RESIDENTIAL

EXISTING RESIDENTIAL

NEW SIDEWALK

PASSIVE GARDEN AREA

ENTRY PLAZA

ACTIVE PLAY AREA

EXISTING STREET

PARKING 6 CARS

NEW SIDEWALK

SEATING

GARDEN

UNDEVELOPED

TREE BOSQUE

PLAY MOUND

PLAYSPACE

LAWN

SEATING

FOUNTAIN

EDGE OF R.O.W.

EDGE OF R.O.W.

WING WALL

SIDE SLOPE

UNDERCROSSING ENTRY

FENCE

SIDE SLOPE

PEDESTRIAN TUNNEL

EDGE OF VERGE

MOTORWAY PAVEMENT

KUWAIT MOTORWAY · KUWAIT

MULTI · USE AREA

DeLeuw, Cather International, by David Linstrum.
Multi-colored, using broad and narrow point markers.

152

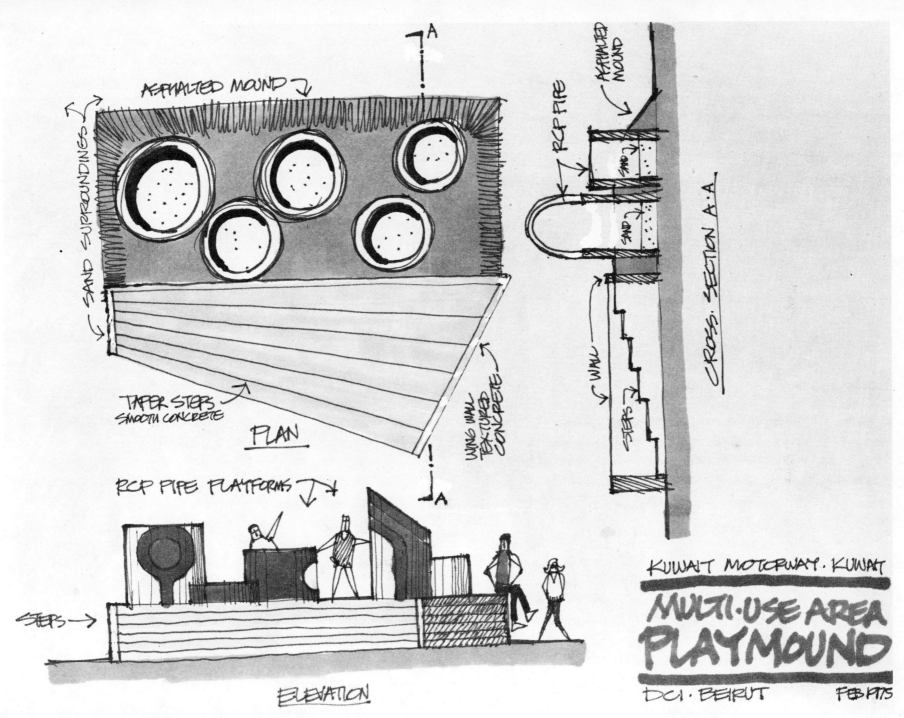

ASPHALTED MOUND

SAND SURROUNDINGS

A

RCP PIPE

ASPHALTED MOUND

SAND

TAPER STEPS
SMOOTH CONCRETE

PLAN

WING WALL
TEXTURED
CONCRETE

WALL

STEPS

CROSS. SECTION A·A

A

RCP PIPE PLATFORMS

STEPS →

ELEVATION

KUWAIT MOTORWAY · KUWAIT

MULTI·USE AREA
PLAYMOUND

DCI · BEIRUT   FEB 1975

DeLeuw, Cather International, by David Linstrum.
Multi-colored, using broad and narrow point markers.

153

FULL SIZE PLANS

Lone Cove. Edward D. Stone, Jr. & Associates, P.A.

PLAZA BOLIVAR

TIENDAS

LOGOS

TIOVIVO

LAGO GURI

BARCO PIRATA

CASA EMBRUJADA

CERVECERIA

ISLA MARGA

LAGO MARACAIBO

VILLA MARACAIBO

TIRO AL BLANCO

PASEO DEL AMAZONAS

MARIONETAS

Theme Park.   Edward D. Stone, Jr. & Associates, P.A.

ZOOLOGICO INFANTIL

TIENDAS

LAS DUÑAS

SERVICIO

AUTOPIAN

MONTAÑA RUSA

MOLINO

TIENDAS

CARROS LOCOS

CAFETERIA

CASA EMBRUJADA

TIENDAS

1430
1420
1410
1400
1390
1380

Theme Park. Edward D. Stone, Jr. & Associates, P.A.

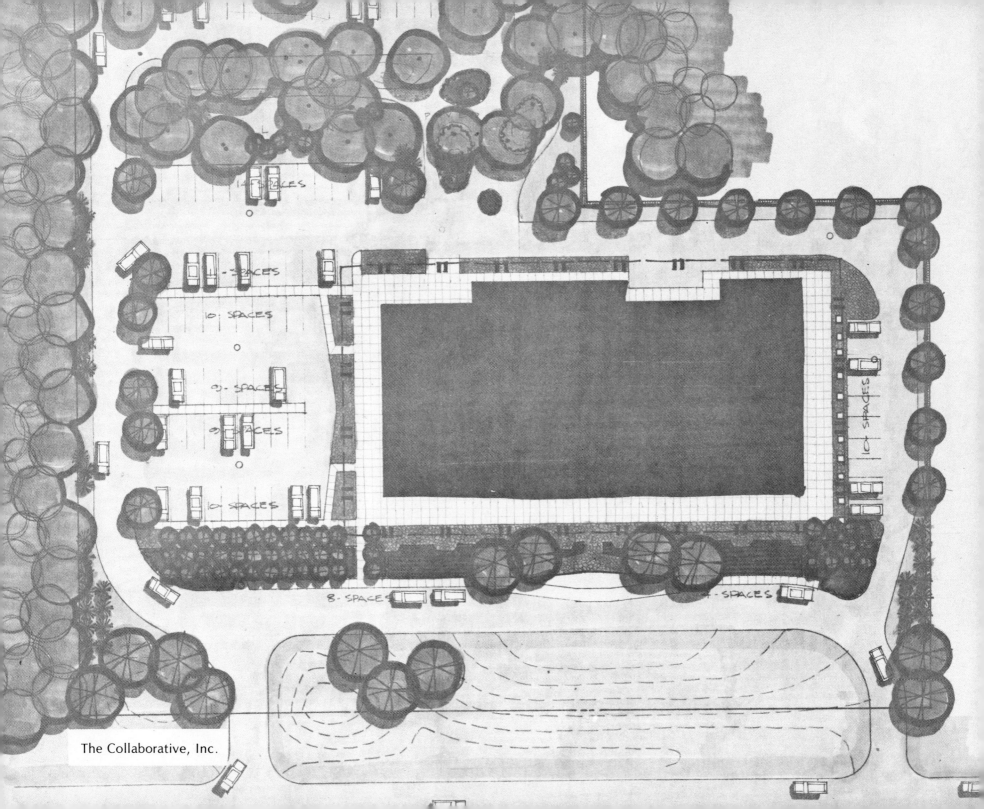

14-SPACES

10·SPACES

9·SPACES

9·SPACES

10·SPACES

10·SPACES

10 SPACES

8·SPACES

4·SPACES

The Collaborative, Inc.

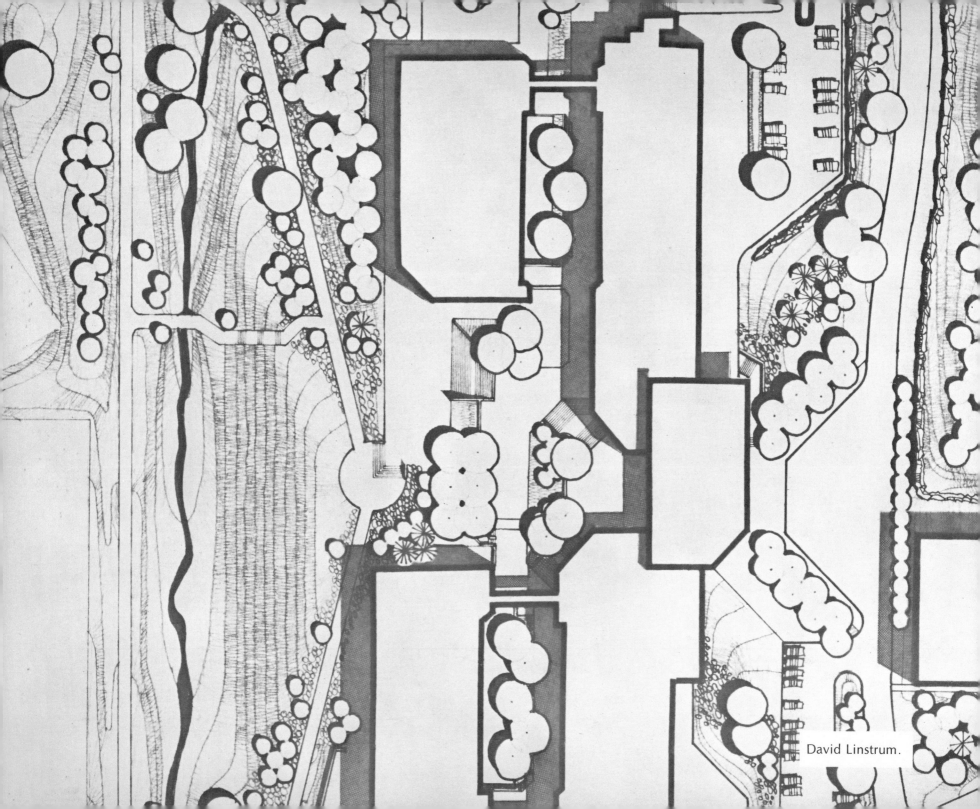

David Linstrum.

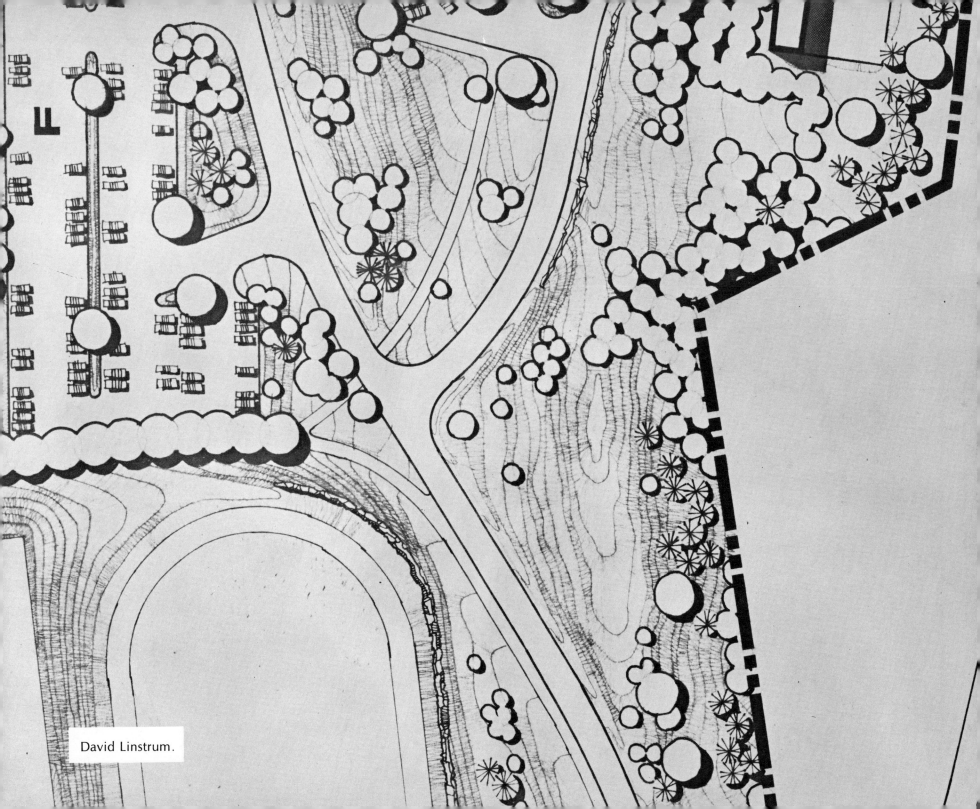

F

David Linstrum.

Tom Balsley.

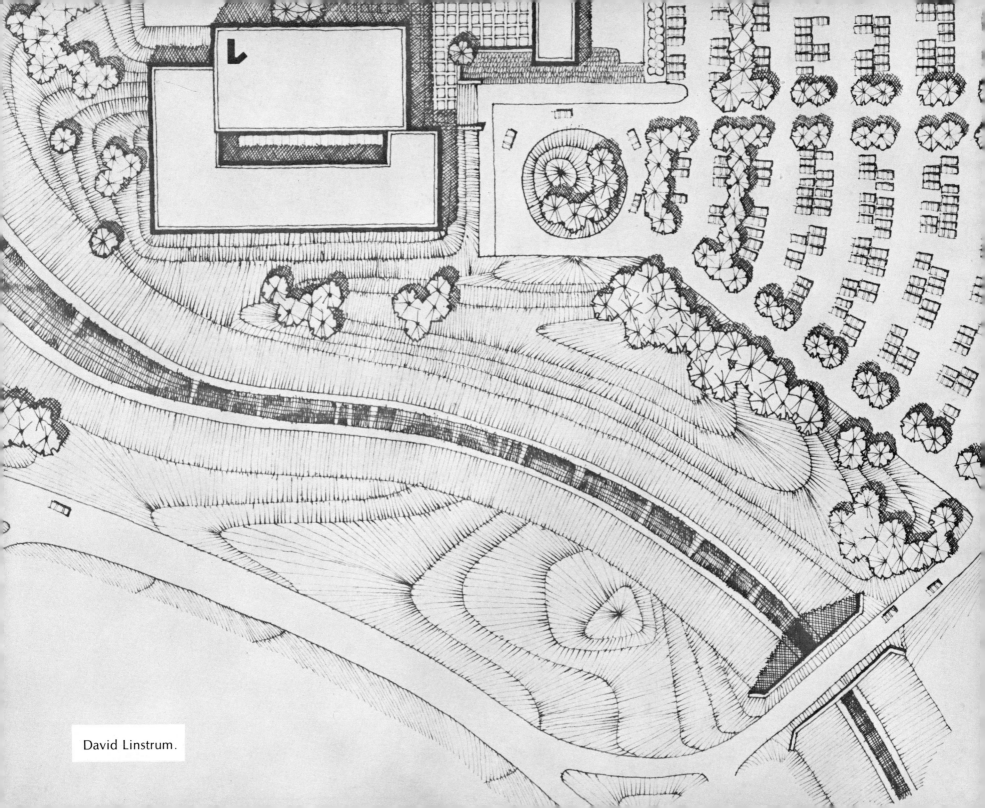

David Linstrum.

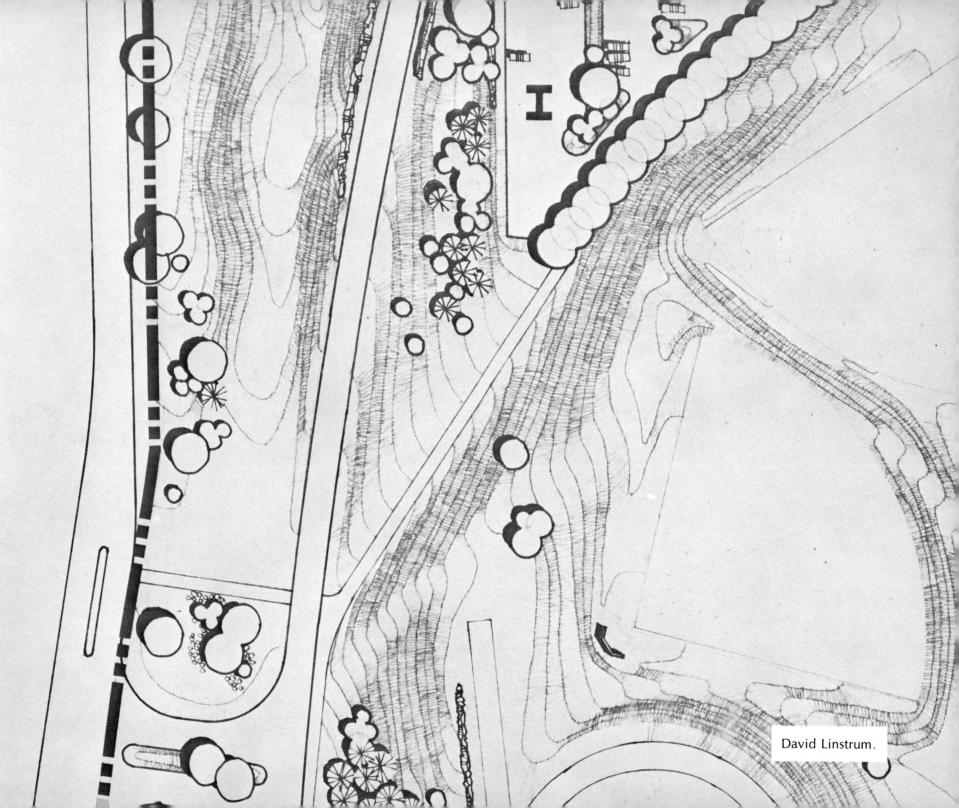

David Linstrum.

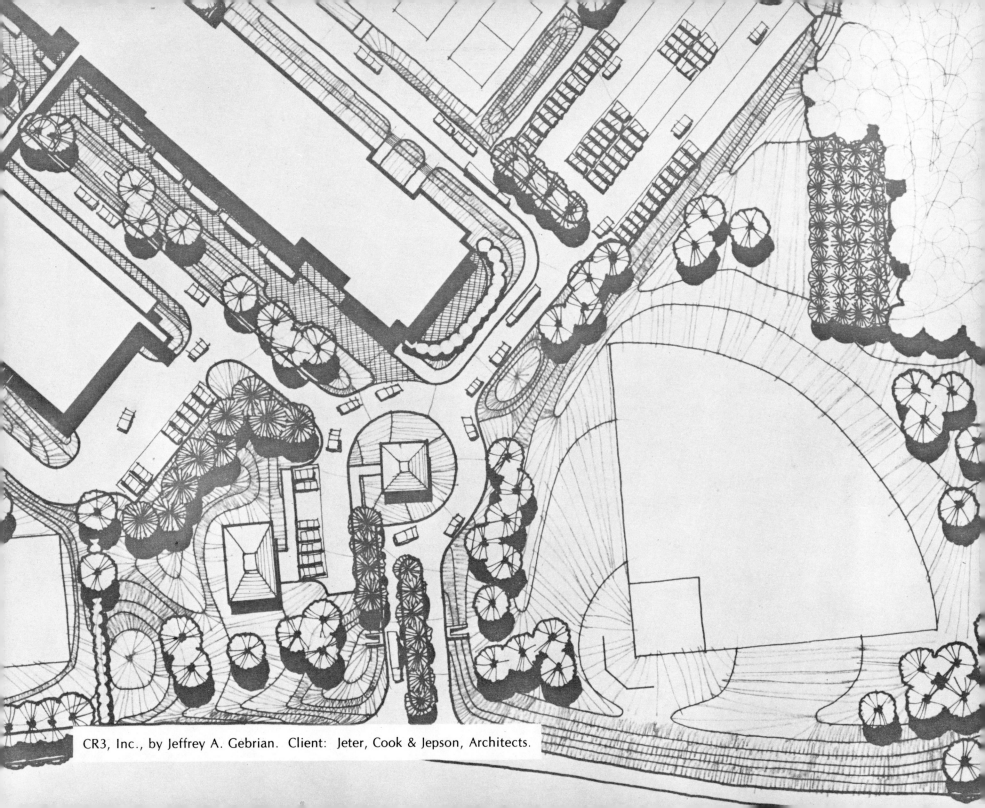

CR3, Inc., by Jeffrey A. Gebrian. Client: Jeter, Cook & Jepson, Architects.

Bristol Harbour. The Reimann-Buechner Partnership, by Cortland Read.

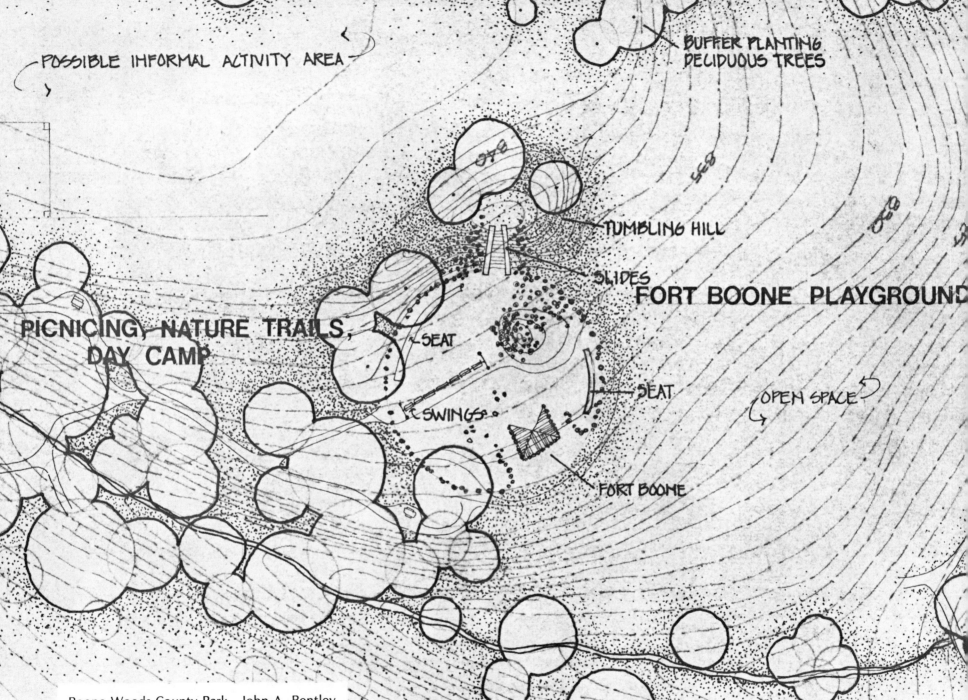

POSSIBLE INFORMAL ACTIVITY AREA

BUFFER PLANTING
DECIDUOUS TREES

TUMBLING HILL

SLIDES

FORT BOONE PLAYGROUND

PICNICING, NATURE TRAILS,
DAY CAMP

SEAT

SEAT

OPEN SPACE

SWINGS

FORT BOONE

Boone Woods County Park. John A. Bentley.

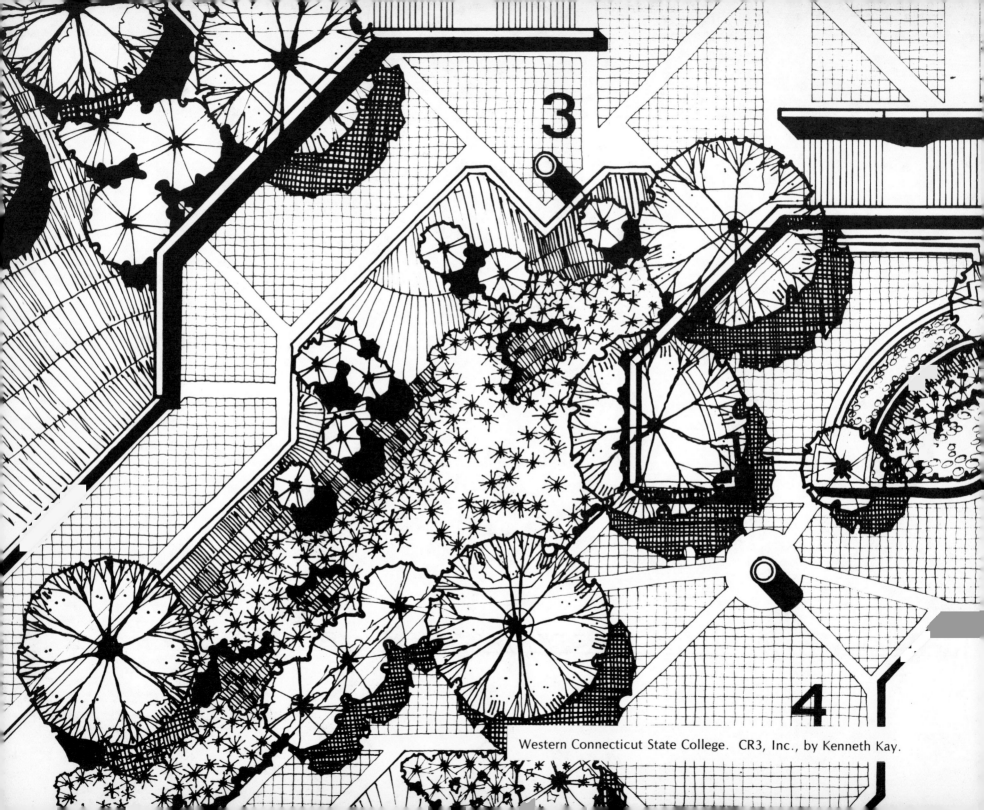

Western Connecticut State College. CR3, Inc., by Kenneth Kay.

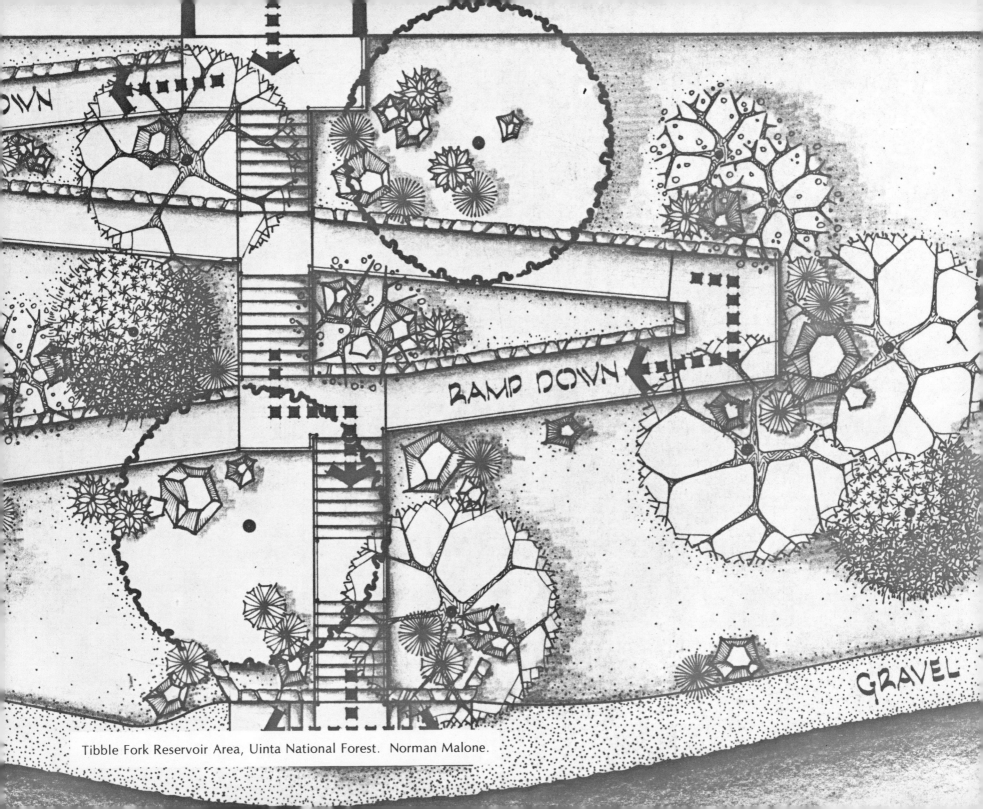

Tibble Fork Reservoir Area, Uinta National Forest. Norman Malone.

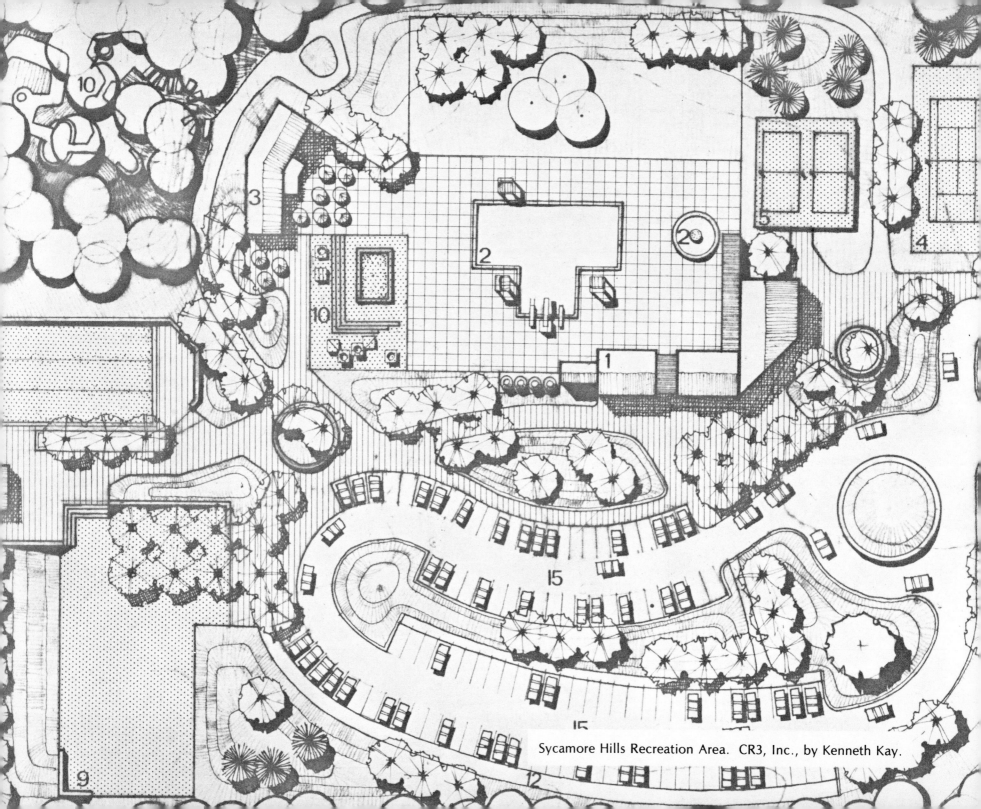

Sycamore Hills Recreation Area. CR3, Inc., by Kenneth Kay.

Chris Macey.

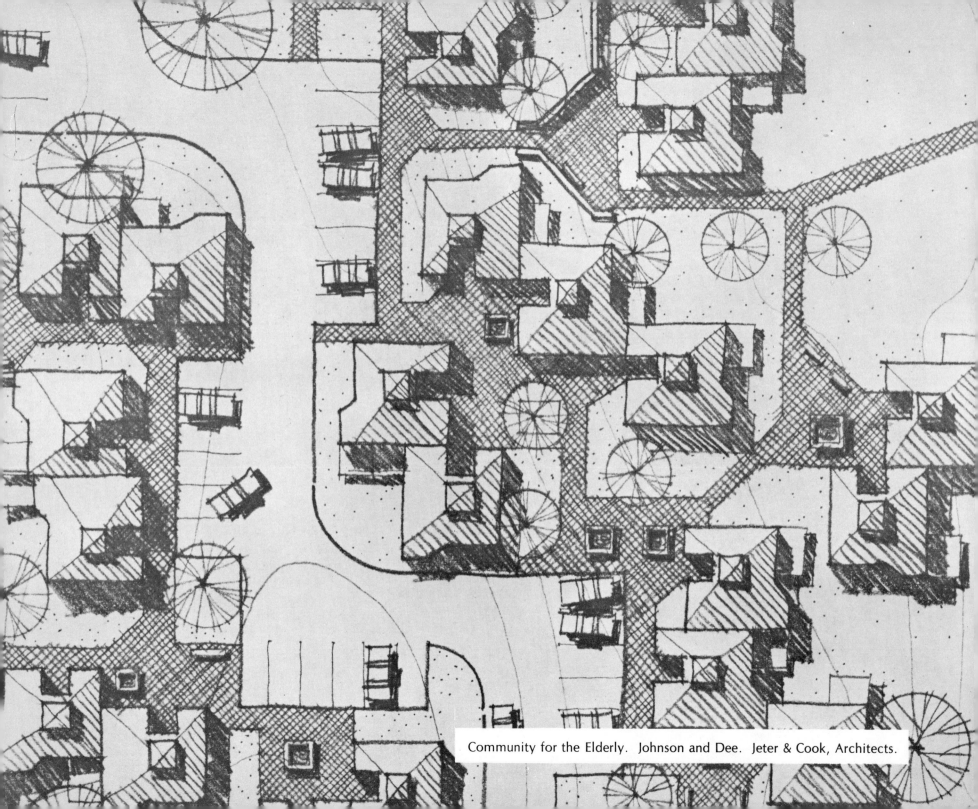

Community for the Elderly. Johnson and Dee. Jeter & Cook, Architects.

Park Master Plan. John A. Bentley.

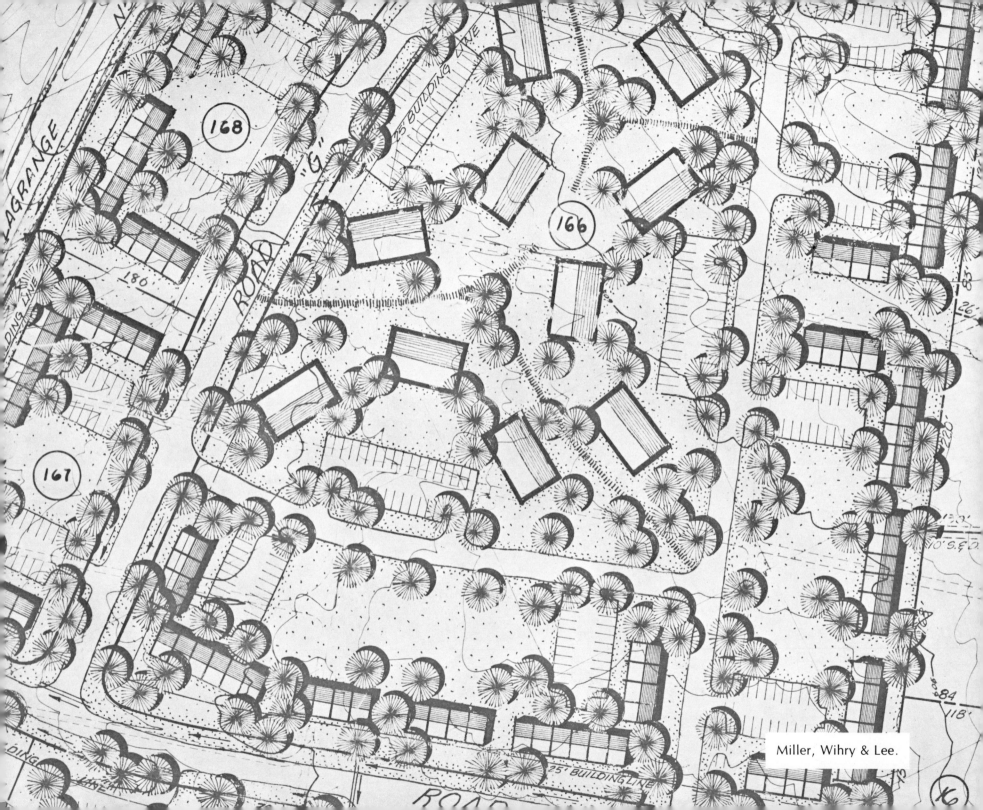

Miller, Wihry & Lee.

Miller, Wihry & Lee.

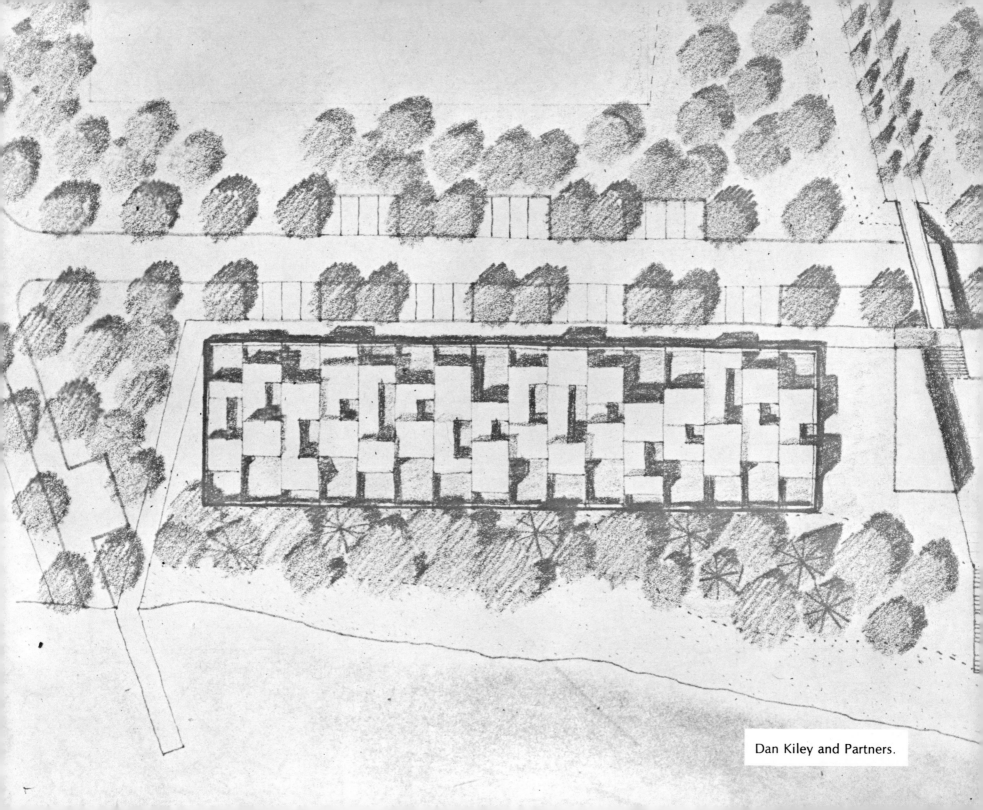

Dan Kiley and Partners.

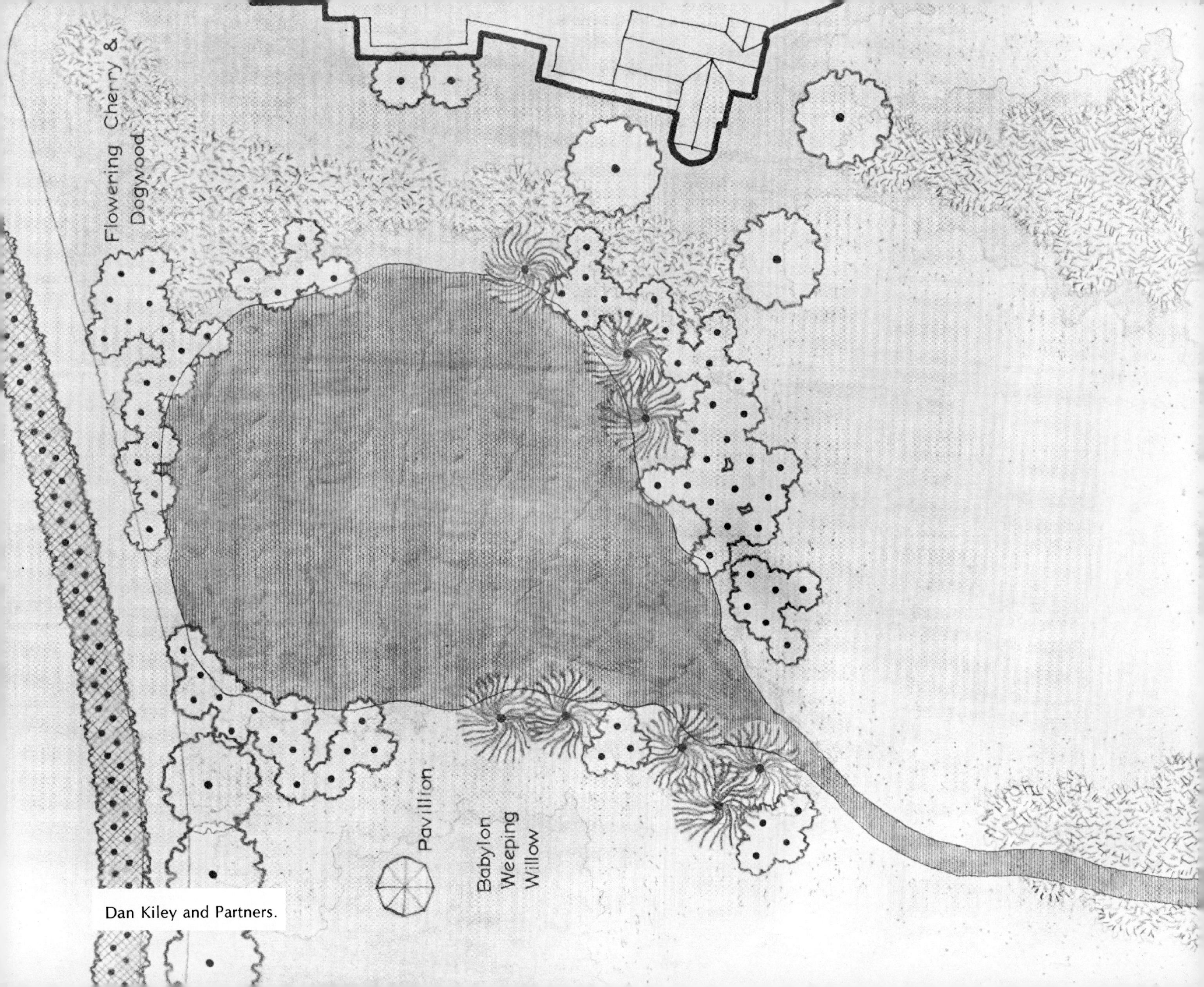

Flowering Cherry & Dogwood

Pavillion

Babylon Weeping Willow

Dan Kiley and Partners.

7

ELEVATIONS AND SECTIONS

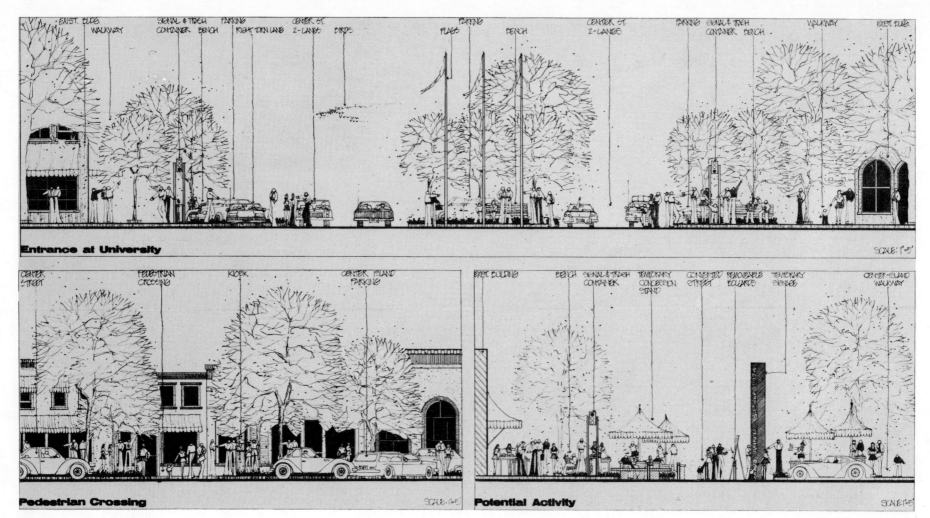

Entrance at University

EXIST. BLDG. / WALKWAY / SIGNAL & TRASH CONTAINER / PARKING BENCH / RIGHT TURN LANE / CENTER ST. 2-LANES / BIRDS / PARKING / FLAGS / BENCH / CENTER ST. 2-LANES / PARKING / SIGNAL & TRASH CONTAINER / BENCH / WALKWAY / EXIST. BLDG.

SCALE: 1"=5'

Pedestrian Crossing

CENTER STREET / PEDESTRIAN CROSSING / KIOSK / CENTER ISLAND PARKING

SCALE: 1"=5'

Potential Activity

EXIST BUILDING / BENCH / SIGNAL & TRASH CONTAINER / TEMPORARY CONCESSION STAND / CONVERTED STREET / REMOVABLE BOLLARDS / TEMPORARY SIGNAGE / CENTER ISLAND WALKWAY

SCALE: 1"=5'

Maas and Grassli.

180

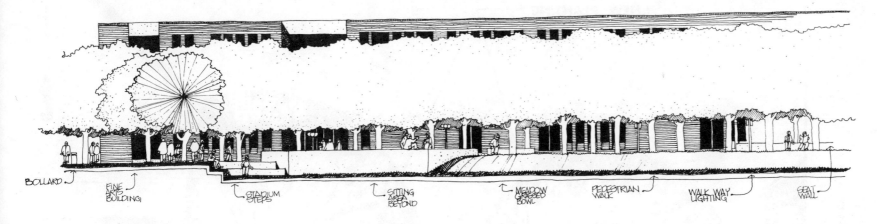

SECTION A·A

BOLLARD | FINE ARTS BUILDING | STADIUM STEPS | SITTING AREA BEYOND | MEADOW GRASSED BOWL | PEDESTRIAN WALK | WALK WAY LIGHTING | SEAT WALL

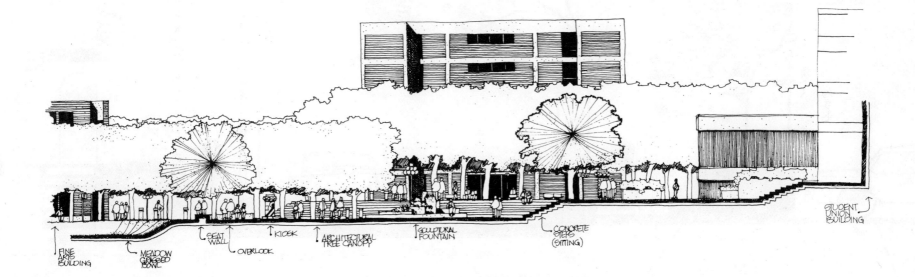

SECTION B·B

FINE ARTS BUILDING | MEADOW GRASSED BOWL | SEAT WALL | OVERLOOK | KIOSK | ARCHITECTURAL TREE CANOPY | SCULPTURAL FOUNTAIN | CONCRETE STEPS (SITTING) | STUDENT UNION BUILDING

Student Center Mall. Miceli, Weed, Kulik.

181

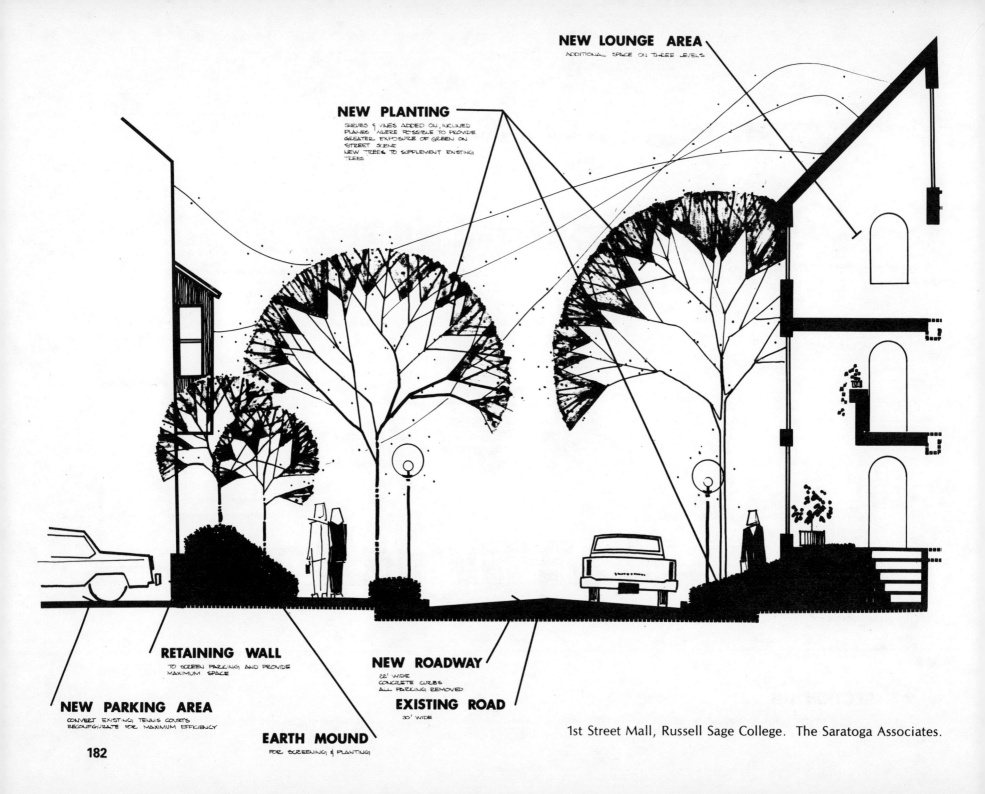

NEW LOUNGE AREA
ADDITIONAL SPACE ON THREE LEVELS

NEW PLANTING
SHRUBS & VINES ADDED ON INCLINED
PLANES WHERE POSSIBLE TO PROVIDE
GREATER EXPOSURE OF GREEN ON
STREET SCENE
NEW TREES TO SUPPLEMENT EXISTING
TREES

RETAINING WALL
TO SCREEN PARKING AND PROVIDE
MAXIMUM SPACE

NEW ROADWAY
22' WIDE
CONCRETE CURBS
ALL PARKING REMOVED

NEW PARKING AREA
CONVERT EXISTING TENNIS COURTS
RECONFIGURATE FOR MAXIMUM EFFICIENCY

EXISTING ROAD
30' WIDE

EARTH MOUND
FOR SCREENING & PLANTING

1st Street Mall, Russell Sage College. The Saratoga Associates.

182

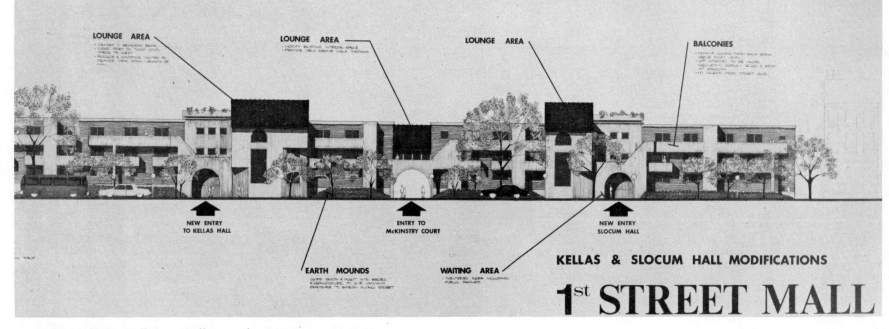

LOUNGE AREA

LOUNGE AREA

LOUNGE AREA

BALCONIES

NEW ENTRY
TO KELLAS HALL

ENTRY TO
McKINSTRY COURT

NEW ENTRY
SLOCUM HALL

EARTH MOUNDS

WAITING AREA

KELLAS & SLOCUM HALL MODIFICATIONS

1st STREET MALL

1st Street Mall, Russell Sage College. The Saratoga Associates.

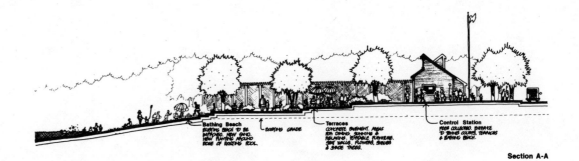

Section A-A

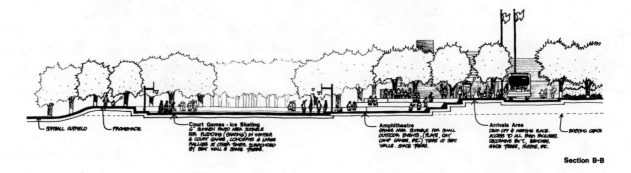

Section B-B

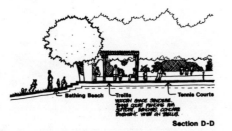

Section D-D

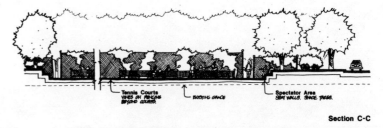

Section C-C

The Hollow Town Park. Miceli, Weed, Kulik.

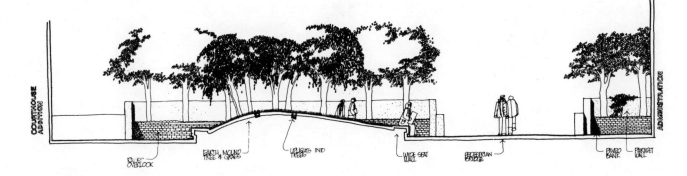

SECTION - GARDEN

SECTION - BOSQUE

Detention Center. Miceli, Weed, Kulik.
Kramer, Hirsch, and Carchidi, Architects.

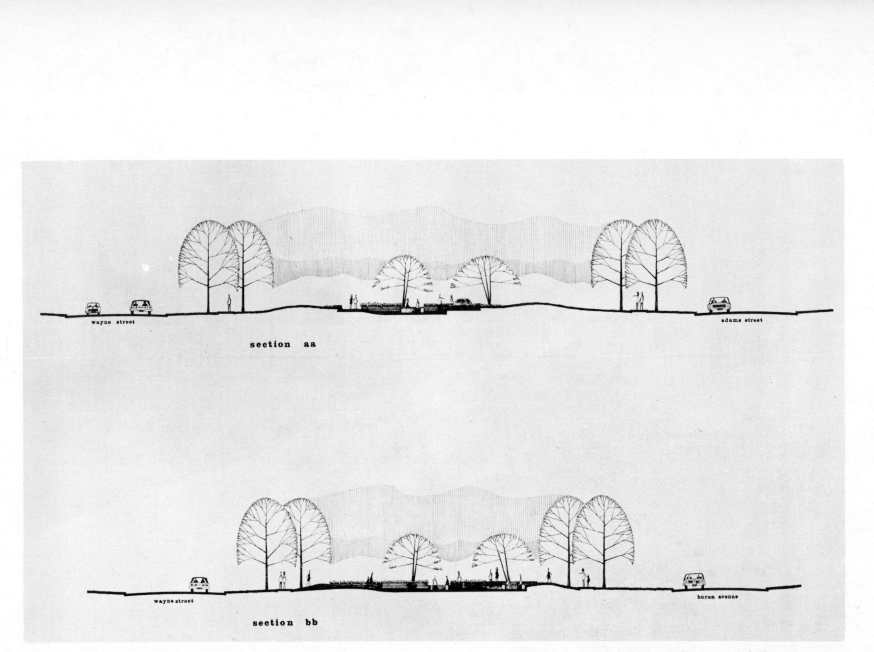

section aa

wayne street

adams street

section bb

wayne street

huron avenue

Dauch Memorial Park. William A. Behnke Associates,
James H. Ness, Associated Landscape Architect.

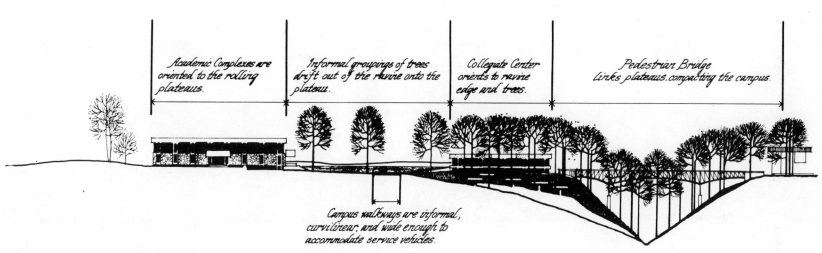

Academic Complexes are oriented to the rolling plateaus.

Informal groupings of trees drift out of the ravine onto the plateau.

Collegiate Center orients to ravine edge and trees.

Pedestrian Bridge links plateaus, compacting the campus.

Campus walkways are informal, curvilinear, and wide enough to accommodate service vehicles.

Grand Valley State College.   Johnson, Johnson & Roy, Inc.

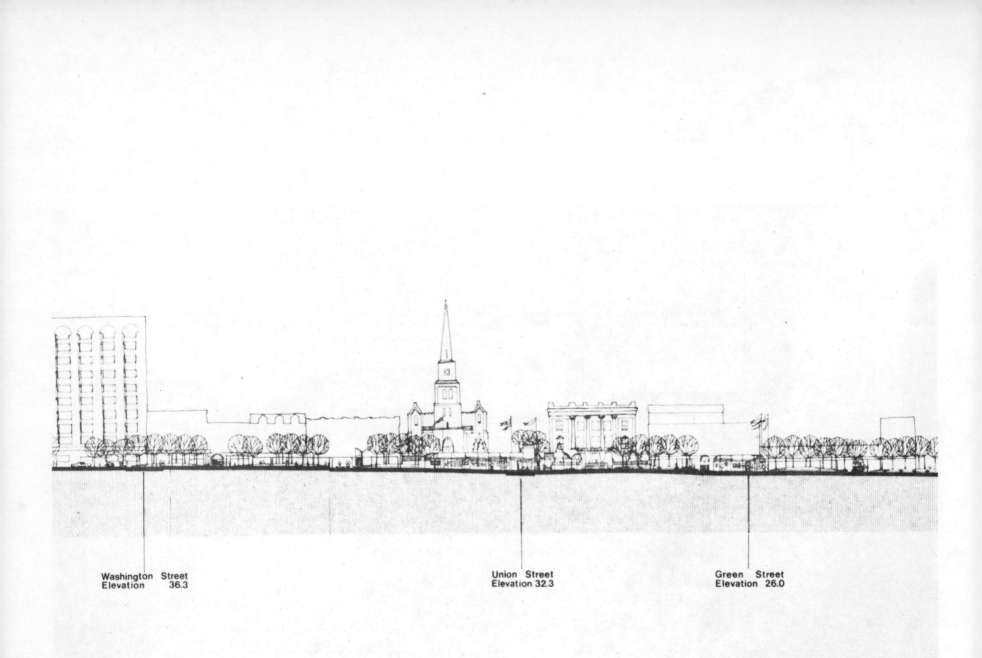

Washington Street
Elevation   36.3

Union Street
Elevation 32.3

Green Street
Elevation 26.0

State Street Semi-Mall. Johnson and Dee.

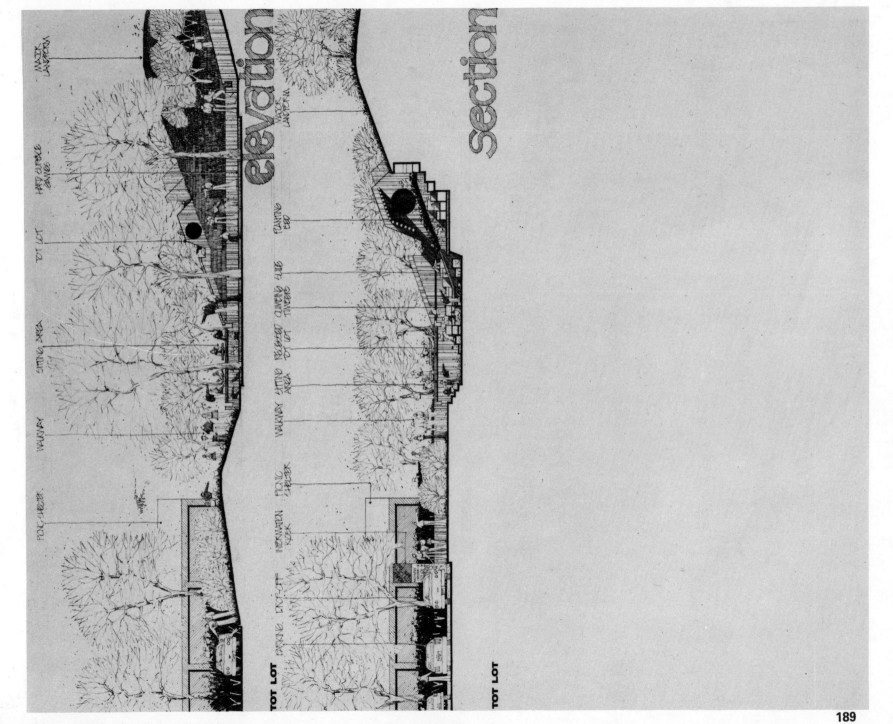

Maas and Grassli.

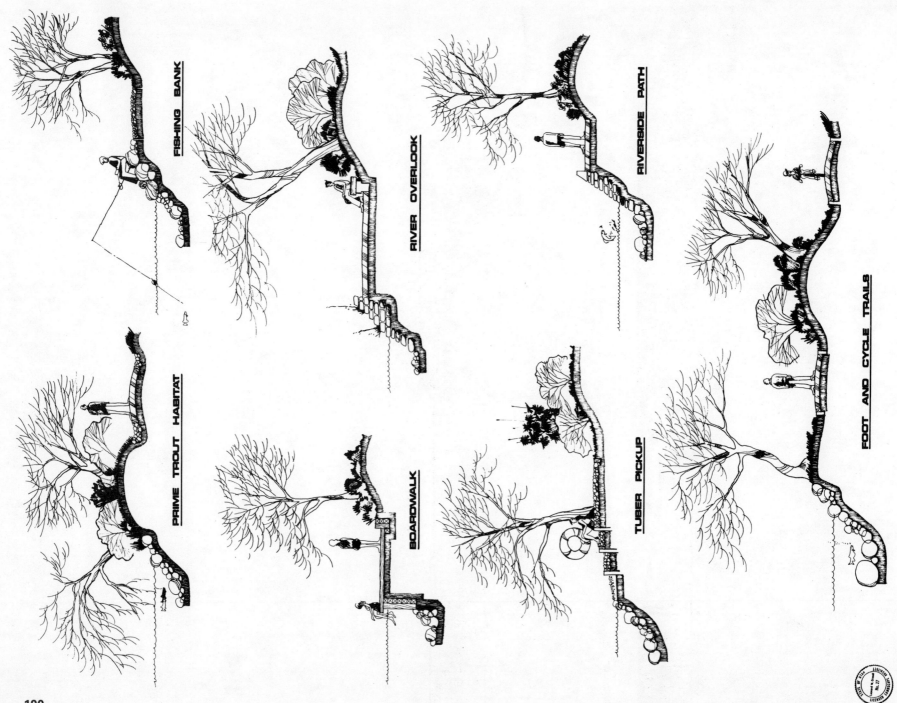

FISHING BANK

RIVER OVERLOOK

RIVERSIDE PATH

PRIME TROUT HABITAT

BOARDWALK

TUBER PICKUP

FOOT AND CYCLE TRAILS

190

Ogden River Parkway. Maas and Grassli.

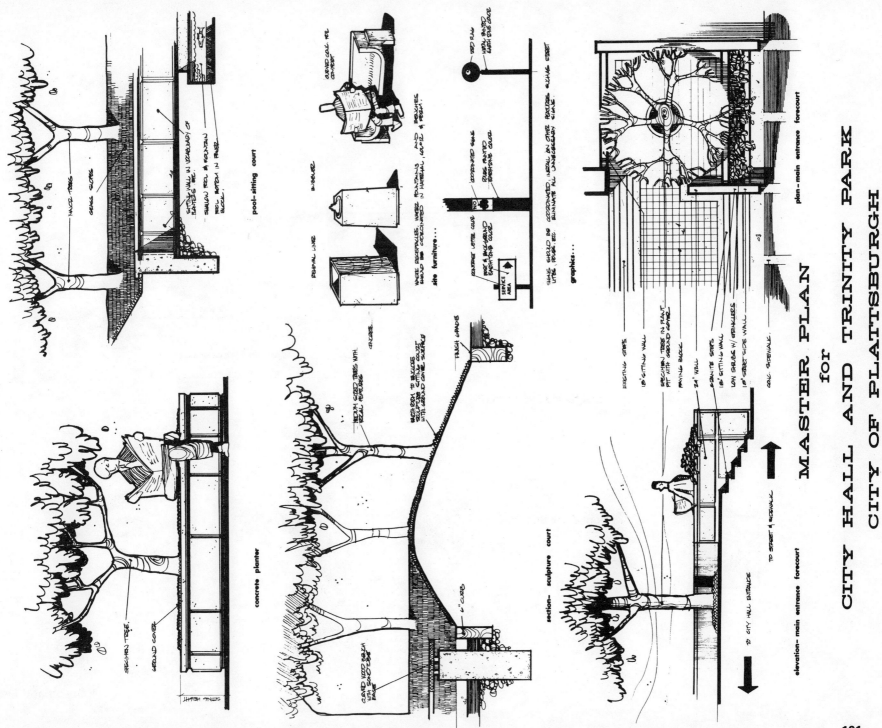

pool-sitting court

concrete planter

section—sculpture court

elevation—main entrance forecourt

plan—main entrance forecourt

site furniture . . .

graphics . . .

MASTER PLAN
for
CITY HALL AND TRINITY PARK
CITY OF PLATTSBURGH

Master plan for City Hall and Trinity Park. The Saratoga Associates.

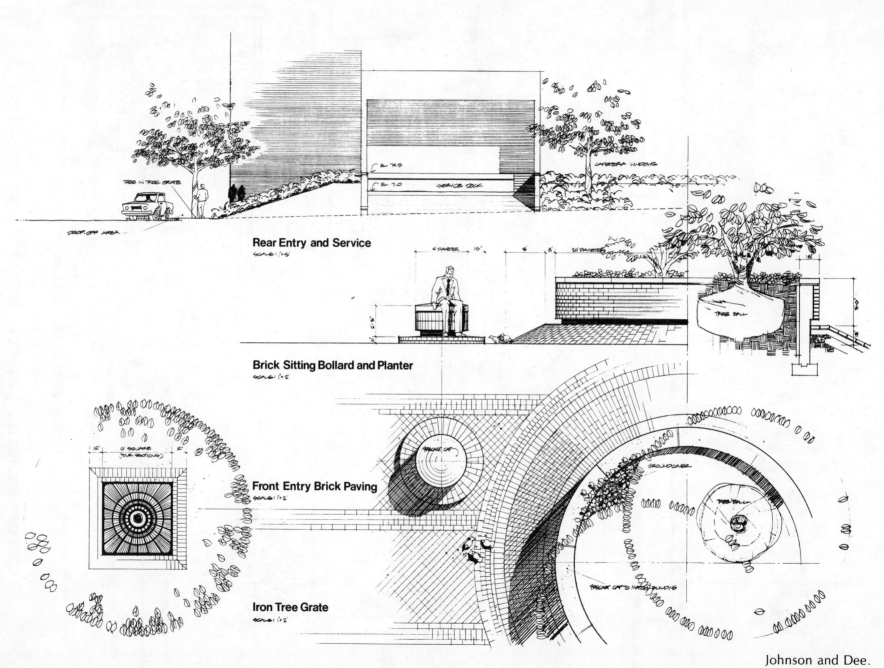

Rear Entry and Service
SCALE: 1"=5'

Brick Sitting Bollard and Planter
SCALE: 1"=2'

Front Entry Brick Paving
SCALE: 1"=2'

Iron Tree Grate
SCALE: 1"=2'

Johnson and Dee.

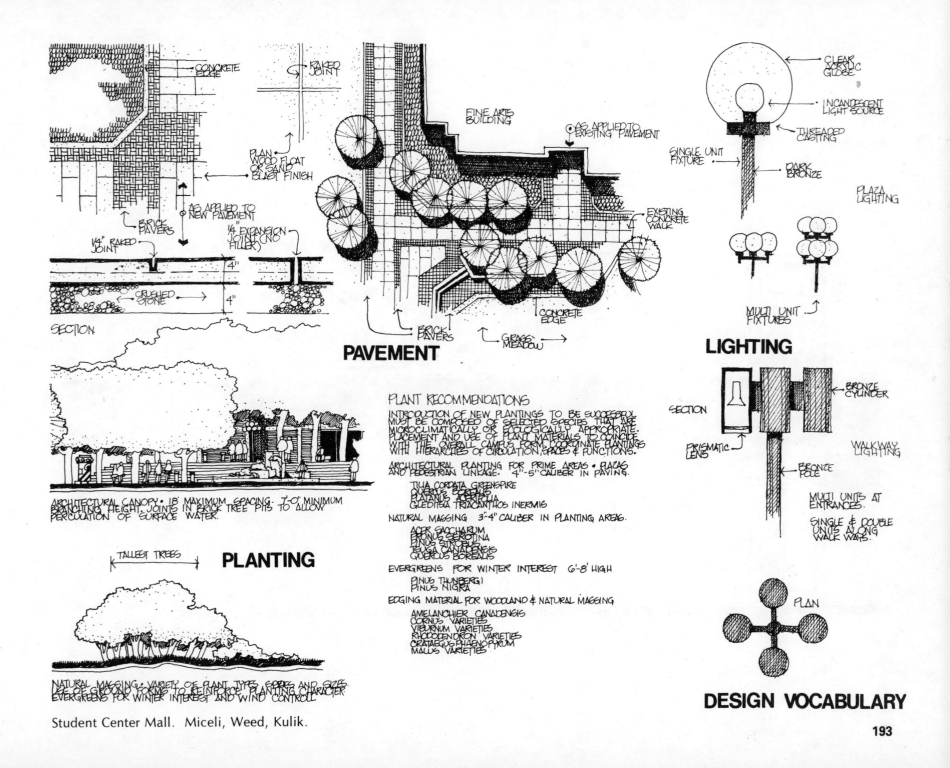

PAVEMENT

CONCRETE EDGE

RAKED JOINT

PLAN WOOD FLOAT OR SAND BLAST FINISH

BRICK PAVERS

AS APPLIED TO NEW PAVEMENT

¼" EXPANSION JOINT (NO FILLER)

¼" RAKED JOINT

4"

4"

CRUSHED STONE

SECTION

FINE ARTS BUILDING

AS APPLIED TO EXISTING PAVEMENT

EXISTING CONCRETE WALK

CONCRETE EDGE

BRICK PAVERS

GRASS MEADOW

LIGHTING

CLEAR ACRYLIC GLOBE

INCANDESCENT LIGHT SOURCE

SINGLE UNIT FIXTURE

THREADED CASTING

DARK BRONZE

PLAZA LIGHTING

MULTI UNIT FIXTURES

SECTION

PRISMATIC LENS

BRONZE CYLINDER

WALKWAY LIGHTING

BRONZE POLE

MULTI UNITS AT ENTRANCES.

SINGLE & DOUBLE UNITS ALONG WALK WAYS.

ARCHITECTURAL CANOPY. 18' MAXIMUM SPACING. 7'-0" MINIMUM BRANCHING HEIGHT. JOINTS IN BRICK TREE PITS TO ALLOW PERCOLATION OF SURFACE WATER.

TALLEST TREES

PLANTING

PLANT RECOMMENDATIONS

INTRODUCTION OF NEW PLANTINGS TO BE SUCCESSFUL MUST BE COMPOSED OF SELECTED SPECIES THAT ARE MICROCLIMATICALLY OR ECOLOGICALLY APPROPRIATE. PLACEMENT AND USE OF PLANT MATERIALS TO COINCIDE WITH THE OVERALL CAMPUS FORM. COORDINATE PLANTINGS WITH HIERARCHIES OF CIRCULATION, SPACES & FUNCTIONS.

ARCHITECTURAL PLANTING FOR PRIME AREAS • PLAZAS AND PEDESTRIAN LINKAGE. 4"-5" CALIBER IN PAVING.

TILIA CORDATA GREENSPIRE
QUERCUS BOREALIS
PLATANUS ACERIFOLIA
GLEDITSIA TRIACANTHOS INERMIS

NATURAL MASSING 3"-4" CALIBER IN PLANTING AREAS.

ACER SACCHARUM
PRUNUS SEROTINA
PINUS STROBUS
TSUGA CANADENSIS
QUERCUS BOREALIS

EVERGREENS FOR WINTER INTEREST 6'-8' HIGH

PINUS THUNBERGI
PINUS NIGRA

EDGING MATERIAL FOR WOODLAND & NATURAL MASSING

AMELANCHIER CANADENSIS
CORNUS VARIETIES
VIBURNUM VARIETIES
RHODODENDRON VARIETIES
CRATAEGUS PHAENOPYRUM
MALUS VARIETIES

NATURAL MASSING • VARIETY OF PLANT TYPES, FORMS AND SIZES. USE OF GROUND FORMS TO REINFORCE PLANTING CHARACTER. EVERGREENS FOR WINTER INTEREST AND WIND CONTROL.

PLAN

DESIGN VOCABULARY

Student Center Mall. Miceli, Weed, Kulik.

DAY

NIGHT

BOLLARD STUDY
XEROX-STAMFORD
BY CR3 INC. SCALE 1"=1'-0" 7·74

Bollard Study — Xerox — Stamford. CR3, Inc.,
by Carl Mueller. Client: Charles Luckman Associates.

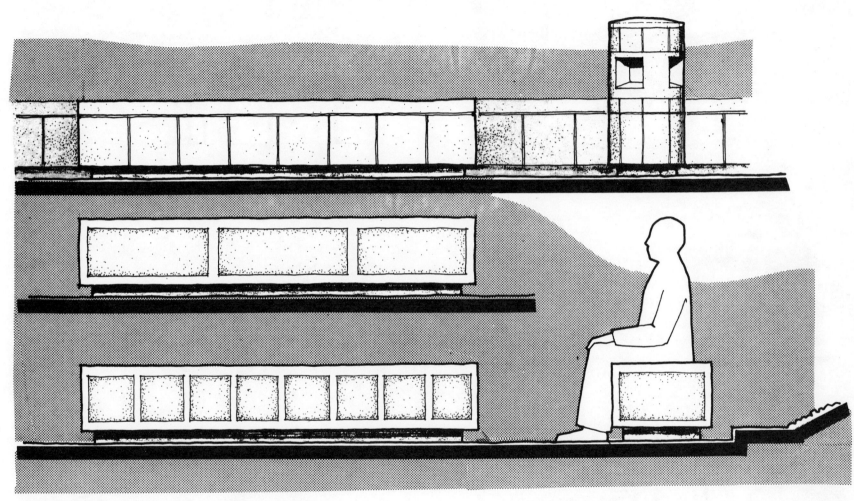

Bench and Wall Study — Xerox — Stamford. CR3, Inc.,
by Carl Mueller. Client: Charles Luckman Associates.

BENCH AND WALL STUDY
XEROX - STAMFORD
BY cr3 INC   SCALE 1"=1'-0"   7·74

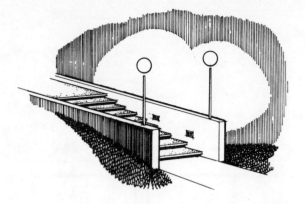

Step lighting

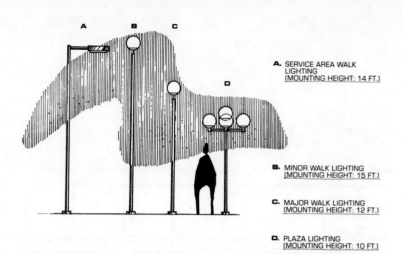

A. SERVICE AREA WALK LIGHTING (MOUNTING HEIGHT: 14 FT.)

B. MINOR WALK LIGHTING (MOUNTING HEIGHT: 15 FT.)

C. MAJOR WALK LIGHTING (MOUNTING HEIGHT: 12 FT.)

D. PLAZA LIGHTING (MOUNTING HEIGHT: 10 FT.)

Pedestrian lighting

Trash receptacle and drinking fountain

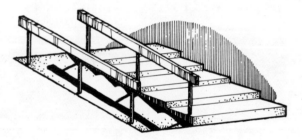

Ramp

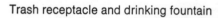

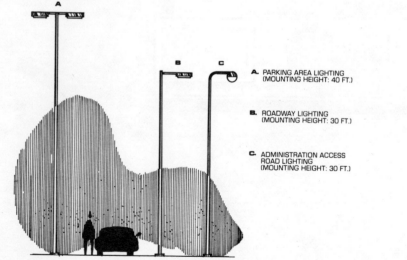

A. PARKING AREA LIGHTING (MOUNTING HEIGHT: 40 FT.)

B. ROADWAY LIGHTING (MOUNTING HEIGHT: 30 FT.)

C. ADMINISTRATION ACCESS ROAD LIGHTING (MOUNTING HEIGHT: 30 FT.)

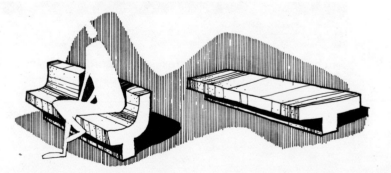

Benches

Parking and road lighting

CR3, Inc., by Cortland Read. Client: Pfohl, Roberts, Biggie, Architects.

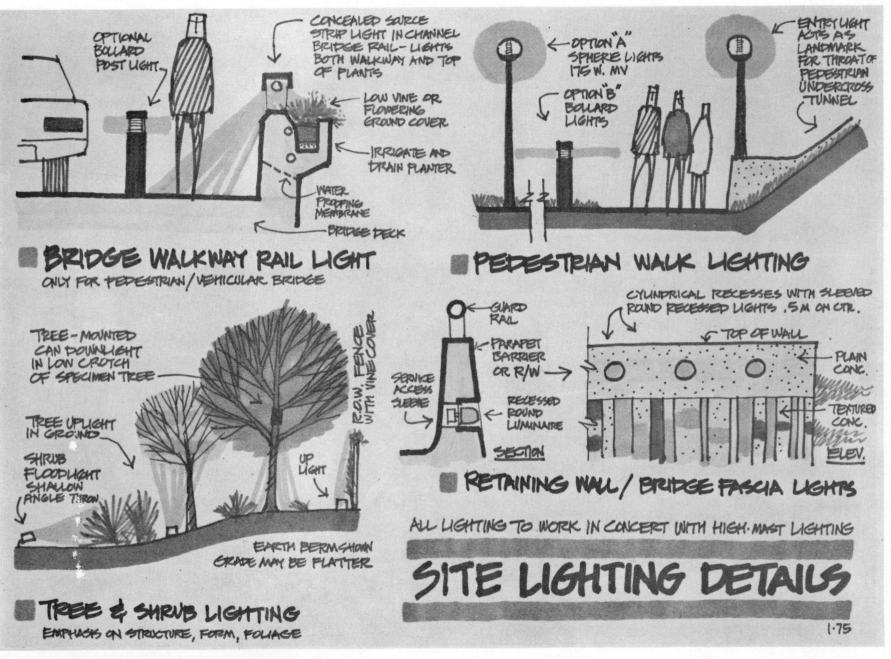

BRIDGE WALKWAY RAIL LIGHT
ONLY FOR PEDESTRIAN / VEHICULAR BRIDGE

OPTIONAL BOLLARD POST LIGHT.

CONCEALED SOURCE STRAP LIGHT IN CHANNEL BRIDGE RAIL — LIGHTS BOTH WALKWAY AND TOP OF PLANTS

LOW VINE OR FLOWERING GROUND COVER

IRRIGATE AND DRAIN PLANTER

WATER PROOFING MEMBRANE

BRIDGE DECK

PEDESTRIAN WALK LIGHTING

OPTION "A" SPHERE LIGHTS 175 W. MV

OPTION "B" BOLLARD LIGHTS

ENTRY LIGHT ACTS AS LANDMARK FOR THROAT OF PEDESTRIAN UNDERCROSS TUNNEL

TREE & SHRUB LIGHTING
EMPHASIS ON STRUCTURE, FORM, FOLIAGE

TREE - MOUNTED CAN DOWNLIGHT IN LOW CROTCH OF SPECIMEN TREE

TREE UPLIGHT IN GROUND

SHRUB FLOODLIGHT SHALLOW ANGLE THROW

R.O.W. FENCE WITH VINE COVER

UP LIGHT

EARTH BERM SHOWN GRADE MAY BE FLATTER

RETAINING WALL / BRIDGE FASCIA LIGHTS

GUARD RAIL

PARAPET BARRIER OR R/W

SERVICE ACCESS SLEEVE

RECESSED ROUND LUMINAIRE

SECTION

CYLINDRICAL RECESSES WITH SLEEVED ROUND RECESSED LIGHTS .5 M ON CTR.

TOP OF WALL

PLAIN CONC.

TEXTURED CONC.

ELEV.

ALL LIGHTING TO WORK IN CONCERT WITH HIGH-MAST LIGHTING

SITE LIGHTING DETAILS

1·75

DeLeuw, Cather International by David Linstrum.
Multi-colored, using broad and narrow point markers.

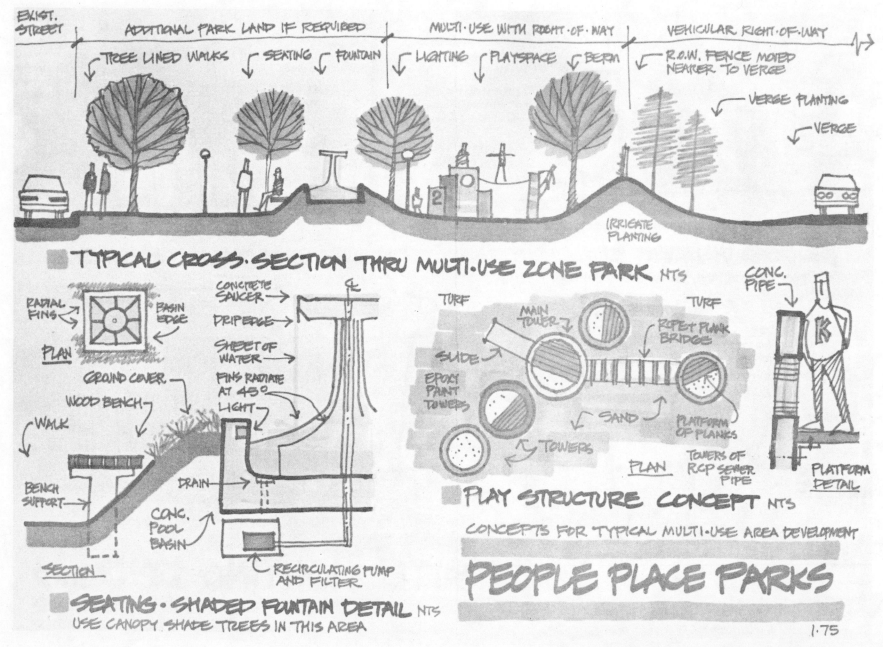

EXIST. STREET | ADDITIONAL PARK LAND IF REQUIRED | MULTI·USE WITH RIGHT·OF·WAY | VEHICULAR RIGHT·OF·WAY

TREE LINED WALKS   SEATING   FOUNTAIN   LIGHTING   PLAYSPACE   BERM   R.O.W. FENCE MOVED NEARER TO VERGE

VERGE PLANTING

VERGE

IRRIGATE PLANTING

TYPICAL CROSS·SECTION THRU MULTI·USE ZONE PARK NTS

RADIAL FINS   BASIN EDGE

PLAN

GROUND COVER

WOOD BENCH

WALK

BENCH SUPPORT

SECTION

CONCRETE SAUCER
DRIPEDGE
SHEET OF WATER
FINS RADIATE AT 45°
LIGHT

DRAIN

CONC. POOL BASIN

RECIRCULATING PUMP AND FILTER

SEATING·SHADED FOUNTAIN DETAIL NTS
USE CANOPY SHADE TREES IN THIS AREA

TURF   TURF

MAIN TOWER   ROPE & PLANK BRIDGE

SLIDE

EPOXY PAINT TOWERS

SAND   PLATFORM OF PLANKS

TOWERS

PLAN   TOWERS OF RCP SEWER PIPE

CONC. PIPE

PLATFORM DETAIL

PLAY STRUCTURE CONCEPT NTS

CONCEPTS FOR TYPICAL MULTI·USE AREA DEVELOPMENT

PEOPLE PLACE PARKS

1·75

DeLeuw, Cather International by David Linstrum.
Multi-colored, using broad and narrow point markers.

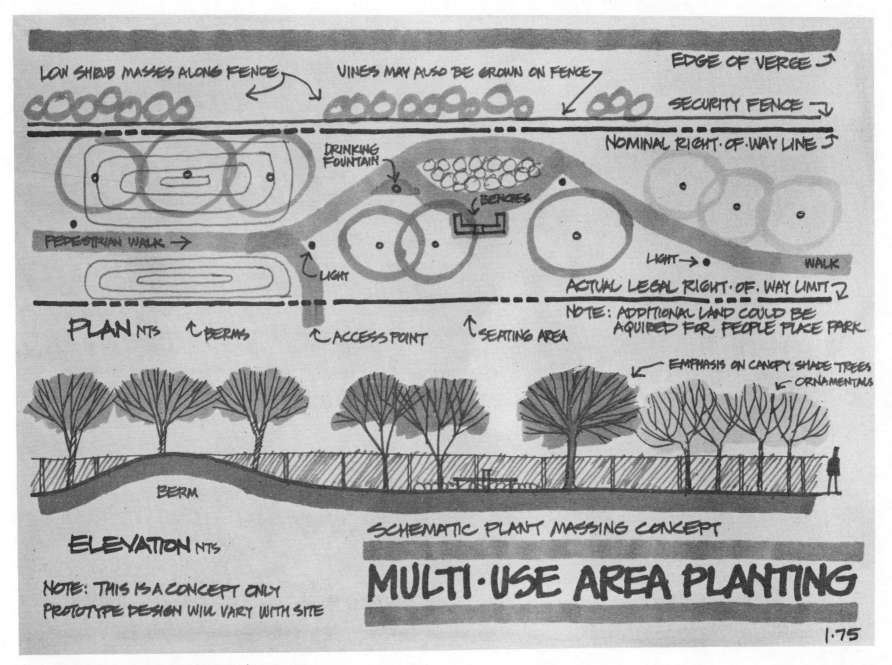

LOW SHRUB MASSES ALONG FENCE

VINES MAY ALSO BE GROWN ON FENCE

EDGE OF VERGE

SECURITY FENCE

NOMINAL RIGHT·OF·WAY LINE

DRINKING FOUNTAIN

BENCHES

PEDESTRIAN WALK →

LIGHT

LIGHT →

WALK

ACTUAL LEGAL RIGHT·OF·WAY LIMIT

NOTE: ADDITIONAL LAND COULD BE AQUIRED FOR PEOPLE PLACE PARK

PLAN NTS   ↑ BERMS   ↑ ACCESS POINT   ↑ SEATING AREA

EMPHASIS ON CANOPY SHADE TREES
ORNAMENTALS

BERM

ELEVATION NTS

NOTE: THIS IS A CONCEPT ONLY
PROTOTYPE DESIGN WILL VARY WITH SITE

SCHEMATIC PLANT MASSING CONCEPT

MULTI·USE AREA PLANTING

1·75

DeLeuw, Cather International by David Linstrum.
Multi-colored, using broad and narrow point markers.

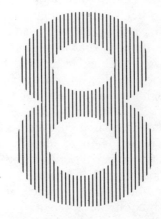

LETTERING

INTRODUCTION

The quality of your work and how it impresses others, especially prospective employers, is largely dependent upon your freehand lettering. The development of a consistent and professional-looking stlye will help you promote your abilities. This section, with its text and illustrations, is intended to provide you with some guidelines and motivation towards that goal.

Please do not be mislead into believing that the press-on style lettering or the use of such mechanical types as the "Leroy" lettering pens will solve your lettering problems. Each has its use in certain situations; none, however, replace freehand lettering. Mechanical lettering is not practical for the amount required on construction drawings and planting plans, whereas freehand lettering is faster and creates an individuality and attractiveness that cannot be achieved with mechanical methods.

Letters and numerals are nothing but symbols which you learn to identify at an early age. When these are grouped together to form words and numbers they acquire meaning which you have also learned and now use freely without much additional thought.

Your freehand lettering will be representative of these common identifiable symbols, which when grouped together will convey important information to your clients and their contractors. Thus, each letter and numeral you form should be a reasonable and readable representation of the original symbol.

ABCDEFGHIJKLMNOPQRSTUVWXYZ 1234567890
AMERICAN SOCIETY OF LANDSCAPE ARCHITECTS

abcdefghijklmnopqrstuvwxyz 1234567890
american society of landscape architects

ABCDEFGHIJKLMNOPQRSTUVWXYZ 1234567890
AMERICAN SOCIETY OF LANDSCAPE ARCHITECTS

abcdefghijklmnopqrstuvwxyz 1234567890
American Society of Landscape Architects

ABCDEFGHIJKLMNOPQRSTUVWXYZ 12345678910
AMERICAN SOCIETY of LANDSCAPE ARCHITECTS

Johnson, Johnson & Roy, Inc.

ELM STREET

RECREATION COMMISSION

Site Location

ISOMETRIC - DROPPED CURB

8/9

NO SCALE

(top) Johnson and Dee, (upper middle) John A. Bentley,
(lower middle) University of Illinois Office for Capital Programs,
(bottom) Browning, Day, Pollak Associates, Inc.

Because a certain attractiveness can be achieved, lettering may also be classified as design. Letters in one style may vary from tall and thin to the wide and broad character of another style. The lines used to form each letter may be narrow and thin, or thick and broad. The spacing between letters may vary, to spread a word out or squeeze it into a small space. Groups of words, and lines of words may be aesthetically placed on the page or drawing.

SUGGESTED TECHNIQUES

1. Always use guidelines when lettering. The spacing of guidelines to each other and between lines of words should always be consistent for the most attractive appearance. A sharp 3H or 4H lead is useful for keeping guidelines light. (Guidelines shown are darker for reproduction purposes only.)

2. Use a soft lead pencil, as it will be easier to control than a hard lead and will glide more easily over the surface of the paper. To start, try an H or HB lead. Later as you become experienced you will select various leads to fit changing situations and different tracing papers. Sharpen your lead frequently to maintain uniform lines in forming your letters and numerals. A sharp lead also provides a cleaner and sharper line, which reproduces better.

3. If you choose to print vertical letters, be sure all vertical lines are consistently vertical. Slanted letters are best when the vertical lines

slant from 15° to 22° right of pure vertical. It will require considerably more practice to keep your letters consistently slanted. (Light guidelines at the desired angle are useful for practicing.)

4. The most popular form of lettering for most situations is all capitals. Lower case letters may be useful, especially for planting plans, if well-done. Script is used occasionally for preliminary plans or freehand style drawings.

5. Because of differences in physical coordination each individual will use a different number of, and direction in the strokes necessary to form each letter or numeral. In your practicing, experiment with a variety of strokes to find those which will fit you best.

6. Be consistent by forming the same letter the same way each time it is used. The height and width of letters should be consistent with each other — each time they are used in the same style. This also applies to the spaces between the letters.

7. As you practice, vary the spacing of your guidelines to give you proficiency in lettering all heights and sizes of letters and numerals.

8. Plan your layout for several lines of lettering on a drawing to create an attractive, balanced and readable arrangement. To achieve this, place an overlay on the final sheet before you start to letter and roughly block out the areas to be lettered. This will also help you to avoid spelling errors.

Concrete Block pillars:

Juniperus communis	COMMON JUNIPER
Rhus trilobata	SKUNK BUSH
Sambucus canadensis	ELDERBERRY

(top) Browning, Day, Pollak, Associates, Inc., (bottom) Blackhawk Scenic Overlook, Uinta National Forest. Lyle B. Gomm.

9. Begin lettering from the top of the sheet and move downward to avoid smudging. If it is necessary to work on top of previously drafted work lay a sheet of clean paper under your hand to protect the drawing and minimize smudging.

10. Perfection requires considerable practice. Print every chance you get — writing letters home, taking class notes, etc. It will take some time to develop a relaxed, swift, and controlled technique.

11. Refrain from attempting to develop several styles at once. Concentrate on and master one style before trying another.

12. Test the readability of your style by asking a friend, who is not a designer or draftsman, to read it. If he has trouble, revise or start over.

EXAMPLES

On the pages which follow you will find several examples of freehand lettering which may give you some ideas and motivation towards creating your own style.

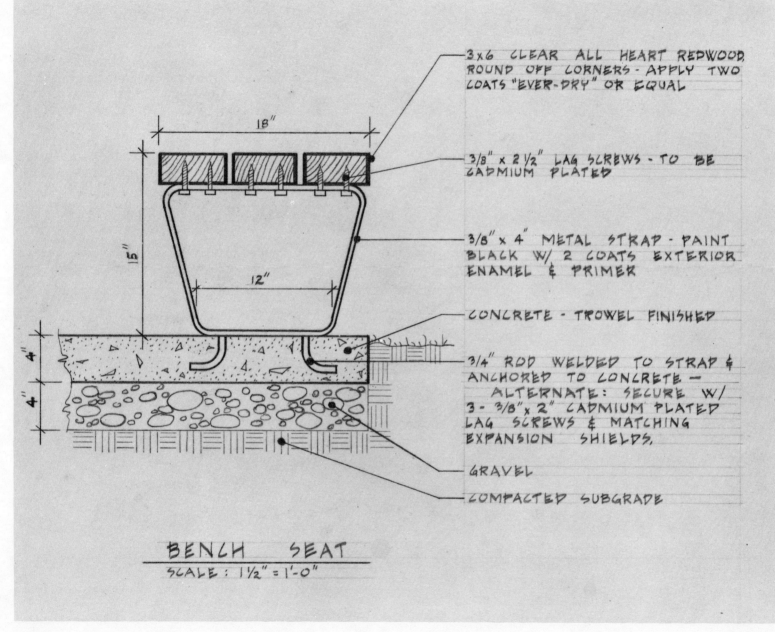

18"

15"

12"

4"

4"

3x6 CLEAR ALL HEART REDWOOD.
ROUND OFF CORNERS - APPLY TWO
COATS "EVER-DRY" OR EQUAL

3/8" x 2 1/2" LAG SCREWS - TO BE
CADMIUM PLATED

3/8" x 4" METAL STRAP - PAINT
BLACK W/ 2 COATS EXTERIOR
ENAMEL & PRIMER

CONCRETE - TROWEL FINISHED

3/4" ROD WELDED TO STRAP &
ANCHORED TO CONCRETE -
    ALTERNATE: SECURE W/
3 - 3/8" x 2" CADMIUM PLATED
LAG SCREWS & MATCHING
EXPANSION SHIELDS.

GRAVEL

COMPACTED SUBGRADE

BENCH SEAT
SCALE: 1 1/2" = 1'-0"

Don Teal.

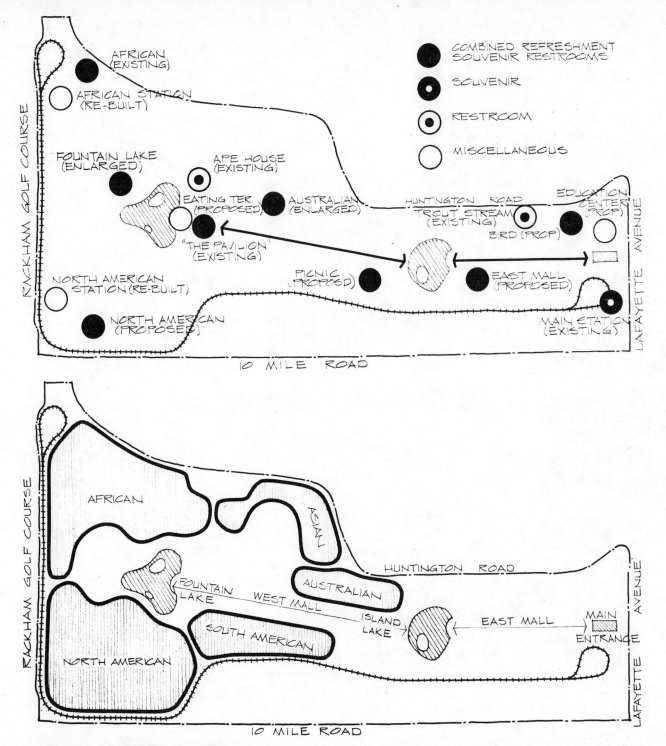

COMBINED REFRESHMENT SOUVENIR RESTROOMS

SOUVENIR

RESTROOM

MISCELLANEOUS

AFRICAN (EXISTING)

AFRICAN STATION (RE-BUILT)

FOUNTAIN LAKE (ENLARGED)

APE HOUSE (EXISTING)

EATING TER. (PROPOSED)

AUSTRALIAN (ENLARGED)

"THE PAVILION" (EXISTING)

HUNTINGTON ROAD

TROUT STREAM (EXISTING)

BIRD (PROP)

EDUCATION CENTER (PROP)

NORTH AMERICAN STATION (RE-BUILT)

PICNIC (PROPOSD)

EAST MALL (PROPOSED)

NORTH AMERICAN (PROPOSED)

MAIN STATION (EXISTING)

RACKHAM GOLF COURSE

LAFAYETTE AVENUE

10 MILE ROAD

AFRICAN

ASIAN

FOUNTAIN LAKE

WEST MALL

AUSTRALIAN

ISLAND LAKE

EAST MALL

MAIN ENTRANCE

SOUTH AMERICAN

NORTH AMERICAN

RACKHAM GOLF COURSE

HUNTINGTON ROAD

LAFAYETTE AVENUE

10 MILE ROAD

Sasaki, Dawson, DeMay Associates, Inc.

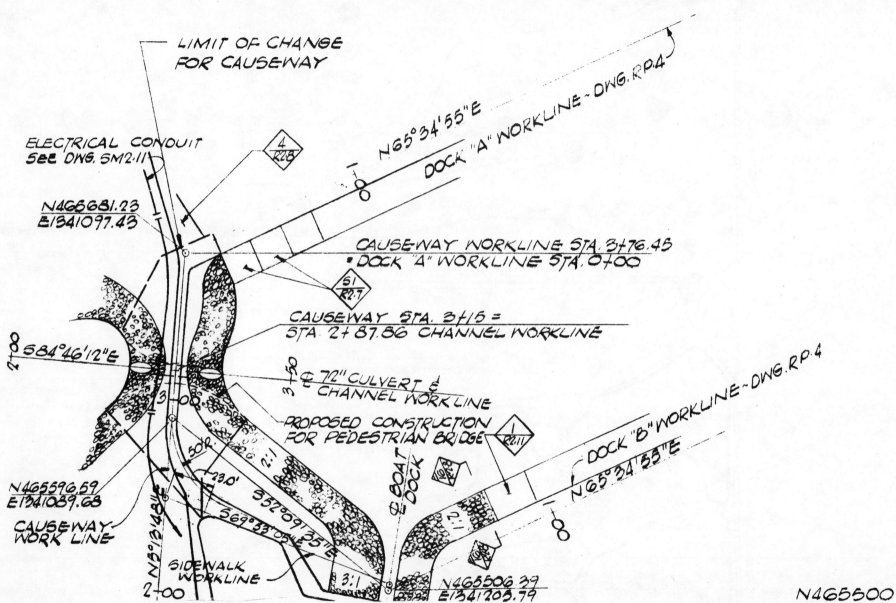

LIMIT OF CHANGE
FOR CAUSEWAY

ELECTRICAL CONDUIT
SEE DWG. SM2-11

N465681.23
E1341097.43

N65°34'55"E

DOCK "A" WORKLINE ~ DWG. R.P.4

CAUSEWAY WORKLINE STA. 3+76.45
= DOCK "A" WORKLINE STA. 0+00

CAUSEWAY STA. 3+15 =
STA. 2+87.86 CHANNEL WORKLINE

₵ 72" CULVERT &
CHANNEL WORKLINE

PROPOSED CONSTRUCTION
FOR PEDESTRIAN BRIDGE

DOCK "B" WORKLINE ~ DWG. R.P.4

N65°34'55"E

S84°46'12"E

N465596.59
E1341089.68

CAUSEWAY
WORK LINE

SIDEWALK
WORKLINE

S57°09'35"E

S69°33'05"E

2:1

₵ BOAT DOCK

3:1

N465506.39
E1341205.79

N465500

Griswold, Winters, Swain and Mullin.

208

COLLINSVILLE, CONNECTICUT

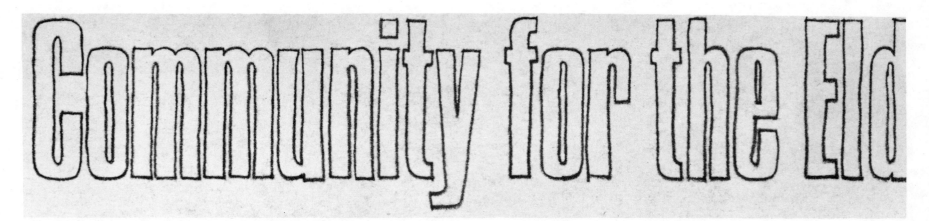

(top) John A. Bentley, (middle and bottom) Johnson and Dee.

209

SECOND EDITION SUPPLEMENT

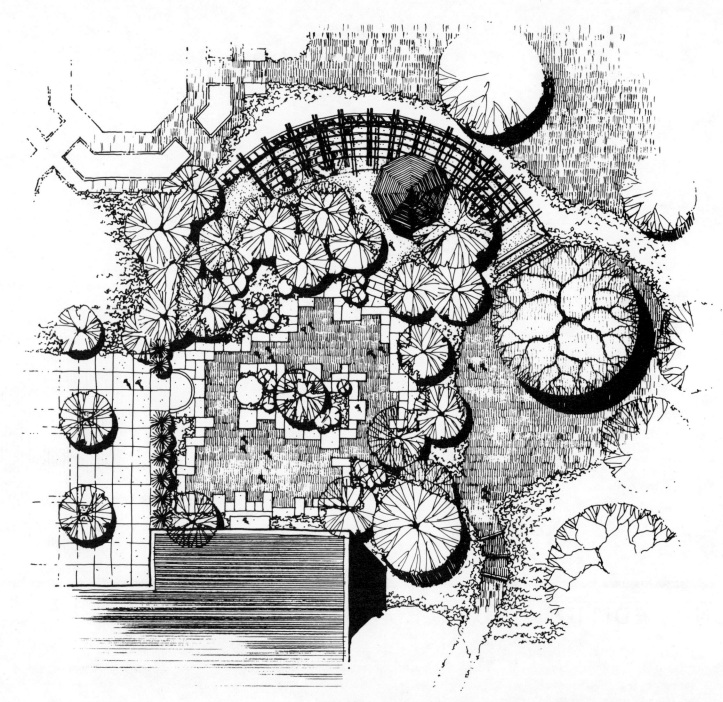

Reading Garden, Cleveland, Ohio. William A. Behnke Associates,
by Russell L. Butler II. Ink and pencil on mylar.

Mawardi — Von Baeyer Residences, Cleveland Heights, Ohio.
William A. Behnke Associates, by Russell L.
Butler II. Ink and pencil on yellow tracing paper.

213

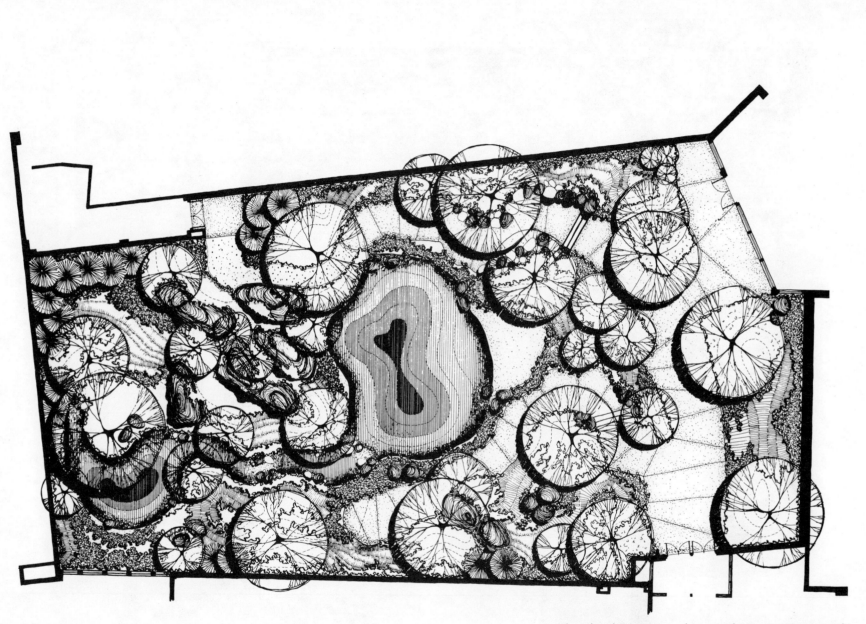

Cleveland Museum of Natural History Courtyard.
William A. Behnke Associates, by Russell L.
Butler II. Ink on yellow tracing paper.

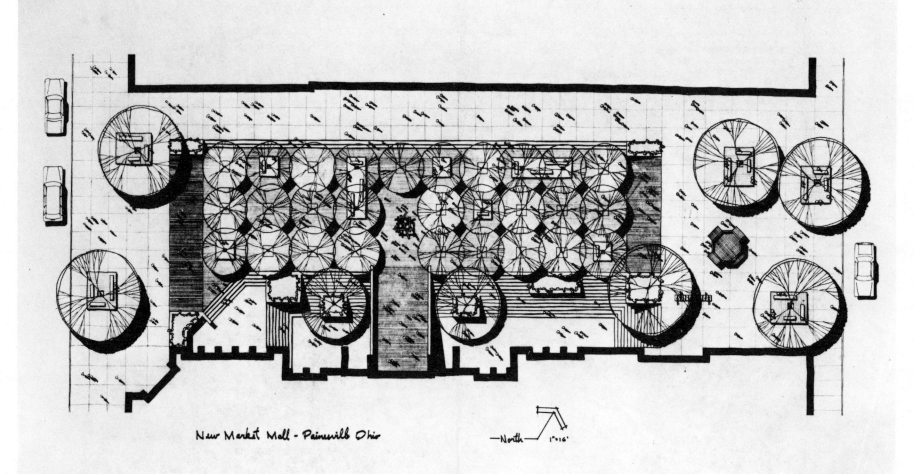

New Market Mall - Painesville Ohio

—North— 1"=16'

New Market Mall, Painesville, Ohio. William A. Behnke Associates,
by Russell L. Butler II. Ink and pencil on mylar.

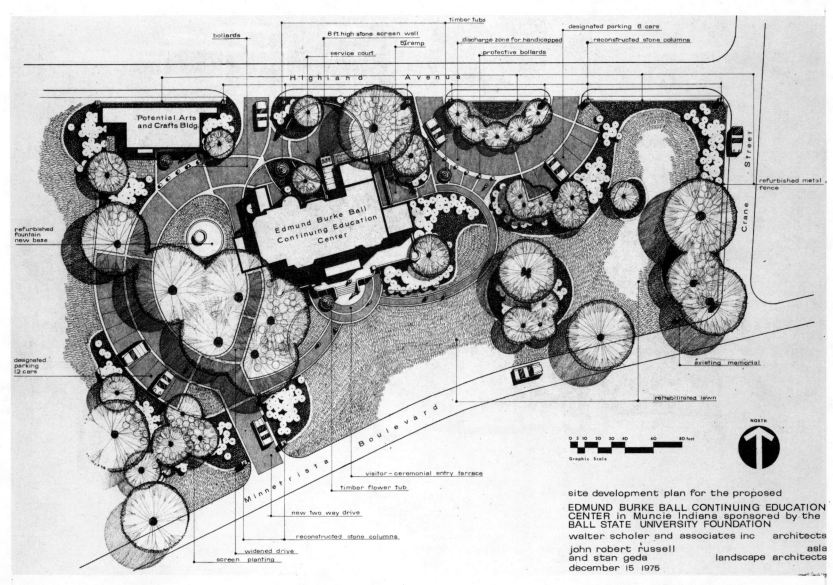

bollards

timber tubs

6 ft. high stone screen wall

service court

5% ramp

designated parking 6 cars

discharge zone for handicapped

reconstructed stone columns

protective bollards

H i g h l a n d   A v e n u e

Potential Arts
and Crafts Bldg.

Crane   Street

refurbished metal
fence

refurbished
fountain
new base

Edmund Burke Ball
Continuing Education
Center

designated
parking
12 cars

existing memorial

rehabilitated lawn

M i n n e t r i s t a   B o u l e v a r d

0 5 10 20   30 40   60   80 feet

Graphic Scale

NORTH

visitor - ceremonial entry terrace

timber flower tub

new two way drive

reconstructed stone columns

widened drive

screen planting

site development plan for the proposed
**EDMUND BURKE BALL CONTINUING EDUCATION
CENTER** in Muncie Indiana sponsored by the
BALL STATE UNIVERSITY FOUNDATION
walter scholer and associates inc   architects
john robert russell   asla
and stan geda   landscape architects
december 15 1975

John Robert Russell and Stan Geda.

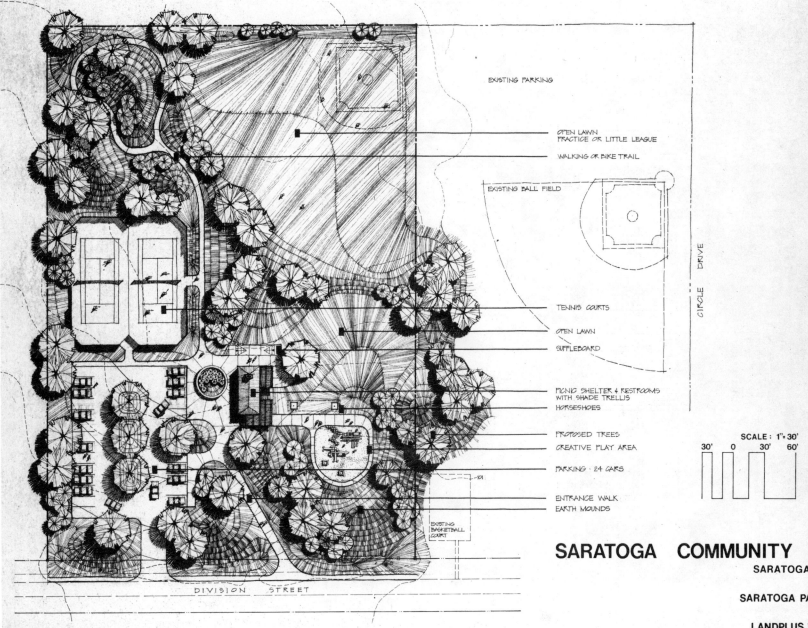

EXISTING PARKING

OPEN LAWN
PRACTICE OR LITTLE LEAGUE

WALKING OR BIKE TRAIL

EXISTING BALL FIELD

CIRCLE DRIVE

TENNIS COURTS

OPEN LAWN

SHUFFLEBOARD

PICNIC SHELTER & RESTROOMS
WITH SHADE TRELLIS

HORSESHOES

PROPOSED TREES

CREATIVE PLAY AREA

PARKING · 24 CARS

ENTRANCE WALK

EARTH MOUNDS

EXISTING
BASKETBALL
COURT

DIVISION STREET

SCALE : 1"=30'

30'   0   30'   60'

SARATOGA COMMUNITY PARK

SARATOGA, INDIANA

Prepared For:
SARATOGA PARK BOARD

Prepared By :
LANDPLUS WEST · LpW

Bruce Alexander/Deane Rundell.

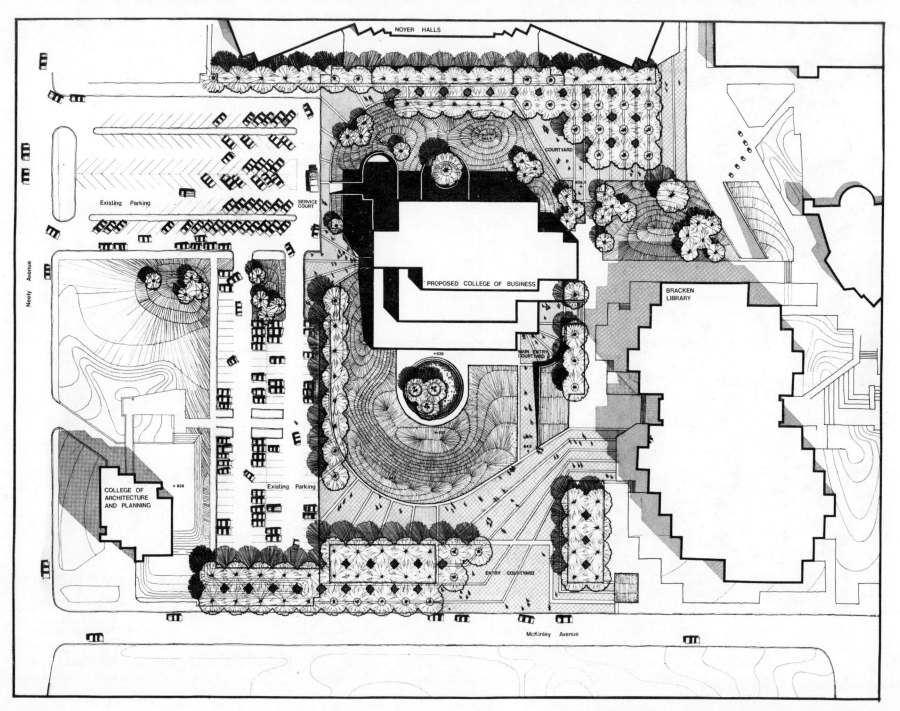

NOYER HALLS

COURTYARD

Existing Parking

Neely Avenue

SERVICE COURT

PROPOSED COLLEGE OF BUSINESS

BRACKEN LIBRARY

+939

MAIN ENTRY COURTYARD

+938

COLLEGE OF ARCHITECTURE AND PLANNING

Existing Parking

ENTRY COURTYARD

McKinley Avenue

College of Business, Ball State University, Muncie, Indiana. Landplus West by Stan Geda.

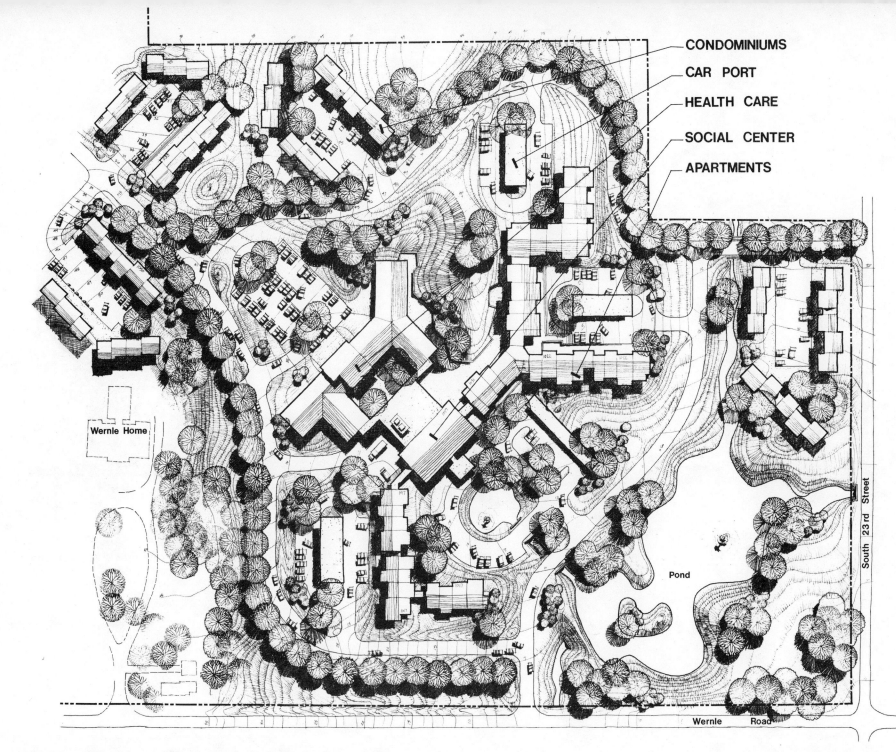

CONDOMINIUMS

CAR PORT

HEALTH CARE

SOCIAL CENTER

APARTMENTS

Wernle Home

South 23 rd Street

Pond

Wernle Road

Vista Pines Retirement Community. Landplus
West by Tom Stearns and Stan Geda.

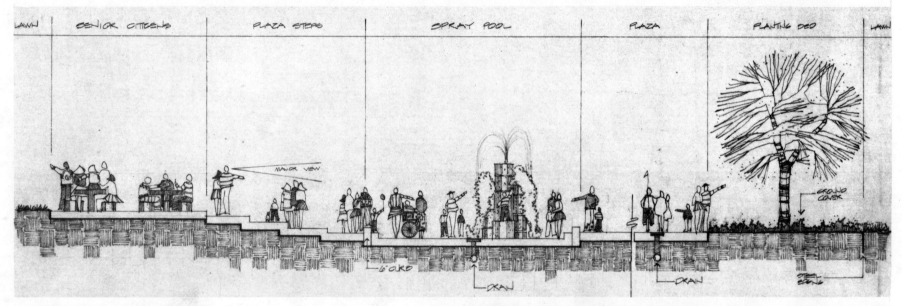

LAWN　SENIOR CITIZENS　PLAZA STEPS　SPRAY POOL　PLAZA　PLANTING BED　LAWN

MAJOR VIEW

GROUND COVER

6" CURB

DRAIN

DRAIN

STEEL EDGING

Wynnefield Park, Philadelphia. Donald R. Knox, Inc., by Francis X. Donnelly.

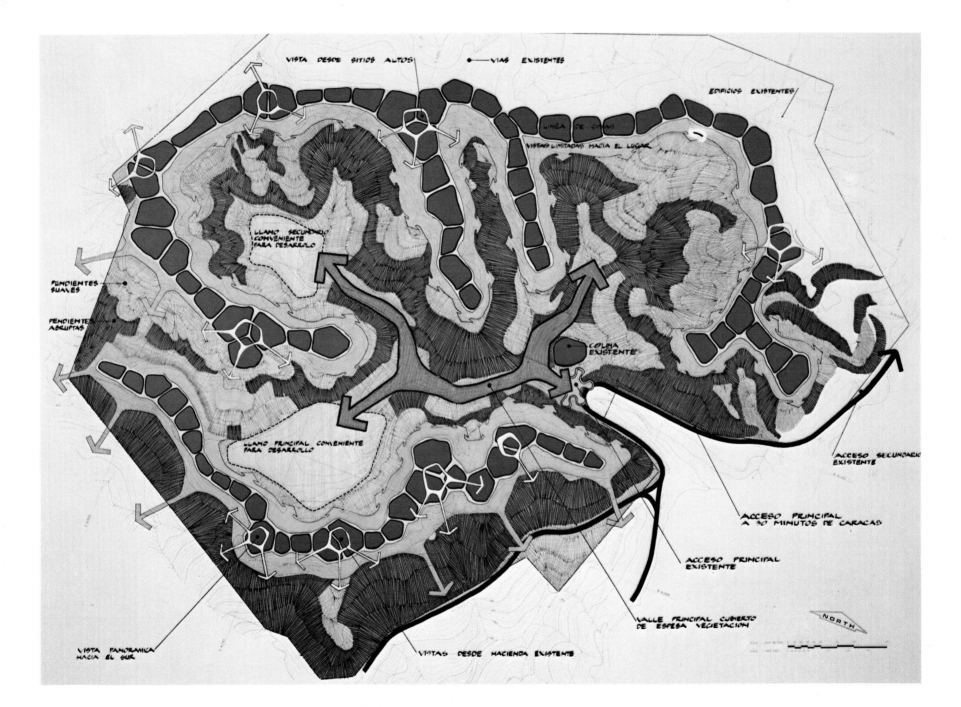

VISTA DESDE SITIOS ALTOS   •—— VIAS EXISTENTES

EDIFICIOS EXISTENTES

LINEA DE CIMAS

VISTAS LIMITADAS HACIA EL LUGAR

LLANO SECUNDARIO
CONVENIENTE
PARA DESARROLLO

PENDIENTES
SUAVES

PENDIENTES
ABRUPTAS

COLINA
EXISTENTE

LLANO PRINCIPAL CONVENIENTE
PARA DESARROLLO

ACCESO SECUNDARIO
EXISTENTE

ACCESO PRINCIPAL
A 30 MINUTOS DE CARACAS

ACCESO PRINCIPAL
EXISTENTE

NORTH

VALLE PRINCIPAL CUBIERTO
DE ESPESA VEGETACION

VISTA PANORAMICA
HACIA EL SUR

VISTAS DESDE HACIENDA EXISTENTE

Theme Park, Caracus, Venezuela. Edward D. Stone, Jr. and Associates.

221

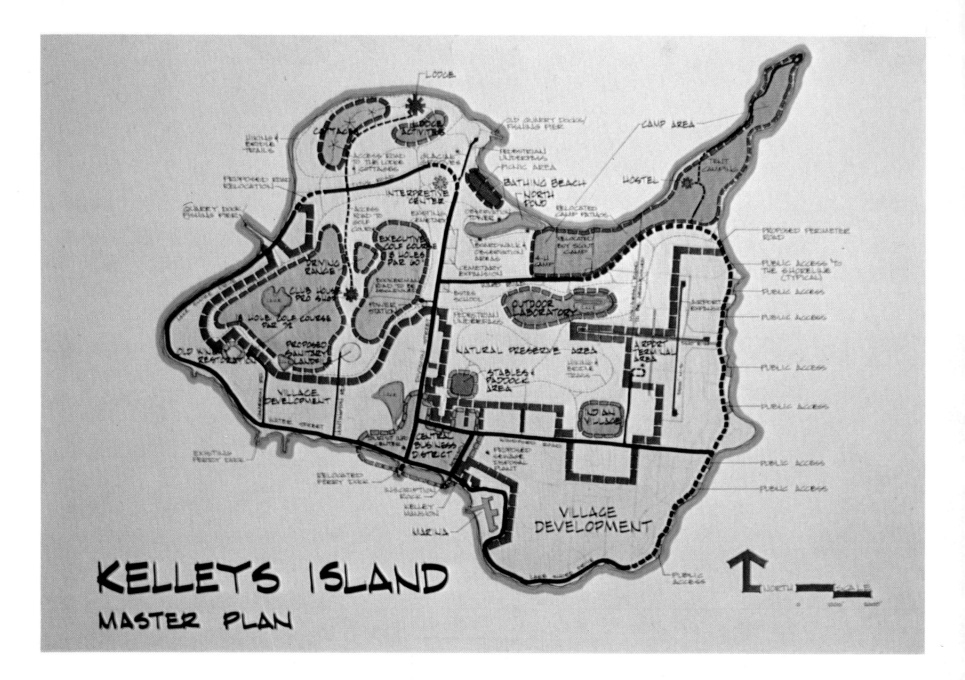

KELLEYS ISLAND
MASTER PLAN

Erie Islands State Park Study. William A. Behnke Associates, by W. Lee Behnke and Russell L. Butler II. Felt markers on print.

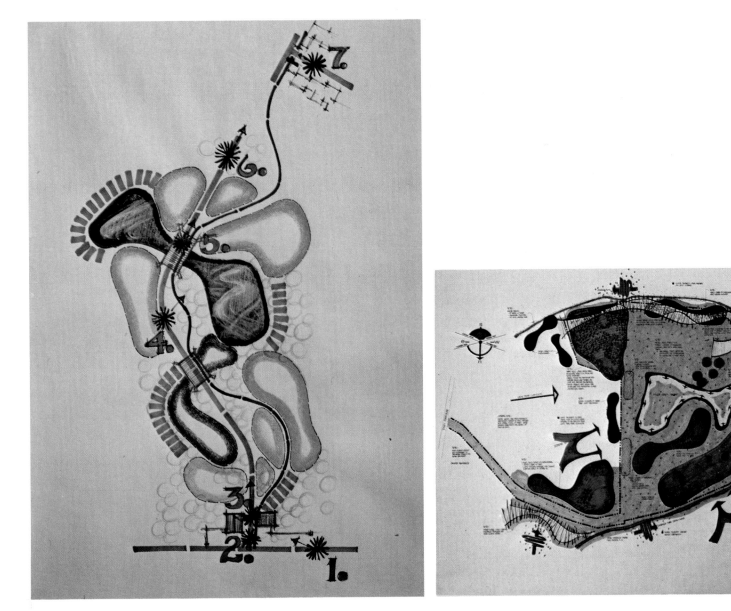

Browning-Day-Pollak, Inc.

CR3, Inc.

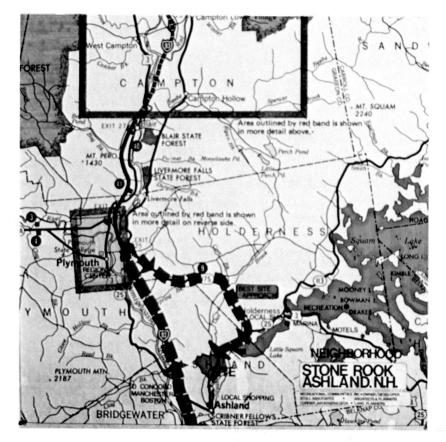

CR3, Inc.

CR3, Inc.

224

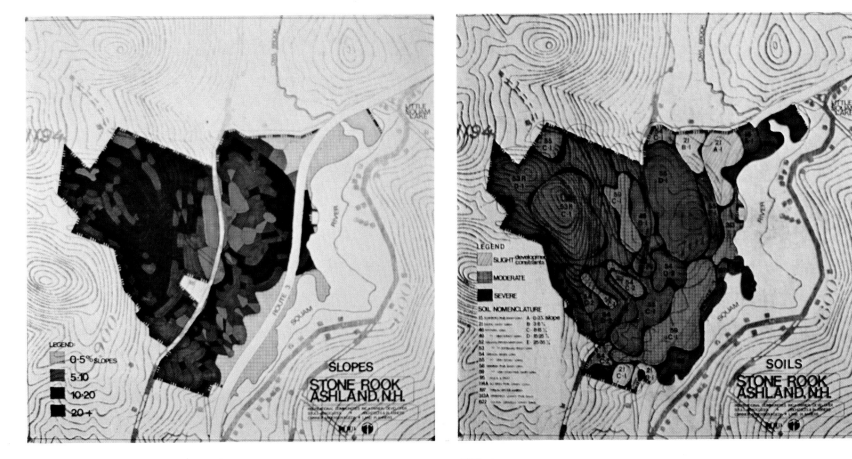

CR3, Inc.

CR3, Inc.

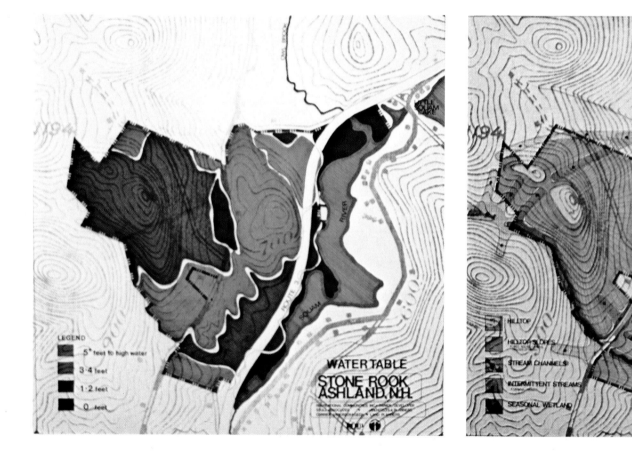

LEGEND

5+ feet to high water

3-4 feet

1-2 feet

0 feet

WATER TABLE
STONE ROOK
ASHLAND, N.H.

HILLTOP

HILLTOP SLOPES

STREAM CHANNELS

INTERMITTENT STREAMS

SEASONAL WETLAND

DRAINAGE
STONE ROOK
ASHLAND, N.H.

CR3, Inc.

CR3, Inc.

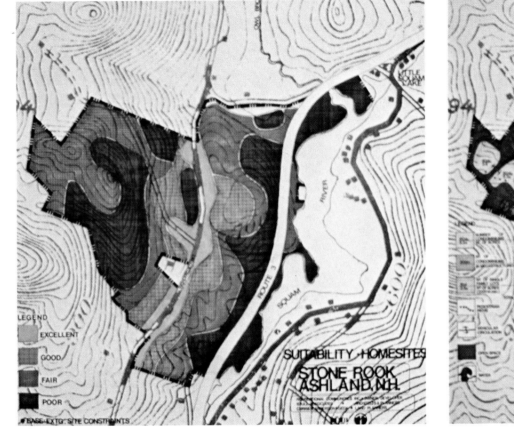

LEGEND

EXCELLENT

GOOD

FAIR

POOR

BASE-EXTG. SITE CONSTRAINTS

SUITABILITY HOMESITES
STONE ROOK
ASHLAND, N.H.

CR3, Inc.

PUD LAND USE PLAN
STONE ROOK
ASHLAND, N.H.

CR3, Inc.

227

CR3, Inc.

CR3, Inc.

228

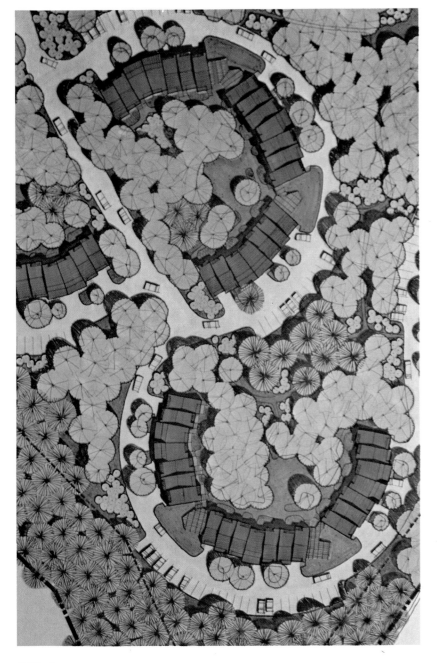

CR3, Inc.

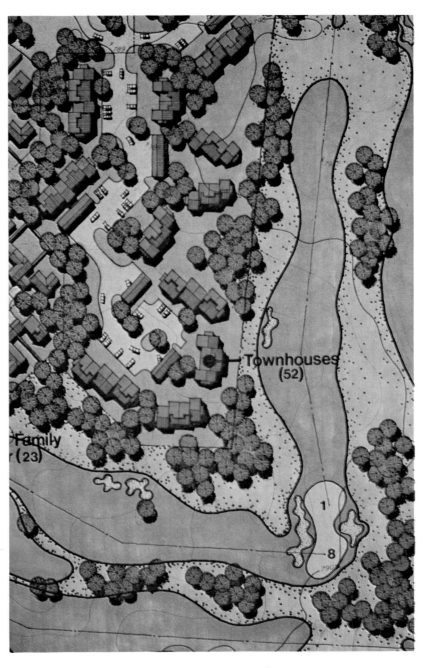

Honeywell Gardens, A Planned Recreational
Community. Landplus West by Deane Rundell.

229

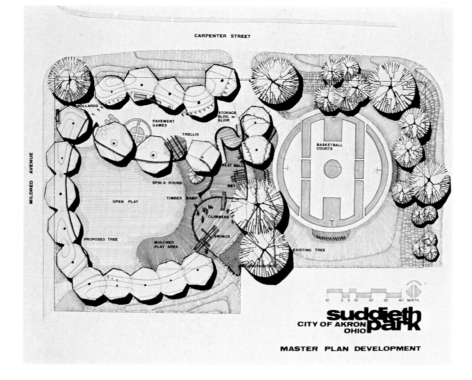

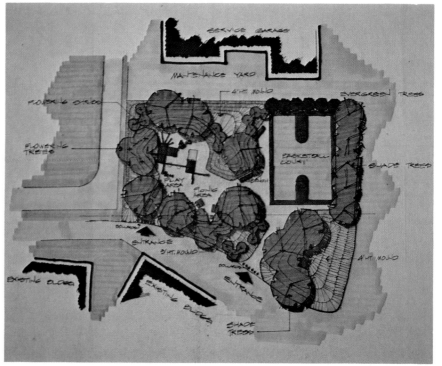

Bonnell & Associates.

Donald R. Knox, Inc., by Francis X. Donnelly.

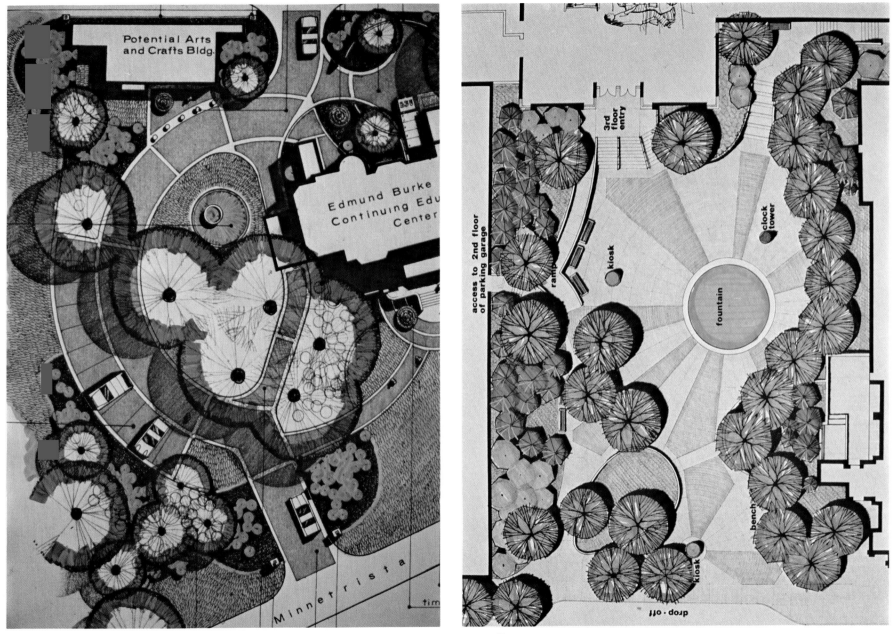

Edmund Burke Ball Center Continuing
Education Center. Stan Geda and John Robert Russell.

Bonnell & Associates.

231

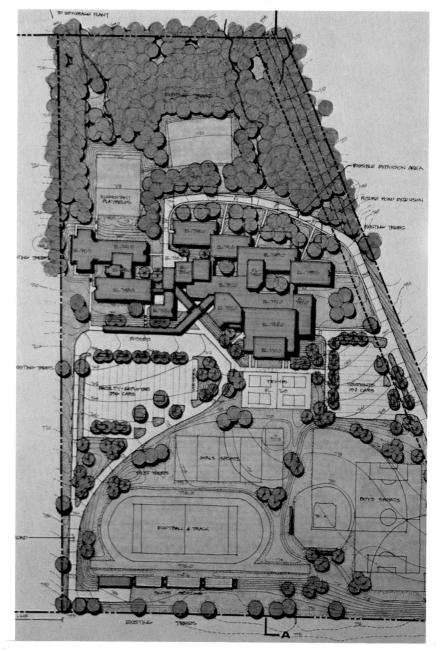

CR3, Inc.

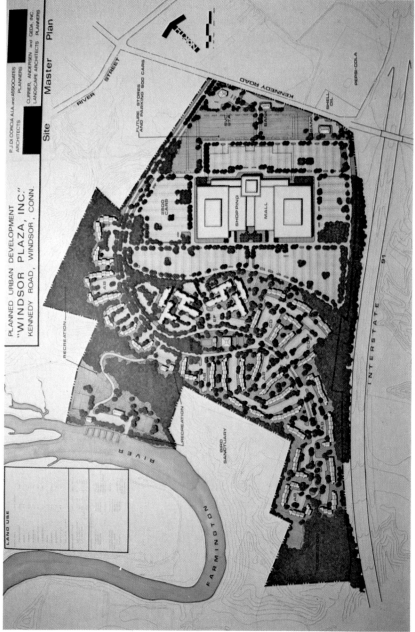

CR3, Inc.

232

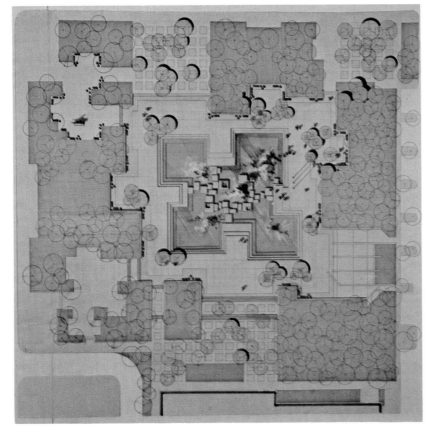

Browning-Day-Pollak, Inc.

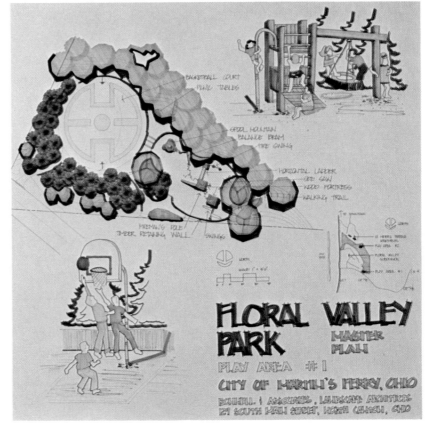

CR3, Inc.